THE CRIMINAL JUSTICE SYSTEM OF THE NETHERLANDS

THE CRIMINAL JUSTICE SYSTEM OF THE NETHERLANDS

Organization, substantive criminal law, criminal procedure and sanctions

Editors:
Piet Hein van Kempen
Maartje Krabbe
Sven Brinkhoff

intersentia
Antwerpen – Cambridge

Intersentia Ltd
8 Wellington Mews | Wellington Street
Cambridge | CB1 1HW | United Kingdom
Tel.: +44 1223 736 170
Email: mail@intersentia.co.uk
www.intersentia.com | www.intersentia.co.uk

Distribution for the UK and Ireland:
NBN International
Airport Business Centre, 10 Thornbury Road
Plymouth, PL6 7 PP
United Kingdom
Tel.: +44 1752 202 301 | Fax: +44 1752 202 331
Email: orders@nbninternational.com

Distribution for Europe and all other countries:
Intersentia Publishing nv
Groenstraat 31
2640 Mortsel
Belgium
Tel.: +32 3 680 15 50 | Fax: +32 3 658 71 21
Email: mail@intersentia.be

Distribution for the USA and Canada:
Independent Publishers Group
Order Department
814 North Franklin Street
Chicago, IL60610
USA
Tel.: +1 800 888 4741 (toll free) | Fax: +1312 337 5985
Email: orders@ipgbook.com

The Criminal Justice System of the Netherlands. Organization, substantive
criminal law, criminal procedure and sanctions
© the editors and contributors severally 2019

The editors and contributors have asserted the right under the Copyright, Designs and Patents Act
1988, to be identified as authors of this work.

No part of this book may be reproduced, stored in a retrieval system, or transmitted, in any form,
or by any means, without prior written permission from Intersentia, or as expressly permitted by
law or under the terms agreed with the appropriate reprographic rights organisation. Enquiries
concerning reproduction which may not be covered by the above should be addressed to Intersentia
at the address above.

ISBN 978-1-78068-962-3
D/2019/7849/152
NUR 824

British Library Cataloguing in Publication Data. A catalogue record for this book is available from
the British Library.

FOREWORD

This publication should have been the fifth edition of my book *The Dutch criminal justice system*. Other projects, however, such as the production of comparative law reports for the new Dutch Code of Criminal Procedure, demanded my attention. In the meantime – eight years after obtaining the status of emeritus – the Dutch criminal legal system went through various changes. A new edition could not be postponed.

In agreement it was decided that my colleague and friend Prof. Dr. Piet Hein van Kempen and his staff (the department of criminal law and criminology of Radboud University) would be free to rewrite a new edition of my book. I am exceptionally delighted with the results.

The Dutch criminal legal system has always been of interest to foreign experts, because of its remarkable differences with other European systems. For example, lay judges are not a part of our system. Also, rules on sentencing are limited. Consequently, Dutch judges have great liberty imposing penalties.

This new edition is an extended version of the previous editions. Not only information on the different doctrines of Dutch criminal law has been supplemented, but also more examples and references to additional sources (literature and case law) have been included. Even more than the previous editions, this book offers thorough knowledge of the Dutch criminal legal system. This will undoubtedly generate opportunities for our system to be included in comparative law projects. All in all, the fact that a group of knowledgeable authors has reshaped this book in its current form, retaining and consolidating its scientific standard, fills me with gladness and contentment.

Prof. em. Peter J.P. Tak
Nijmegen, December 2019

PREFACE

Before you lies the first edition of *The criminal justice system of the Netherlands. Organization, substantive criminal law, criminal procedure and sanctions.* This book is based on its prequel: *The Dutch criminal justice system* (Wolf Legal Publishers, 2008) by Prof. Dr. Peter Tak, professor emeritus at Radboud University in Nijmegen, the Netherlands. Professor Peter Tak has been so generous to make his text available to us, so we could build upon his work. We owe him many thanks for his generosity and for the confidence he gave us.

We are also very thankful to the co-authors of this book: Joeri Bemelmans, Masha Fedorova, Roel Klaar, Maarten Kuipers, Sjarai Lestrade, Geert Pesselse, Henny Sackers, Martine van der Staak and Mikhel Timmerman. Many thanks go out to them, not only for their contributions but also for your patience.

The authors of this book are all specializing in the field of Dutch criminal law. Their common denominator is that they work or, at some point in time, have worked at the department of Criminal Law & Criminology of Radboud University. More information on individual authors is available at the beginning of each chapter, where a bibliographical note is included.

We wrote this book not only for students, but also for foreign researchers and everybody else who is interested in the general basics of the criminal justice system of the Netherlands. The topics discussed in this book are the doctrines of our Bachelor curriculum. However, we aim to bring these topics to you from a 'foreign perspective'. That is, while writing this book the authors thought of aspects of our criminal justice system that would be of specific interest to foreigners. For example, the powers of the Dutch public prosecutor, the Dutch anti-terrorism legislation and our drug policy.

We included a modest amount of references to case law, websites and more detailed (if possible English) texts, in order to support readers who desire a more thorough understanding of a specific topic in the field of Dutch criminal law. References to Dutch case law in this book not only mention journals, but also the so called 'ECLI numbers'. An ECLI number looks like this: ECLI:NL:HR:2016:2418. By inserting this number into a search engine (preferably rechtspraak.nl, but Google will also do) the court decision can be found easily.

This book also offers references to literature, including the two major handbooks of Dutch criminal law: *Materieel strafrecht* by J. de Hullu (Wolters Kluwer, 7th edition, 2018) on substantive criminal law and *Het Nederlands strafprocesrecht* by G.J.M Corstens, M.J. Borgers & T. Kooijmans (Wolters Kluwer, 9th edition, 2018) on criminal procedure. In order to avoid an overkill of detailed footnotes, references to these works are usually clustered at the beginning or end of a specific section.

The book furthermore contains many references to parliamentary documents (*Kamerstukken*) and to the Bulletin of Acts (*Staatsblad*).

We could go on with reading instructions for quite a while, but it is probably better for you to start reading. We hope this book will introduce you to the basic concepts of Dutch criminal law and will trigger your enthusiasm for further exploration of our fascinating legal system.

Nijmegen, December 2019
Piet Hein VAN KEMPEN, Maartje KRABBE & Sven BRINKHOFF

CONTENTS

PART II
SUBSTANTIVE CRIMINAL LAW

PART III
CRIMINAL PROCEDURE LAW

5. Criminal Procedure Law

PART IV
SANCTIONS

6.   Sentencing

PART I
CRIME, LAW AND POLITICS

1. THE STRUCTURE OF THE STATE

Martine VAN DER STAAK[*]

1.1 GENERAL ORGANIZATION OF THE STATE STRUCTURE

The Netherlands (*Nederland*) is located in North-western Europe, west of the Federal Republic of Germany, north of Belgium and east and south of the North Sea. The present boundaries of the country were established with the separation of Belgium from the Netherlands in 1830. As of 2010 the Kingdom of the Netherlands (*Koninkrijk der Nederlanden*) includes four separate countries: the Netherlands (Europe), Aruba, Curacao, and Sint Maarten (which are all Caribbean islands).[1] The Netherlands is furthermore part and founding member of the European Union (28 Member States) as well as of the Council of Europe (47 Member States).

Although formally and principally incorrect, The Netherlands is often referred to as Holland. North and South Holland in the western part of The Netherlands are only two of the twelve provinces within the Netherlands. Another linguistic matter concerns the adjective of the noun 'the Netherlands'. In English that adjective is the word 'Dutch', which term thus refers to the inhabitants, the language, and anything pertaining to the Netherlands. Consequently, the criminal law discussed in this book should be referred to as *Dutch* criminal law.

The Netherlands is a constitutional monarchy. The Constitution charges the Government – the Monarch and Her ministers – with the responsibility for governing the country. The Monarch, although part of the Government, cannot be held accountable for political decisions (The King can do no wrong, Article 42 Constitution). Consequently, the powers of the King are primarily symbolic.[2]

The Netherlands is a parliamentary democracy, which means that the Government may hold office only as long as it has the confidence of Parliament. Once this is lost, or an individual member of Government loses this confidence,

---

[*] Mrs. M.G.J.M. van der Staak is an attorney at law, specialized in privacy law, and a judge *at litem* at the district court of Limburg.
[1] See further P.P.T. Bovend'Eert & C.A.J.M. Kortmann, *Constitutional Law in the Netherlands*, Alphen aan de Rijn: Kluwer Law International, 2018, pp. 38–43.
[2] Idem, pp. 76–77.

the Government or the minister must resign. Dutch governments as a rule are formed by coalitions of a number of political parties owing to the electoral system of proportional representation. Ministers or deputy ministers are not themselves members of Parliament.

The Dutch Parliament (*Staten-Generaal*) consists of two houses: the Lower House (*Tweede Kamer der Staten-Generaal*) and the Upper House or Senate (*Eerste Kamer der Staten-Generaal*). The 150 members of the Lower House are elected every four year by the general population of Dutch citizens. The 75 members of the Senate are elected by the members of the provincial councils, of which there are twelve.

The main task of the Lower House is to supervise the Government in their day-to-day running of the country. Members of the Government can, under the responsibility with which they are charged under the Constitution, be ordered to appear before the Lower House and to answer questions as to their decisions and any actions taken. The Lower House is frequently the scene of heated political debate.

The Dutch Parliament, acting jointly with the Government, may pass Acts of Parliament. As a rule, the Government takes the initiative in the legislative process by drafting bills. Following the adoption of a bill in the Lower House, it is discussed by the Senate and, if adopted, the bill becomes an Act of Parliament through the signature of the Monarch and the Minister responsible for the field to which the bill relates.

The Lower House also has the right to take the initiative in the legislative process as well as possessing the right to propose amendments to a governmental bill. The minister proposing a bill may adopt or reject any such amendments or may submit these to a vote. The Lower House may reject the bill or adopt it by majority vote. The Senate does not have the right of initiative or amendment but shares other rights such as the right of interpellation and the right of inquiry with the Lower House. Although without the right of initiative or amendment, the Senate has the right to reject a bill adopted in the Lower House. The bill in such a case will be withdrawn by the Government. As such, the Senate has limited tools to influence political debate and is therefore sometimes also known as the 'House of reflection'. There is a separation of powers between the legislature, the administration and the judiciary. This separation is, however, not very strict; e.g. an Act of Parliament can only be adopted by agreement between Government and Parliament.[3]

The constitutional organization of the Netherlands is that of a decentralized unitary state. One type of decentralisation concerns the division of state

---

[3]   See for a more elaborate description of the form of government: P.P.T. Bovend'Eert & C.A.J.M. Kortmann, 2018, pp. 57–116, and L. Besselink, 'The Kingdom of the Netherlands', in: P.P. T. Bovend'Eert, H. Broeksteeg, R. de Lange & W. Voermans (Eds.), *Constitutional law of the EU member states*, Kluwer: Deventer 2014 (first edition), pp. 1187–1242.

powers over territorially-decentralized entities: the twelve provinces and the approximately 450 municipalities. These decentralized entities have restricted legislative and executive powers. The Netherlands has three administrative layers: the State, the provinces and the municipalities. At the state level, administrative powers are held by the Government (the ministers and their ministries). By Act of Parliament the Government can be empowered to issue rules giving shape to those Acts.

The supreme organ of a province is the provincial council, which is directly elected. The supreme organ of a municipality is the municipal council, which is also directly elected. These bodies have mainly local legislative powers. They may issue city or province regulations. Non-compliance with these regulations constitutes a minor offence that carries a statutory sentence of a fine of the third category (see section 8.4).

In municipalities, the executive powers are vested mainly in the board of mayor and aldermen (*college van burgemeester en wethouders*). In the provinces, the so-called States Deputies (*Gedeputeerde Staten*) chaired by the Queen's Commissioner (*Commissaris van de Koningin*) are vested with executive powers. The Mayor and the Queen's Commissioner are appointed by the Government by Royal decree.

State powers may also be divided between functionally decentralized entities such as water boards and public law industrial regulatory bodies. Water boards and public law industrial regulatory bodies, such as the Social and Economic Council as well as the commodity boards (*productschappen*) and industrial boards (*bedrijfsschappen*), have the power to issue regulations, non-compliance with which constitutes a criminal offence.[4]

1.2 LEGISLATIVE POWER RELATED TO CRIMINAL JUSTICE

The primary form of legislation is an Act of Parliament (*Wet in formele zin*) enacted jointly by Government and Parliament. Article 81 of the Constitution provides that the legislative power is exercised by the Government and the Parliament jointly. As a rule, a bill is prepared by the Government – specifically, the legislative department of the Ministry of Justice and Security which has competence over the subject dealt with – and discussed in legislative committees of the Parliament. During the final discussion in a full session of the Parliament, amendments to the bill may be proposed. The bill and any amendments are adopted by majority vote. The Act may include a delegation of further legislation on the subject to the Government or to an individual minister. On this basis,

---

[4] See further P.P.T. Bovend'Eert & C.A.J.M. Kortmann, *Constitutional Law in the Netherlands*, Alphen aan de Rijn: Kluwer Law International, 2018, pp. 44–56.

the Government may issue rules (*Algemene maatregel van bestuur, Ministeriële regeling*), which may declare a certain act an offence. The precise penalties for these offences must however be defined in the Act of Parliament itself.[5]

Furthermore, organs of territorially decentralized bodies holding legislative power– the provinces and municipalities – as well as functionally decentralized bodies can take decisions of a legislative nature, the non-compliance with which may constitute a criminal offence. These decentralized bodies derive such legislative powers from an Act of Parliament.

All bodies mentioned above have legislative powers in the field of substantive criminal law. Only an Act of Parliament, however, may define of crimes. Any other legislative regulations may only contain definitions of criminal infractions.[6]

Procedural criminal law rules may be enacted only by Act of Parliament. However, Parliament may decide to delegate the authority to issue elaborative rules of a procedural nature to the Government or an individual minister. This is also to penitentiary law and the law relating to the execution of sentences.[7]

1.3 MINISTERIAL RESPONSIBILITY FOR THE MAIN ORGANS OF THE CRIMINAL JUSTICE SYSTEM

The judiciary comprises both judges and public prosecutors. The Minister of Justice and Security is responsible for the judiciary as far as it concerns the prosecution service (public prosecutor). Judges on the other hand are independent and no Minister has authority over them. The budget for the courts' operation is nevertheless part of the wider budget of the Ministry of Justice and Security. This budget is allotted to the courts by the Council for the Judiciary (*Raad voor de Rechtspraak*)[8] and the courts are accountable to the Council for the Judiciary with regard to how they utilize their resources. The Minister is only thus responsible for the functioning of the judiciary as a whole.

Since the 2012 Police Act, the Netherlands has a national police force with three organisational levels: the national level, the level of the units and the level of the municipalities.[9] The Minister of Justice and Security is responsible for

---

5   See Article 89 of the Constitution.

6   This is how Article 107 of the Constitution is interpreted. See J. de Hullu, *Materieel strafrecht*, Deventer: Wolters Kluwer 2018, p. 66. The differences between crimes and infractions are discussed in chapter 4, section 3.2.

7   Article 1 CCP.

8   More information on the Council for the Judiciary can be found in chapter 2 section 20.

9   J. Terpstra, 'Police reform in the Netherlands and Scotland compared', *Scottish Justice Matters*, June 2015, pp. 31–32; see also J. Terpstra & N.R. Fyfe, 'Mind the implementation gap? Police reform and local policing in the Netherlands and Scotland', *Criminology & Criminal*

the police forces when it comes to criminal investigations, while the Minister of Home Affairs is responsible for their other police tasks, such as upholding the public order. The police budget is controlled by the Minister of Home Affairs.

The prosecution service is a nationwide organization with offices at district court level and at the level of the Courts of Appeal. It is hierarchically organized and is headed by the Board of Prosecutors General. The service functions under the responsibility of the Minister of Justice and Security but is, however, not an agency of the Ministry.

On a day-to-day basis, the police forces, prosecution services and courts are directed by, respectively, the chief police officer, the chief public prosecutor or the board of the court. Instructions to ensure that certain investigation and prosecution policies are enforced may be issued by the chief public prosecutor or by the Board of Prosecutors General. No actor has the authority to issue instructions to the courts. Instructions with regard to the division of the case load within the court are given by the head of a court's section.

1.4 RULE OF LAW AND THE RELEVANCE OF HUMAN RIGHTS

The Netherlands is a *Rechtsstaat* – i.e. a state of justice – and is thus governed by the rule of law. International human rights treaties play an important role in that regard. The Netherlands accepts the monistic view with respect to the status of international law in the Dutch legal order: all international law applicable to the Netherlands is part of the domestic legal order. No translation into domestic legislation is needed.[10] International and regional human rights and humanitarian law treaties have power over national law (even over statutes and the Constitution).[11]

The Kingdom of the Netherlands is party to most of the important international and European human rights treaties and endorses many soft law codifications of human rights, such as declarations, sets of rules and principles, and codes of conduct.[12] As regards criminal procedure, the European Convention on Human Rights (ECHR) is of especially great significance. The right to liberty (Article 5 ECHR), the right to a fair trial (Article 6 ECHR), and the right to privacy (Article 8 ECHR) are most frequently invoked by the

---

Justice, 2015, pp. 1–18, and J. Terpstra & N.R. Fyfe, 'Policy processes and police reform: Examining similarities and differences between Scotland and the Netherlands', *International Journal of Law, Crime and Justice,* 2014, vol. 42, iss. 4, pp. 366–383.

10 See Articles 93 and 94 of the Constitution.

11 Piet Hein van Kempen, 'The Protection of Human Rights in Criminal Law Procedure in The Netherlands', *Electronic Journal of Comparative Law,* 2009, Vol. 13.2 www.ejcl.org/132/art132-1.pdf, pp. 1–37, p. 2.

12 Idem, pp. 1–37, p. 2.

defense in criminal proceedings and exert a daily influence on criminal justice proceedings.[13] Fundamental rights that are relevant to criminal procedure in the Netherlands cannot only be found in the ECHR; several of these rights are contained in chapter 1 (Articles 1 to 23) of the Constitution of the Kingdom of the Netherlands.

---

[13]   Idem, pp. 1–37, pp. 1 and 5.

2. THE MAIN ORGANS OF THE CRIMINAL JUSTICE SYSTEM

Masha FEDOROVA[*]

2.1   INTRODUCTION

The main organs of the criminal justice system of the Netherlands are the police force, the public prosecution service, the courts, the probation service, the sentence enforcement agencies and the defense. These will now be discussed respectively.

A   THE POLICE FORCE

2.2   THE 2012 POLICE ACT

The formal organization of the police (*de politie*) is laid down in the 2012 Police Act (*Politiewet 2012*), which entered into force in January 2013. Prior to this Act, the police force was divided into 25 relatively autonomous regional forces and a small national police force with only very specific tasks and powers (1993 Police Act). In addition to the regional and national police forces, there was a Royal Dutch Military Police, a small force which, under the supervision of the Minister of Defense, exercised the primary general role of policing within the Dutch armed forces. The regionalized structure of the police was viewed as fragmented, lacking coordination and consequently as ineffective in approaching major crimes, such as organized crime and terrorism.[1]

The introduction of the 2012 Police Act was meant to address these shortcomings. The main structure of the police now consists of 10 Regional Units (*regionale eenheden*), a National Unit (*Landelijke eenheid*) and the National Police Services (*politiedienstencentrum*). The leadership lies with the national

---

[*]   M.I. Fedorova (Ph.D.) is full professor of Criminal law and Criminal Procedure at Radboud University Nijmegen. She is also a judge *at litem* at the district court of 's-Hertogenbosch.

[1]   For background information see J. Terpstra, 'Towards a National Police in the Netherlands – Background of a Radical Police Reform', in: N.R. Fyfe, J. Terpstra & P. Tops (eds.), *Centralizing Forces?*, The Hague: Eleven International Publishing, 2013, pp. 137–155.

chief of police (*korpschef*). The 10 Regional Units operate on regional level and are in turn divided into 43 districts on a local level. These districts again consist of 167 basic teams. The National Unit deals with specialized police tasks and tasks that go beyond regional units. The National Police Services clusters all the administrative tasks of the police. The national police operates under the authority of the Ministry of Justice and Security.

2.3 TASKS OF THE POLICE

In accordance with Article 3 of the 2012 Police Act, the task of the police force is to enforce the legal order and to render assistance to those who need help. The enforcement of the legal order comprises the enforcement of criminal law, the enforcement of public order and the performance of judicial services. When enforcing public order, the police operates under the authority of the mayor of the municipality in which the police acts (Article 11 2012 Police Act). The mayor can issue instructions in this respect. For the enforcement of public order, the legal regime of the Police Act is applicable.

When enforcing criminal law and performing judicial services, the police acts under the authority of the Public Prosecution Service competent at the place of action (Article 12 2012 Police Act). The enforcement of criminal law comprises the effective prevention, termination and investigation of criminal offences. The public prosecution can give instructions to the police for the enforcement of criminal law.

There is no organizational separation or distinction within the police force between the investigation of criminal acts and the prevention thereof. Both are tasks of the police. Within the police force some departments concentrate on the investigation of crimes, while others concentrate on prevention. For the enforcement of criminal law, regardless of whether it is prevention or investigation, the Code of Criminal Procedure is applicable.

As noted above, the political responsibility depends on the nature of the police action, but in cases in which the enforcement of the legal order and the enforcement of criminal law coincide, the mayor and the public prosecutor will confer on the steps to be taken. This applies in particular when large scale risk events (football matches etc.) take place (Article 13 2012 Police Act).

Unlike in systems such as that of England and Wales, the Dutch police do not play any role in the prosecution of crimes. A police officer has jurisdiction *ratione loci* in the whole of the Dutch territory, but as a rule he will restrict his actions to the region where he is stationed, unless an action outside this region is reasonably necessary or is authorized by law or the competent authority (Article 6 2012 Police Act). In order to carry out judicial services, all senior police officers have the role of auxiliary to the public prosecutor (*hulpofficier van justitie*). In this capacity, they may carry out a number of tasks on behalf of the public prosecutor.

2.4 ORGANIZATION OF THE POLICE FORCE

The national police consists of 10 Regional Units (*regionale eenheden*), a National Unit (*Landelijke eenheid*) and the National Police Services (*politiedienstencentrum*).[2]

Regional Units

The 10 Regional Units all consist of a unit management staff, five services (discussed below) and several districts, which in turn are divided into several 'basic teams'. Each regional unit is run by a regional police chief.

The five services are the following:

(1) *The regional operational center service* connects the organization and the tasks the police officers perform on the street. The service includes a control center and a central information point.

(2) *The regional investigation service* focuses on criminal organizations and criminal acts with a high impact on the victim. The service covers issues such as environmental crimes, fraud, child pornography, crimes involving the sexual integrity of a person, cybercrime and human trafficking. The service is moreover responsible for the enforcement of the law with regard to aliens and supports investigation in the areas of observation, interception and forensic, digital and financial investigations.

(3) *The regional information organization service* focuses on the collection and supply of the latest intelligence. The service issues threat assessments and advises. It incorporates a team for criminal intelligence (*team criminele inlichtingen*) and a team for public order intelligence (*team openbare orde inlichtingen*). The criminal intelligence team collects information on serious crimes. Informants form an important source of that information. In addition, the regional information service provides support on a local and regional level to the General Intelligence and Security Services (*Algemene Inlichtingen- en Veiligheidsdienst*) operating under the authority of the Ministry of Home Affairs.

(4) *The regional operational cooperation service* consists of several support departments, such as the department for Conflict and Crisis Management that provides support for police involvement during events and the organization of the police's mobile unit, or the regional service center that answers non-urgent telephone calls from citizens.

(5) *The regional unit management service* focuses on a limited number of managerial issues that directly relate to operational police work in the region, such as scheduling of the regional team and public information.

---

2   Information for this section is mainly retrieved from www.politie.nl.

Every Regional Unit is divided into several districts, which form the connection between the regional level of the unit and the local level on which the 'basic teams' operate. Every district consists of an investigation unit, a 'flex-team' and a central information point.

The district investigation unit is responsible for the handling of criminal acts with high impact on the victim and provides support to the 'basic teams'. The 'flex-team' works on a problem-based basis and provides temporary additional men-power to the 'basic teams'. The central information point provides most recent information around the clock.

The bottom of a regional police force consists of the so-called 'basic teams' – the smallest territorial unit – which are responsible for daily surveillance, help in emergencies, the registration of criminal offences, contact with the population in their territory and smaller criminal investigations. The 'basic teams' operate on the level of (a part of) a municipality or several municipalities. The local police officer (*wijkagent*) plays a central role.

National Unit

In addition to the regional units, a national police unit exists. Next to tasks that ensure the unity of the national police, the national unit has several autonomous tasks, such as tackling major organized crime and terrorism, guarding and ensuring security of the Royal Family and other dignitaries, and investigation on highways, railways, waterways and aviation. It supports other police units by providing specialists in the area of investigation and forensics, as well as police dogs, police horses and helicopters. The National Unit consists of seven services:

(1) *The national operational center service* streamlines all ongoing operations and ensures a permanent and complete overview with regard to the current societal issues and the means available to the police.
(2) *The national investigation service* focuses on serious and organized crime, and on specific areas such as human trafficking, environmental criminality, terrorism and high-tech crime. In addition, it is also responsible for the investigation of serious, organized crime committed abroad whenever nationals or property of the Netherlands are involved.
(3) *The national information organization service* performs specific tasks such as coordination of national information and international exchange of police information; and ensures an overview of the (inter)national security situation for the benefit of police operations. Furthermore, the service forms a front office for organizations such as Europol and Interpol and maintains contact with Dutch liaison officers abroad.
(4) *The national operational cooperation service* provides operational support and (technical) innovation for the police with regard to, for example, covert

operations and witness protection, phone taps or trained police animals. The national forensic service center is part of this service.

(5) *The infrastructure service* addresses criminality concentrated on the Dutch main infrastructure such as highways, water, railways and aviation.

(6) *The Guarding and Securing service* ensures the security of persons, objects and services on national, regional and local levels and works closely with the National Coordinator for Security and Counterterrorism and the Public Prosecution Service.

(7) *The special interventions service* focuses on all forms of serious violence and terrorism. The service controls all special units of the police and the defense. The Arrest and Support teams that consist of regional police officers and military police, act in life threatening situations. The Intervention Unit consists of police and military officers and focuses on small scale operations that present a high risk due to the presence of heavy weaponry, explosives or dangerous substances. The Expertise and Operational Support Unit, consisting of police and military officers, provides for snipers.

National Police Services

The National Police Services manages the national police, including its finances, general and technical support services, information management, ICT, communication and human resources. Centralizing the management of the national police was deemed necessary to better accommodate the day-to-day practice of the police officers within their units.

2.5 INVESTIGATIVE POWERS

On the basis of the *generally* phrased Article 3 of the 2012 Police Act, the police have the power to perform limited invasions of someone's privacy by means of surveillance, for example, or by taking pictures of persons in public.[3] This provision does not suffice as a basis for the use of investigative powers if the power used – considering the place where it is used, its duration, intensity and frequency, and whether it involves the use of technical aids – is suitable for obtaining a more or less complete picture of certain aspects of the personal life of the person concerned. Therefore, more invasive powers, related to the task of detecting and investigating criminal offences, can be found in *specific statutory powers* such as arrest, police custody, seizure and intrusive special investigative

---

[3] See recently, e.g., Supreme Court, 6 November 2018, ECLI:NL:HR:2018:2050 (Lawful surveillance with GSM tracking device places under a car on the basis of Article 3 of the Police Act). See furthermore, e.g., Supreme Court, 21 March 2000, ECLI:NL:HR:2000:AA5254, and Supreme Court, 13 November 2012, ECLI:NL:HR: 2012:BW9338.

powers such as systemic surveillance, infiltration, systemic gathering of information and the interception of communication. Some powers may only be exercised by senior police officers who have been designated as auxiliary to the public prosecutor (*hulpofficier van justitie*). An auxiliary is not a member of the prosecution service, nor vested with the powers of a public prosecutor. He may, however, use certain coercive measures, such as search and police custody.

2.6   INVESTIGATION POLICY

On the basis of Article 148(2) CCP (Dutch Code of Criminal Procedure) the Board of Prosecutors General[4] has issued general instructions for investigation of criminal acts (*Aanwijzing voor opsporing*). The most recent instruction entered in force on 1 January 2014 (no. 2013A020, *Staatscourant* 2013, 35757). This general instruction for investigation serves five objectives: (1) the correct use of available capacity (limited investigation capacity should be used in the right cases: the viability of the case should be determined as soon as possible i.a. depending on the seriousness of the case); (2) advancing equal treatment of similar cases; (3) providing for criteria to screen cases; (4) defining the lower threshold of what is expected from investigating authorities; and (5) accounting for the choices made with regard to criminal investigations.

On a general level, the criteria for prioritizing cases which must be investigated are (1) knowledge about the identity of the suspected person; (2) the relative seriousness of the crime; and (3) the impact on the victim. The instruction introduces four investigation frameworks for different kinds of criminality:

(1) The so-called "ready-made" cases where the suspect is caught red-handed or similar cases where the identity of the suspect is known to the complainant. As a rule, these cases should be dealt with, unless there are weighty reasons not to take on a case. These reasons can be based on the public interest more generally (disproportionate use of available capacity due to high occurrence of such cases) or on interests involved in the concrete case (for example because an intervention outside criminal law is deemed more effective in that case).

(2) For cases occurring on a large scale, such as shoplifting, bicycle theft, destruction, assault and defamation, but not being "ready-made", two criteria are guiding in determining the priority for investigation: the clues available for investigation and the chance to find evidence to proof the case. As a rule, cases that fall within the national or local security policy, where there are enough indications to base an investigation on and that have a high chance of proof should always be investigated.

---

[4]   The Board of Prosecutors General is the head of the Public Prosecution Service in the Netherlands. See chapter 5 for more information on this institution.

(3) The so-called high-impact crime, serious crime that has high impact on the specific victim and the feeling of insecurity among the population more generally. As a rule, such crime should always be investigated and the decision-making should always be coordinated with the public prosecution.

(4) The so-called 'undermining cases' (*ondermijningszaken*) that concern less visible criminality that has a highly disruptive impact on society more generally. Categories concern criminality related to weapons and drug production and trafficking, human trafficking and smuggling, the environment, money laundering, and large-scale fraud. In these cases, an integrated and coordinated approach is preferred, whereby the public prosecution is involved in the decision-making on the necessary intervention in a specific case. More concrete elements for prioritizing criminal intervention are, for example, the level of undermining the integrity of certain systems (such as the monetary system); the extent to which it is possible to confiscate illegal money; the extent to which a criminal investigation is necessary in order to use other possible interventions; the impact on the victim and society; and the extent to which the choice for a specific investigation would generate public debate.

2.7 PROSECUTORIAL POWERS

The police in the Netherlands has the power to dismiss a case without any further involvement of the criminal justice system. When an offence has been investigated and the investigation has been concluded, the police has various possibilities of action towards the offender. The police can caution the offender or give him an oral or written admonition. This may be a preferred option when dealing with juvenile offenders, first offenders or those committing either domestic violence or minor crimes. Furthermore, the police can mediate between the offender and the victim[5] by suggesting that the former compensate for the damage done or offer an apology, all of which may be an appropriate reaction in cases of bodily injury, damage to property or embezzlement.

In addition, the police can issue a so-called 'penal order' imposing a fine for misdemeanors (Article 257b(1) CCP). For crimes which carry a statutory term of imprisonment not exceeding six years and which are of a non-complex nature and have been committed by persons who have reached the age of eighteen years, the police can impose a 'penal order' imposing a fine of a maximum of 350 euro (Article 257b(2) CCP). The criminal offences for which the police can issue a penal order concern minor traffic offences and minor cases concerning theft and embezzlement.

---

[5] Article 51h (1) CCP determines that "The Public Prosecution Service shall see to it that the police inform the victim and the suspect of the option of mediation at the earliest possible stage."

2.8   RECRUITMENT AND APPOINTMENT

The selection criteria for joining the police force at the lower level – assistant police officer and police officer – are age (> 17 years), a driving license, Dutch nationality, the absence of a criminal record and a good physical condition. An initial police education (basic training) is provided. For the higher police ranks, post-initial education is provided through management courses (operational management, tactical management and strategic management) as well as specialist courses (technical and tactical detective, specialist, graduate detective or specialist). Part of the career development concept is to encourage police officers to take post-initial courses for the purpose of specialization or for the acquisition of management skills. The Netherlands Police Academy is the education and research institute of the police. The Academy provides the initial courses at Bachelor and Master level, as well as the post-initial courses.

The national chief of police is appointed for a period of six years (which can be prolonged by subsequent three years terms) by the Crown (Article 28 2012 Police Act). The regional mayor and the Board of Prosecutors General may advice on the appointment. The regional police chief is appointed by the Crown and the regional mayor. The chief prosecutor may advice on the appointment (Article 38 2012 Police Act).

2.9   SPECIAL INVESTIGATING UNITS OUTSIDE THE POLICE FORCE

In addition to the police services, there exist special criminal law enforcement agents and agencies vested with the right to monitor and investigate a restricted category of offences (Articles 141(d) and 142 Code of Criminal Procedure). According to Article 141 Code of Criminal Procedure special investigating officers, appointed by special acts or by the Minister of Justice and Security, can be charged with the investigation of specific criminal offences. These special investigating officers operate in areas covered by, for example, the Authority for Consumers and Markets, the Dutch Authority for Financial Markets, the Netherlands Gambling Authority, provinces, municipalities and Dutch water boards. Moreover, there are four special investigative agencies under the control of governmental departments (Article 2 Special Investigative Agencies Act):

(1) the Economic Control Agency and the Customs and Excise Investigative Office of the Inland Revenue Ministry (FIOD);
(2) the Social Information and Investigation Agency of the Ministry of Social Affairs and Employment;

(3) the Investigative Agency of the General Inspectorate of the Ministry of Agriculture, Nature and Food Quality;

(4) the Information and Investigation agency of the Ministry of Housing, Spatial Planning and the Environment.

These special agencies have investigative powers only for criminal offences related to matters of immediate concern to these Ministries. The Public Prosecution Service supervises the criminal investigations of these agencies.

B THE PUBLIC PROSECUTION SERVICE

2.10 INVESTIGATIVE AND PROSECUTORIAL POWERS

The main task of the Public Prosecution Service is to administer, by means of criminal law, the legal order. It is no exaggeration to say that the Dutch prosecution service has enormous powers, at least in dealing with criminal cases. It has a monopoly over prosecutions and employs the expediency principle in this connection. Article 167 CCP forms the legal basis for the principle of expediency by providing that the Public Prosecution Service can decide not to prosecute on grounds of public interest. It is common understanding that this power is interpreted, more positively, to imply that the prosecutor should prosecute a case if and when public interest so requires. Furthermore, the Public Prosecution Service makes use of its hierarchical structure to pursue a coordinated policy. In this way, the prosecution service is able to systematically determine what cases should be prosecuted and what sentences the courts should be asked to impose.

Since the introduction of the current Code of Criminal Procedure in 1926, the decision to initiate criminal proceedings has been reserved exclusively to the prosecution service. Approximately half of the crimes that reach the public prosecutor's office through the intermediary of the police are not brought to trial, but are disposed of by the prosecution service itself. Usually this involves a decision not to prosecute through a dismissal due to technicalities, or through a dismissal applying the expediency principle, or by a settlement out of court by means of a transaction or by issuing a penal order.

If the prosecution service decides to refer a matter to a criminal court, suspects in simple, less serious types of crimes will generally be summoned by the public prosecutor exclusively on the basis of the information obtained in the police investigation. In cases of a more complicated nature or a serious crime, the public prosecutor may apply to the investigating judge to exercise certain investigating powers. Complicated and serious crime cases are cases in which more intrusive investigative methods are required (such as searches, interception of communication by technical means et cetera). For the use of those intrusive methods, the police and public prosecutor need to seek permission of the investigating judge. Some methods can, as a rule, only be authorized by an investigating judge who has powers which the police and prosecutor lack. He may order a witness to appear before him and make a witness deposition or he may order a psychiatric examination of the suspect or initiate a bodily examination. When the preliminary investigation, conducted either by the police or by the examining judge, is completed, it is once again the public prosecutor who will decide whether or not to prosecute or to continue the prosecution.

In case the public prosecutor notifies the suspect that no charges will be brought (either conditionally or otherwise), the case is closed and cannot be prosecuted again, unless fresh incriminating evidence is subsequently discovered (Article 255 CCP). In case the public prosecutor decides to prosecute (i.e. if a notification of further prosecution or a summons is issued), the accused can file a written notice of objection against this summons with the district court within eight days after he has been served with the summons (Article 262 CCP). This objection procedure enables the suspect to challenge in a non-public setting (i.e. *in chambers*) what may be a rash or unjust prosecution, and thereby avoid the exposure of a public trial. Such a judicial review of the decision to prosecute is fairly marginal.

The grounds on which the prosecution may be dismissed are limited to four (Article 262(5) CCP):

- where the case is to be dismissed because the prosecutor no longer has the right to prosecute, e.g. due to the statute of limitations;
- where there is insufficient indication of guilt;
- where the act does not constitute a criminal offence; and
- where the accused is not criminally liable, e.g. due to self-defense.

In all other cases the district courts shall declare either the objection of the suspect inadmissible or the notice of objection ill-founded and indicate, if necessary, the amendments to the indictment that need to be made (Article 262(6) CCP). In the vast majority of cases, the notice of objection procedure results, after a brief investigation, in a decision by the judge *in chambers* that the case should go to trial after all.

2.11 SUPERVISION OVER THE POLICE

The prosecution service is ultimately responsible for all criminal investigations. Historically, the prosecution service did not perform its supervisory role over the police in an adequate manner. The police enjoyed too much autonomy in their investigative activities, in particular in the fight against organized crime. Since the adoption of statutory rules on investigative police methods in 2000 and the reorganization of the prosecution service, the services' supervisory role over the police has been improved. For the use of covert policing methods, prior consultation with the prosecution service or its explicit approval is mandatory.

2.12   ORGANIZATION OF THE PROSECUTION SERVICE

General Prosecution Service

The prosecution service is a nation-wide organization of prosecutors.[6] It is organized hierarchically. At the top is the Board of Prosecutors General. The service functions under the political responsibility of the Minister of Justice and Security, but is not an agency of the Ministry. The Minister of Justice and Security together with the Board of Prosecutors General determines the priorities in relation to criminal investigation and prosecution. The organization of the prosecution service is regulated by the 1827 *Wet op de Rechterlijke Organisatie* (Judicial Organization Act). In 1999, the prosecution service underwent a thorough reform in terms of its organizational structure, the line of command and the power of the Ministry of Justice and Security to give instructions in individual cases.

The prosecution service is organized on two levels, corresponding to the courts of first instance and the courts of appeal. There are ten prosecution services at the district court level (*arrondissementsparket*)[7] while at the appeals level, the prosecution service (*ressortparket)* has four locations.[8] The *arrondissementsparket* consists of prosecutors holding the rank of chief prosecutor, senior prosecutors, prosecutors, substitute prosecutors and prosecutors acting in single court sessions. The latter is vested with all powers of a prosecutor with one exception: he may only act as prosecutor in single judge court sessions. In these sessions, only simple criminal cases are tried. The single judge is vested only with the power to impose prison sentences of one year maximum.

The public prosecutors are supported by clerks of the prosecution service (*parketsecretaris)* who may hold a mandate to summon a suspect in simple cases. They assist the prosecutor in preparing prosecutorial decisions. As a rule, these clerks check the police files to see whether there is sufficient evidence for a prosecution, and draft the charge and wit of summons. Clerks of the prosecution service may hold a mandate to summon an arrested suspect prior to his release. The mandate is restricted to criminal cases to be tried in single judge court sessions. A mandate, under the law of the Netherlands, means that the public

---

6   For more information see also www.om.nl.

7   Amsterdam, The Hague, Limburg, Central Netherlands, North Holland, North Netherlands, East Brabant, East Netherlands, Rotterdam and Zeeland-West-Brabant.

8   Amsterdam, Arnhem-Leeuwarden, 's-Hertogenbosch and The Hague.

prosecutor remains at all times competent to withdraw the summons issued by his clerk.

At the level of the four courts of appeal, the prosecution service consists of the chief Advocates-General and the Advocates-General. Their main task is to deal with charges in appellate cases.

National public prosecution office

In addition to the ten district prosecution offices, there are two offices on national level which are not linked to any district or appeal court: the National Public Prosecutor's Office (*landelijk parket*) and the National Public Prosecutor's Office for serious fraud and environmental crime and asset confiscation (*functioneel parket*).

National Public Prosecutor's office

The public prosecutors of the national public prosecution office (*landelijk parket*) are vested with the same powers as the prosecutor at district court level. Their main task is to investigate and prosecute serious (organized) crimes – crimes which due to their seriousness or frequency constitute a serious threat to the legal order and nation-wide or international crimes (such as terrorism, human smuggling and trafficking, et cetera). The office supervises the National Police Services Agency (KLPD) for the fight against (inter)national organized crime and prosecutes cases investigated by this unit. Furthermore, the national prosecution office develops investigation and prosecution policies with regard to (international) organized crime. An operational task of the office is the coordination and handling of foreign requests for legal assistance. The structure of the national prosecution office is similar to the prosecution office at district court level.

Functional prosecution office

A separate office exists within the prosecution service for the prosecution of criminal offences investigated by the four special investigative agencies (see section 5.7) under the control of governmental departments such as fiscal, economic and fraud crimes, social security crimes, health crimes and environmental crimes. In this functional prosecution office, special expertise in these fields is concentrated, which is beneficial for a proper prosecution of these, generally speaking, rather complicated crimes.

Central processing unit

A substantive amount of relatively simple standard cases, such as drunk driving, driving without insurance and also minor traffic appeals are handled by the

Central Processing Unit (*CVOM*). The goals of this central processing are the enhancement of quality and maximization of the number of processed cases.

Service Center for the Public Prosecution Service

Products and services in the field of facilities and information management, finance and staffing are provided for by the service center for the public prosecution service (*DVOM*). This service center is a shared service provider which performs operational management tasks for the offices of public prosecution at district, appeal and national levels.

Office for Criminal Law Studies

The office for criminal law studies (*WBOM*) is responsible for legal documentation for the public prosecution office generally. Moreover, the office for criminal law studies conducts research or commissions external research.

National Police Internal Investigations Department

The national police internal investigations department (*Rijksrecherche*), a small, highly specialized investigation unit, is responsible for handling complaints about improper conduct of state officials and public servants. The department investigates, for example, allegations of fraud and corruption against the police, public prosecutors and municipal, provincial and central government officials. Moreover, the department investigates cases of use of firearms by police officers and death in detention.

The Board of Prosecutors General

There is no hierarchical relation between prosecution services of the courts of first instance or of the national prosecution office and the prosecution services of the courts of appeal. All are subordinated to the Board of Prosecutors General in The Hague. The Board directs the prosecution service as one organization.

The prosecution service is headed by a Board of three to five Prosecutors General (*College van procureurs-generaal*). The Crown appoints the chairman of the Board (Article 130 JOA). He can be re-appointed once for a second term of three years. The members of the Board (maximum five) are appointed by the Minister of Justice and Security for an indeterminate term. The Board has its office (*het parket generaal*) in The Hague. The Board of Prosecutors General may give instructions to the members of the prosecution service concerning their tasks and powers in relation to the administration of criminal justice and other statutory powers, e.g. supervision of the police. Such an instruction may be of a general policy nature or of specific nature. Prosecutors are legally bound by these instructions. The highest authority over investigations and prosecutions rests with the Board. The Board ultimately supervises the implementation of a proper prosecution policy by the prosecution service, and a proper investigation policy by the police. The Board meets on a regular basis with the Minister of Justice and Security. The Board of Prosecutors General is advised by a number of advisory bodies, consisting of public prosecutors and high-ranking police officers. One of these bodies is the serious crime committee, which functions as a policy making body concerning organized crime, and which filters recommendations about organized crime control. The advisory bodies initiate the issuing of national prosecution guidelines.

2.13 POLITICAL ACCOUNTABILITY

The prosecution service is not an independent body in the sense that the Minister of Justice and Security is politically accountable for the policy of the prosecution service and can be held accountable in Parliament for intervening or failing to intervene in this policy. He can be questioned by Parliament both on the prosecution policy at large and on individual prosecutorial decisions. This political accountability is one of the core elements of the Rule of Law (Rechtsstaat) in the Netherlands. The Minister of Justice and Security is hence involved in the formulation of the prosecution policy at large. There are regular contacts between the Minister and the Board of Prosecutors General in this respect. The Board of Prosecutors General is responsible for the proper realization of the prosecution policy, as agreed with the Minister of Justice and Security. The Board issues instructions in this respect. The Minister may be involved in the decision making in individual cases as well. He may be consulted by individual prosecutors in cases where the prosecutorial decision may have an impact on the general prosecution policy, or where his political accountability is at stake. The final responsibility rests with the Minister of Justice and Security.

Article 127 of the Judicial Organization Act (JOA) empowers the Minister of Justice and Security to issue general and special instructions on the exercise of the tasks and powers of the prosecution service. Those instructions are legally binding for the prosecution service as a whole as well as individual public prosecutors. This section underlines that the Minister is politically accountable for the policy of the prosecution service at large and for individual prosecutorial decisions. Before the Minister can issue an instruction concerning the investigation or the prosecution in an individual case, a special procedure is to be applied (Article 128 JOA).When the Minister of Justice and Security considers issuing an instruction in an individual case, the Board of Prosecutors General shall be given the opportunity to express its views concerning the instruction: it is sent to the Board, which gives its reasoned views. The instruction must be reasoned and issued in a written form. In very urgent cases, the instruction may be issued orally if it is issued in writing within one week. The instruction together with the considered instruction and the views of the Board shall be added to the case file unless this is contrary to state interest. In the latter case, a notification that an instruction has been issued is added to the case file. In this way, the court is informed that an instruction to prosecute the case or an instruction on what sentence to request has been given to the public prosecutor. The court will certainly consider this when giving its judgment.

The Minister of Justice and Security is not only empowered to instruct that an individual case is to be investigated and prosecuted, but can also issue an instruction that a case is not be investigated or prosecuted. In that case the Minister shall notify Parliament (both Chambers of the States-General) that such an instruction has been issued. His instruction together with the considered instruction and the views of the Board of Prosecutors General shall be sent to Parliament. This procedure ensures democratic control over the Minister's decision. Through this procedure, openness over the involvement of the Minister in prosecutorial decisions is guaranteed. This openness, however, is absent when the prosecution service agrees with the considered instruction and takes such a prosecutorial decision so that an instruction does not need to be issued. The reason of the legislator to adopt Article 128 JOA was that there shall be a restricted use of instructions in individual cases by the Minister. Until now, the Minister has not made use of this power.

2.14 RECRUITMENT AND DISMISSAL OF PUBLIC PROSECUTORS

The statutory requirements for becoming a public prosecutor are possession of Dutch nationality and a university law degree (Article 1c and 1d Legal Position of Judicial Civil Servants Act). Supplementary professional requirements are laid down in the Royal Decree concerning the Education of Judicial Civil Servants.

The training for a public prosecutor takes – depending on knowledge and experience – from eighteen months up to a maximum of four years. After an introductory period, the trainees follow an individualized training of theoretical education to improve professional skills, abilities and knowledge and practical experience through working experience both with the public prosecutor's office (at both district and appellate level), at a district court (as law clerk or substitute judge) or at an external organization such as the police or a law firm. An annual assessment is part of the training. Before an applicant is selected to follow the internship program, the National Selection Committee for the Judiciary will ask for written information about the applicant from referees, will interview the applicant and will take note of the results of a psychological test by the applicant. Public prosecutors are, dependent on their rank, appointed either by the Minister of Justice and Security or by the Crown. Substitute public prosecutors are appointed by the Minister and all other prosecutors are appointed by the

Crown by Royal Decree (Article 1a Legal Position of Judicial Civil Servants Act). Public prosecutors are appointed for an unlimited period. When they do not function well, they can be dismissed.

Since public prosecutors are civil servants, the grounds for dismissal are laid down in Article 98 of the General Rules for Civil Servants (a Royal Decree). The main grounds are:

a. the loss of a statutory prerequisite to become a public prosecutor;
b. a court decision that he is placed under legal restraint;
c. a prison sentence for a crime;
d. disability to exercise his tasks properly due to illness for more than two years;
e. disability to exercise his tasks properly due to other reasons;
f. retirement at the age of 70; and
g. providing irregular or restricted information which otherwise would not have led to an appointment as public prosecutor.

The dismissal can be both honorable and dishonorable. The grounds for dismissal under a, d, e, f are honorable.

2.15 SELF-PERCEPTION

The aim of the prosecution service is to bring those criminal cases to trial that the service cannot itself dispose of by applying its discretionary powers in conformity with the law and guidelines issued by the Board of Prosecutors General. The overall aim is to pursue a criminal policy in order to reduce the crime rate.

Individual members are expected to work objectively, to take well considered prosecutorial decisions and to present to the court both evidence against the suspect and evidence in his favor, and to request a sentence which is appropriate. Rather than being merely a crime fighter, a prosecutor in the Netherlands should take up a magisterial attitude similar to judges. The international standards and norms for prosecutors as well as the principles laid down in human rights instruments are considered by the service to work with their endeavors to promote an effective, fair, impartial and efficient prosecution of criminal offences.

2.16 THE OFFICE OF THE PROCURATOR-GENERAL AT THE SUPREME COURT

The office of the Procurator-General at the Supreme Court is not part of the prosecution service. It forms an independent office with special tasks and powers. The office consists of the Procurator-General and the Advocates-General. The Procurator-General and the Advocates-General at the Supreme Court are independent officials appointed for life with mandatory retirement at the age of seventy (Article 117 Dutch Constitution and Article 1a Position of Judicial Officials Act).

The main statutory tasks of the Procurator-General are:

– to prosecute members of Parliament, ministers and deputy ministers for criminal offences committed in the exercise of their function. No *ex officio* prosecution is allowed. An order to prosecute has to be given either by Royal Decree or by decision of the Lower House (Article 119 Dutch Constitution);
– to advise the Supreme Court in all cases before it, and to give his legal opinion on disputed legal questions;
– to appeal in cassation in the interest of the proper application of criminal law;
– to submit cases of malfunctioning judges to the Supreme Court (Article 111 JOA).

The tasks of advising the Supreme Court and of giving a legal opinion on disputed legal questions is primarily carried out by the Advocates-General. The Procurator-General is charged in particular with the supervision of the enforcement and implementation of statutory rules by the courts.

C   THE COURTS

2.17   ORGANIZATION OF THE COURT SYSTEM

The organization of the court system is regulated by the JOA, which was enacted in 1827. This statute underwent a major reform in 2002. At present, there is a total of approximately 2,200 (FTE) judges in the Netherlands, of whom around 450 deal with criminal cases. Approximately 65% of judges are female.[9]

Criminal offences are dealt with by the criminal sections of the courts on three levels. The first instance level are district courts (*rechtbanken*). There are eleven such courts in ten districts (*arrondissementen*).[10] The district courts differ in size, depending mainly on the number of inhabitants in their district. Most district courts have a so-called cantonal sector (chamber for cantonal cases or cantonal judge). The cantonal sectors process civil cases up to 25,000 euro, labor

---

9   www.rechtspraak.nl (Rechtspraak in cijfers). Most information below on the courts can also be found on this website.
10   Amsterdam, Noord-Holland, Midden-Nederland, Noord-Nederland, Oost-Nederland, Den Haag, Rotterdam, Limburg, Oost-Brabant, Zeeland-West-Brabant.

cases, rent and consumer cases, consumer credit cases and minor criminal cases such as traffic cases (speeding). The second level is the court of appeal (*gerechtshof*), of which there are four.[11]

The highest level is the Supreme Court (*Hoge Raad*) in The Hague. Unlike the other courts, the Supreme Court does not deal with the facts of a case, but reviews only the lawfulness of the judgments of lower courts and the manner of proceedings. In exceptional circumstances, the Supreme Court is the court of both first and last instance. Where members of Parliament, ministers and deputy ministers are to be tried for offences committed in the exercise of their functions, only the Supreme Court is competent to try these cases. Up until now, no such trial has ever taken place.

Not all judges are strictly professional judges. Legal scholars, lawyers and other persons holding a law degree and who possess knowledge of and experience in the criminal justice system may be appointed as substitute (part-time) judges (judges *at litem*). In such capacity, they participate on a more or less regular basis in the administration of criminal justice, for which they receive a small remuneration. Through their participation, the case load of professional judges is reduced and courts may also benefit from their specific expertise.

There is no jury system in the Netherlands. Criminal justice is administered by legally qualified career judges and public prosecutors. Thus, there is no participation by lay persons except in a single instance: the penitentiary division of the court of appeal in Arnhem, which hears penitentiary issues such as the refusal of early release, consists of three professional judges and two experts in behavioral sciences. Judges are independent and no administrative body has competence or authority to influence court decisions. No administrative body is empowered to issue guidelines or to formulate and enforce a criminal policy directed at the judiciary. In the criminal justice system in the Netherlands, penal order procedures by judges are unknown, as are guilty plea procedures or plea-bargaining procedures.

2.18   GENERAL COURT SERVICE

Infractions are tried by a single cantonal judge (*kantonrechter*) of the cantonal sector of a district court. These are often infractions for which either the police or the public prosecutor have offered a settlement out of court but which has not been accepted by the offender. The judge pronounces his sentence orally and immediately following the closure of the public trial.

Crimes are tried either by a full bench of three judges, or by a single judge of a district court. The more complex and serious cases for which the public prosecutor requests a sentence exceeding one year of imprisonment are dealt with

---

[11]   Amsterdam, Arnhem-Leeuwarden, Den Haag, 's-Hertogenbosch.

by a full bench. If the public prosecutor considers the case to be a comparatively minor one, he can prosecute before the police judge (*politierechter*): a single judge chamber of the district court. The police judge may not impose prison sentences exceeding twelve months. He is entitled to refer a case to the full bench of the criminal division if he is of the opinion that a full bench would be more appropriate. Furthermore, nearly all economic crimes and environmental crimes such as infringement of the Trading Hours Act or the Commodities Act are tried by a single judge (economic police court), and nearly all juvenile crimes are tried by a single judge of the juvenile court (*kinderrechter*), except in serious cases where a full bench specialist chamber deals with economic crimes and juvenile crimes.

The court of appeal sits in a three judge or one judge bench and reviews judgements issued by the district courts. The review may lead to an acquittal, a more severe sentence or a confirmation of the sentence. As a rule, the Supreme Court hears a case in last instance with a bench of five judges. It may hear a case with a bench of three judges as well, where the Supreme Court deems that the review of the case cannot result in cassation, or when no legal questions are at stake (Article 75 JOA).

As a result of the 2002 reorganization of the judicial system, integral management has been introduced within each of the courts. Each court has its own collegial council, chaired by the court's president. This council is charged with the general management and day-to-day running of the court. New members of the collegial council are appointed by Royal Decree and nominated by the Minister of Justice and Security. The Council for the Judiciary (*Raad voor de Rechtspraak*) drafts a shortlist after consultation with the collegial council. The collegial council further consists of the heads of the various sectors who may give directions as to how judges should go about their work. They allocate the case load for individual judges or court chambers. Furthermore, the director of operations is a member of the council. This ensures unity within the court management. Within this framework, the sector heads are charged with the day-to-day running of their sector. The collegial council decides on the number of sectors and allocates cases to those sectors. The collegial council may issue instructions and directions in order to improve the operation of the court. Tasks and powers of the collegial council are laid down in Articles 15–28 of the JOA.

The courts are accountable to the Council for the Judiciary with regard to how they utilize their resources. They are, however, not accountable to the Council for the way in which judicial decisions are adopted. In its turn, the Council reports to the Minister of Justice and Security for the way in which resources are utilized. This autonomy of the judicial system ensures that the Minister is less directly involved. As a result, he is politically responsible only for the functioning of the judicial system as a whole.

2.19   THE SUPREME COURT

The highest court in criminal matters is the Criminal Chamber of the Supreme Court. It is competent to review a decision (cassation) in cases where the law has been improperly applied, or the rules of due process and fairness of the procedure have been violated (Article 79 JOA). Both the defendant and the prosecution service have the right to appeal in cassation to the Supreme Court against all criminal judgments of lower courts against which no other remedy is open, or against which such remedy has been open. Since 2002 the ban on cassation against an acquittal has been overturned. Where the Supreme Court quashes the judgment due to an error of law, the case, as a rule, is remitted to the court whose judgment was quashed. In cases of a procedural error, the Supreme Court remits the case to another court. The court of remittance is bound by the decision of the Supreme Court.

The Supreme Court can also give a decision in cases in which the parties themselves have not submitted an appeal in cassation. This is possible when the Procurator-General at the Supreme Court *sua sponte* submits a case to the Supreme Court to decide a matter of principle. This so-called cassation in the interests of law *(cassatie in het belang van de wet)* is intended to ensure uniformity in the application of criminal law by the courts.

Furthermore, the Supreme Court can be seized upon the request of the procurator general or of a convicted person, that his case, in which a final judgment has already been rendered, be reviewed for the benefit of the person. Such review of a case is only possible if contradictory judgments in a case exist; if the European Court of Human Rights (ECtHR) has determined that there has been a violation in the proceedings leading up to the conviction; or new, previously unknown, facts in favor of the convicted person have emerged that cast serious doubt on the validity of the final judgment. This review is an extraordinary remedy against miscarriages of justice. The retrial is conducted by the court of appeal to which the case is referred (Articles 457–481 CCP).

Since 2013 the Supreme Court is also empowered to review a case to the disadvantage of the former suspect who has been acquitted or against whom charges have been dismissed. Such review can take place if it is necessary for the proper administration of justice and if there is (1) a new, previously unknown fact, which gives reason to believe that had this fact has been known during the hearing of the case it would have resulted in a conviction for an intentional crime that resulted in the death of another person; or (2) the first judgment is based on false material or (3) a witness has committed perjury or (4) the former suspect is guilty of corruption, use or threat of violence or extortion, and there is a strong believe that this information would have led to a conviction at the initial trial. The retrial is conducted by a district court that has not handled the case before (Article 482a–482i CCP).

Precedents

The Supreme Court can play a guiding role in the application of criminal law at large through its powers to give decisions of principle on criminal law issues. Although there is no statutory rule on precedents and although due to their status as independent courts, lower courts are not compelled to follow the views of the Supreme Court, they will generally do so, since the Supreme Court does not readily deviate from previous rulings.

2.20 COUNCIL FOR THE JUDICIARY

With the 2002 reorganization of the judicial system in the Netherlands a Council for the Judiciary was established at the national level, while courts throughout the country were made responsible for the management of their own organization on the basis of an integral management structure. The Council for the Judiciary is part of the judicial system but does not administer justice itself. It has assumed responsibility for a number of tasks of the Minister of Justice and Security. These tasks are operational in nature and include the allocation of budgets, supervision of financial management, personnel policy, ICT and accommodation. The Council supports the courts in executing their tasks in these areas. It was also given the task of promoting the quality of the judicial system, while it also acts as a spokesperson for the judiciary in public and political debates.

The Council has a pivotal role in terms of preparing, implementing and accounting for the judicial system's budget. The budget system is based on a workload measurement system maintained by the Council. The Council encourages and supervises the development of operational procedures in the day-to-day running of the courts. The specific tasks in question are personnel policy, accommodation, ICT and external affairs. The Council has a range of formal statutory powers that enable it to carry out these tasks. For instance, the Council is empowered to issue binding general instructions with regard to operational policy, although it prefers to exercise this power as little as possible.

The Council is responsible for the recruitment, selection and training of judicial and court officials. It carries out its tasks in these areas in close consultation with the court councils. The Council has a significant say in appointing members to the court council. The Council's task relating to the quality of the judiciary system involves promoting the uniform application of the law and enhancing judicial quality. In view of the overlap with the content of judicial rulings, the Council has no powers of compulsion in this area. The Council also has a general advisory role. It advises the Government on new laws that have implications for the judicial system. This process takes place in ongoing consultation with the members of the court councils.

Although the Council has formal powers at its disposal, the relationship between the Council and the courts should not be seen as hierarchical. The Council sets itself the primary goal of supporting the courts in their tasks. In order to ensure that the various tasks are carried out properly, the Council consults regularly with court presidents, directors of operations, sector heads and the Board of Representatives (an advisory body made up of representatives from the courts). The organization of the Council for the Judiciary is laid down in Articles 84–90 of the JOA, and the tasks and powers of the Council are laid down in Articles 91–104a JOA.

2.21 RECRUITMENT

The main prerequisite to being eligible for training to become a judge is a law degree and relevant legal work experience outside the judiciary. There are two trainings for magistrates: an elaborate training for candidates with a minimum two years and a maximum of six years of legal relevant work experience and a restricted training for candidates with a minimum of six years working experience. The candidates must pass a psychological examination, as well as interviews with the National Selection Committee for the Judiciary, which consists of legal and non-legal professionals. The psychological test is an analytical/cognitive one, testing individual intelligence; whereas the interviews with members of the selection committee test communicative skills and the ability to make and motivate sound decisions.

Candidates who are selected are appointed by the Minister of Justice and Security as trainee at one of the eleven district courts. An elaborate training takes four years, while the restricted training takes from fifteen months up to a maximum of three years, depending on working experience. The training is a mix of theory and practice. The theory consists of courses provided by the magistrate's academy, the so-called study center for the administration of justice in Utrecht (*Stichting Studiecentrum Rechtspleging (SSR)*).

The training consists of a preliminary phase (three months) and a main phase (maximum of three years and nine months). The nature of the preliminary phase is introductory: the trainee judges get acquainted with the court and other trainees and formulate their study goals. During the main phase, the focus is on working and learning at the court within particular legal areas (usually three) or themes. This phase includes at least three internships: a society-oriented internship, an internship at an appellate institution and a short internship at an international institute or abroad. Criminal law trainees are required to intern at the Public Prosecutor Service.

The promotion of judges to higher positions such as vice-president of the court or appellate judge is mainly based on work experience and outstanding legal and managerial skills. The same is also true for promotion within the prosecution service. There are no criteria for promotion laid down by law. Judges are appointed for life, until their retirement at the age of seventy. Life tenure is seen as a means to support their independency.

D   THE PROBATION SERVICE

2.22   ORGANIZATION OF THE PROBATION SERVICE

The Dutch Association for the Moral Improvement of Prisoners was established in 1823 as a private initiative, since which time the Dutch probation system has been extended by a number of (sometimes religious) associations, all of which have focused on the three main tasks of the probation service: cell visits, the provision of social enquiry reports, and the provision of aftercare. In the past decades, reorganizations of the probation service (*reclassering*) have taken place in order to increase their efficiency in spite of regular budget cuts.

The present probation services cooperate in the Foundation for Probation Services in the Netherlands (*Stichting Reclassering Nederland*)[12] established in 1994, which divides the budget for probation activities between the three probation agencies: the probation department of the Salvation Army (in particular dealing with homeless people and juveniles in multi-problem situations)[13], the probation department of the Mental Health Care Organization (*GGZ Nederland*) (dealing with alcohol and drug addicted clients)[14] and the National Probation Service (*Reclassering Nederland*).[15] A reorganization in 2012 incorporated the ten regional offices into five. Nowadays each of the five regional offices is run by a regional director and supervised by a national directorate in Utrecht. In the regions, the professionals (1,928 in total in 2016) work within different specialized units, focusing on *inter alia* supervision, writing advisory reports, community service execution and providing behavioral trainings. The Foundation is governed by the 1995 Probation Rules (*Reclasseringsregeling 1995*). The Foundation's responsibility is to ensure that in each of the court districts the statutory probation activities are performed by professional probation officers that possess an (academic) education in social work.

Main functions

The main functions of the probation service are laid down in Articles 8–12 of the 1995 Probation Rules:

---

[12]   www.reclassering.nl.
[13]   www.legerdesheils.nl/reclassering.
[14]   www.fivoor.nl.
[15]   www.reclassering.nl.

- providing early support, consisting of provisional social enquiry reports on the offender to the police, the prosecution service and the judge in case the person in question has been arrested by the police and pre-trial detention is considered;
- providing social enquiry reports at the request of the criminal justice agencies, of the offender or on the initiative of the probation service in order to enable the agencies to make decisions;
- providing assistance and supervision for suspects or convicted persons;
- assisting someone with a suspended sentence or a conditional pardon to comply with the conditions imposed and to report to the judicial authorities on this compliance. The probation officer can, in case of failure to comply, propose to revoke the suspension of the sentence or the conditional pardon;
- providing probation activities during aftercare;
- preparing and implementing community service and alternatives to imprisonment, such as electronic surveillance. This includes supervision of the compliance with the imposed community services and providing information to the competent authorities on this compliance.

The probation service no longer offers probation activities in penitentiary establishments.

Role of volunteers

There are two kinds of volunteers assisting in probation activities:

- individual volunteers who, at the request of the probation foundation, cooperate in carrying out the statutory probation tasks; and,
- organizations of volunteers who initiate and develop projects which are closely related to the statutory probation activities.

E SENTENCE ENFORCEMENT AGENCIES

National Agency of Correctional Institutions

The enforcement of custodial sentences is a statutory task of the prosecution service (Article 553 CCP) but is actually carried out by the National Agency of Correctional Institutions of the Ministry of Justice and Security (*Dienst Justitiële Inrichtingen*).[16] It is the Agency's task to ensure the safe, efficient and humane enforcement of custodial sentences and measures. The Strategic prison policy is developed by the Minister of Justice and Security, who is politically accountable

---

[16] www.dji.nl.

for the development of a prison policy. The National Agency of Correctional Institutions translates this strategic prison policy into an operational one. The policy is implemented by the prison governor and his assistants. The distinction between policy making and policy implementation enables prison management teams to make their own decisions in personnel, financial and material matters, as each of the penitentiary establishments is required to manage its own budget.

Central Fine Collection Agency

The enforcement of fines is carried out by the Central Fine Collection Agency (*Centraal Justitieel Incassobureau*)[17] under the supervision of the prosecution service. The agency collects fines for traffic violations and fines imposed by the courts. It furthermore implements the penal orders or transactions by the police or the prosecution service.

Crime should not pay. Therefore, the public prosecutor may request the court to confiscate the proceeds from crime. The prosecution service has a special office in Leeuwarden – the proceeds of crime office – to advise public prosecutors in these matters. In case the court decides to confiscate the proceeds of a crime, recovery is carried out by the Central Fine Collection Agency.

F   THE DEFENSE

2.23   INTRODUCTION

Although the defense lawyer is not an officer of the court, defense is considered vital for the proper administration of criminal justice in so far as the crime charged is a serious one. For the defendant, defense counsel is of crucial importance. One of the main tasks of the defense counsel is to legally support his client during the pre-trial, trial and appeal stages and to ensure that his client receives a fair trial. The defense lawyer is his client's counsel and the relation is based on trust. The aim of the defense is to provide his client with the best chance of realizing his legal rights as one of the parties in the proceedings. The defense cannot be obliged to actively cooperate in the investigation of the case, nor to provide the court with information on the case unless this is in the interest of his client. A code of conduct exists for defense lawyers.[18] As a rule, the defense lawyer will represent the points of view of his client. He shall perform his task independently and shall not act in a way as to jeopardize his freedom and independence in the exercise of his profession.

---

[17]   www.cjib.nl.

[18]   http://regelgeving.advocatenorde.nl.

2.24 THE BAR

Assistance in criminal matters and legal aid is provided by lawyers registered with a district court. A university degree in law and further professional training is required in order to register. Early 2017, the number of registered lawyers in the Netherlands was more than 17,000, with a slight female minority. There are more than 5,000 law firms, the majority of which are small (< 20 lawyers). Relatively few lawyers specialize solely in defense work.[19] All registered lawyers must be members of the Dutch Bar Association (*De Nederlandse Orde van Advocaten, NOvA*).[20] The General Board of the Association, under the presidency of the Dean, is elected by the members of the Assembly of Deputies, who are elected by the regional bar associations. The General Board and the local bar associations promote the ethical practice of law by registered lawyers, and may take disciplinary measures in this respect.

All registered lawyers are subject to disciplinary law regulations issued by the Association. Disciplinary jurisdiction is exercised by Disciplinary Councils in first instance, and by the Court of Discipline in appellate cases. Disciplinary sanctions may be imposed for a registered lawyer's acts and failures that are in conflict with the proper care lawyers have to provide to those whose interests have to be served, as well as for acts and failures that are unbecoming of a professional in a situation of trust etc.

Admission to the profession, the powers and duties of registered lawyers, the organization of the Bar and disciplinary law are regulated in the 1952 Bar Act (*Advocatenwet*). Strictly speaking, defense counsels are not bodies under public law, or even an official part of the criminal justice system. Institutions such as public defenders are unknown in the Netherlands. All lawyers are independent in the pursuance of their profession.

2.25 LEGAL AID

Under the Code of Criminal Procedure, a defendant is at all times entitled to choose one or more defense counsels. In principle, the defendant has to pay for any defense counsel chosen in this way. The rules on legal aid are contained in the 1993 Legal Aid Act (*Wet op de Rechtsbijstand*). Legal aid is provided in cases where the suspect has been arrested for a crime where detention on remand is possible. Once a suspect has been detained in police custody, he is awarded legal assistance by the counsel on duty. Whenever a suspect has been invited to the police station for interrogation or the crime does not fit the category of crimes for which pre-trial detention can be issued, there is no right to free legal assistance.

---

[19]   *Jaarverslag NOvA 2017* at www.advocatenorde.nl.
[20]   https://www.advocatenorde.nl.

2.26 QUALIFICATIONS OF DEFENSE LAWYERS

The qualifications of defense lawyers are the same for all defense lawyers regardless whether they are state paid or privately paid lawyers. They must be in possession of a law degree and must have completed a further three years of professional training. After completing a master's degree at a university law faculty, prospective lawyers can apply to a law firm for employment as a trainee lawyer. The term of a traineeship is three years, during which the trainee may act as a lawyer under the direction of an experienced lawyer, his mentor, in order to improve knowledge, acquire the necessary skills and experience. At the beginning of the traineeship one is sworn in by the district court as a lawyer so that one has the right to pursue litigations in civil law suits or to serve as defense lawyer in criminal cases. The implementation of the training program is entrusted to the implementation organization consisting of the Center for Post Academic Legal Education (*Centrum voor Postacademisch Juridisch Onderwijs*) en Dialogue (*Advice, Coaching, Mediation and Training Bureau*). NOvA has established the Foundation Professional Training for Lawyers (*Stichting Beroepsopleiding Advocaten*) which evaluates the quality and the implementation of the professional training for lawyers.

The professional training for lawyers is split in three possible tracks: civil law, administrative law and criminal law. The trainee lawyer chooses a track that fits her or his preference best. That track is called a major. In addition, a minor in one of the other two legal areas is to be chosen and trainees have the possibility to choose between several subjects. Most subjects are finally concluded with an examination. During the traineeship, a Continued Education Program for Trainees is to be followed. This Program encompasses a number of courses which deepen legal and practical knowledge. Courses are offered on various subjects such as bankruptcy law, European law and environmental law. There are furthermore, a number of other educational requirements, such as participation in plea competitions and attendance of lectures. Such courses usually represent several educational points. According to the Regulation on Legal Profession (*Verordening op de Advocatuur*) a lawyer has to collect at least twenty educational points (of which at least ten have to be in relation to the chosen major track (criminal law, administrative law and private law)).

3. CRIMINAL POLICY AND CRIMINAL JUSTICE STATISTICS

Piet Hein van Kempen[*]

The Dutch criminal justice system has long been known for its mildness. In support of this view, reference is usually made to its tolerant criminal policies towards societal and morally controversial criminal offences like drugs or euthanasia, and to the low prison rate in the Netherlands compared to other European countries. This chapter deals with these and other characteristics as well as with relevant statistics in order to find out whether the Netherlands still has a relatively mild criminal climate. Since both criminal policy and criminal justice statistics are at least partly dependent on the demographic situation of the Netherlands, that situation deserves attention first.

3.1 DEMOGRAPHIC INFORMATION[1]

Being a geographically low-lying country, most of the Netherlands exists of low and flat lands, with only some minor hills in the east and south. About one fifth of its area and of its population are located below sea level. That also applies to the three biggest cities of the Netherlands: Amsterdam (which is the capital, and has a population of 0.86 million inhabitants), Rotterdam (which has one of the largest ports in the world, and has a population of approximately 0.64 million inhabitants), and The Hague (which is the seat of the Dutch government, the national parliament, the Supreme Court of the Netherlands, the Council of State, and the National Ombudsman; it is also the residential city of the Dutch Royal House, and has a population of approximately 0.53 million inhabitants).

---

[*]   P.H.P.H.M.C. van Kempen (Ph.D.) is full professor of Criminal law and Criminal Procedure at Radboud University Nijmegen and Dean of the Faculty of Law. He is also justice *at litem* at the court of appeal of 's-Hertogenbosch and Secretary General of the International Penal and Penitentiary Foundation (IPPF).

[1]   This paragraph is partly an update of Aya Gruber, Vicente de Palacios & Piet Hein van Kempen, *Practical Global Criminal Procedure: the United States, Argentina, and the Netherlands*, Durham, North Carolina: Carolina Academic Press 2012, pp. 9–12.

With a total population of over 17 million (2018)[2], the Netherlands belongs to the most densely populated countries in the world.[3] The Netherlands has an average of around 505 inhabitants per square kilometer land. In the western part of the Netherlands, an area called the Randstad, the population density is more than twice as high. Relative to the statistics presented below, it merits attention that the population of the Netherlands was approximately 14.1 million in 1980, 16.3 million in 2005, and 16.6 in 2010.

The Gross Domestic Product of the Netherlands in 2017, according to the IMF, was 832 billion dollars. With that it has the 18th largest economy in the world. The Netherlands ranks 12th in GDP nominal per capita in 2017. According to figures from the European statistics office Eurostat, 13.2% of the Dutch live below the official poverty line. With this score the Netherlands belongs to the six countries within the European Union with the lowest such percentage (the other countries are: Denmark, Slovakia, Finland, Norway, Czech Republic).[4] A similar percentage is established by the CIA World Factbook (8.8% in 2015).

The Netherlands is a multicultural society and has a racially and ethnically diverse population, but less so than for example the United States of America. According to figures of CBS Statistics Netherlands, the Netherlands has almost 3.8 million immigrants, which is 22.6% of the population (2017). Slightly less than half of them (43,7%) are western immigrants, the others (56.3%) being non-western immigrants (individuals are regarded as immigrants if at least one parent is born in a foreign country). According to an estimate of CBS Statistics Netherlands, 78,3% of the population is Dutch, 2.2% German, 2,2% Indonesian, 2.3% Turkish, 2,1% Surinamese, 2,3% Moroccan, 0.9% Netherlands Antilles & Aruba, and 9,7% from other states (2015). Approximately 53% of the population regards itself to belong to a religion or religious group. Approximately 25% of them are Catholics, around 16% Protestants and 5% Islamic, which means that the Netherlands has almost 842,000 Muslims. Some 6% consider themselves to belong to another religious denomination or religious group, including Jewish (0.1%), Hindu (0.6%) and Buddhist (0.4%) (all figures by the CBS Statistics Netherlands for 2014).

Approximately 4.1% of the working population (8.7 million, between 15 and 75 years) is unemployed according to CBS Statistics (end of 2017). More than 161,000 people have been unemployed for longer than twelve months.

---

[2]   See the Population counter at: https://www.cbs.nl/en-gb/visualisaties/population-counter.

[3]   It holds position 16 on the Wikipedia List of countries and dependencies by population density (1 May 2019).

[4]   http://appsso.eurostat.ec.europa.eu.

3.2 PENAL POLICY AND STATISTICS

In the 1970s and early 1980s the criminal justice system of the Netherlands belonged to the most liberal and mild ones in the world. Sentences and prison rates were quite low. For example, hardly anyone was ever convicted to life imprisonment, and the prison rate in the seventies was around 20 per 100,000 of the national population (23 in 1980). The qualification as a liberal and mild system is deserved, even if one takes into consideration that the low prison rate in the 1970s and the early 1980s was to some extend cosmetic, because in practice there was a considerable difference between actual prison capacity and the need for capacity, giving rise to 'waiting lists'. From the mid-1970s, the backlog in execution of prison sentences and thus of the waiting lists was increasing. The prison department of the Ministry of Justice and Security had failed to anticipate the mismatch between the actual capacity of the prison system and the need for capacity. Only at the beginning of the 1980s a wide scale extension of prison capacity was initiated. Still, both criminal procedure and the prison system were very much directed at the protection of suspects and the rehabilitation of inmates.

Quite a bit has changed, as the data below illustrate. Repression and retribution have become more important than before. Particularly since 1990 the prison population numbers have increased. Especially numbers related to prison sentences and pre-trial detention have grown almost constantly up till 2005 in the Netherlands. The total number of people that are in Dutch prisons on the basis of a criminal law decision increased from 6,890 in 1990 to 15,206 in 2005. Since then, the number has been decreasing to 11,736 in 2010 and has been slightly further decreasing since to 8,806 in 2016. It slightly increased to 9,138 in 2017, according to statistics of the WODC Research and Documentation Center and CBS Statistics Netherlands (WODC & CBS Statistics Netherlands).[5] Only around 5.4 percent of detained persons are women (2017).[6]

Before going deeper into these statistics, it deserves to be noted that as a result of different definitions and calculation methods, the prison rates and detention rates may vary considerably between different sources. For example, statistics of WODC & CBS Statistics Netherlands imply a prison rate of 52 for 2016 (and 54 for 2017)[7], the Council of Europe's SPACE I finds a higher rate for the Netherlands of 51 in 2016[8], and the World Prison Brief mentions a prison rate for the Netherlands of 59 for 2016 (and 61 for September 2018). The problem

---

5   See *Criminaliteit en rechtshandhaving 2017. Ontwikkelingen en samenhangen*, WODC, CBS & Raad voor de Rechtspraak, The Hague, 2018, chapter 7; see also the tables at: https://www.cbs. nl/nl-nl/publicatie/2018/42/criminaliteit-en-rechtshandhaving-2017.

6   See also Peter J.P. Tak, 'Women in prison in the Netherlands', in: P.H.P.H.M.C. van Kempen & M.J.M. Krabbe (eds.), *Women in Prison. The Bangkok Rules and Beyond*, Cambridge/ Antwerp/Portland: Intersentia 2017, pp. 541–564.

7   The numbers are 8,806 prisoners on a population of 16.9 million in 2016 (and 9,138 on 17 million in 2017).

8   The numbers are 8,726 prisoners on a population of 16.9 million in 2016.

of varying numbers applies even more to detention rates, which in principle refer to persons who, in connection with an alleged offence or offences, are deprived of their liberty following a judicial or other legal process but have not been definitively sentenced by a court for the offence(s).[9] For 2015 the number of pre-trial and trial detainees is 3,874 (on the aforementioned total of more than 9,100), and was 6,194 in 2005, 5,623 in 2010 and also 3.874 in 2015, according to WODC & CBS Statistics Netherlands.

This increase in prison numbers since the 1970s and early 1980s has been mainly due to the rise of crime and the handing down of more severe sentences. The average prison sentence imposed has become much longer. In 1985, almost 16,000 (partly) unsuspended prison sentences were imposed, while in 2005 there were over 31,000 such sentences and in 2015 this was 23,158. There is furthermore a decrease of sentences up to a year from 2005 to 2017, and an increase of sentences of 12 years and over in that same period: 292 such sentences for 2005, against 364 in 2017. The proportion of custodial sentences in case of guilty verdicts was in 2017 almost the same as about ten years before: around 35% of the sentences are custodial sentences.[10] However, as such the number of custodial sentences including youth detention is dropping: 37,000 in 2017, which is 14% lower than in 2007 and only slightly higher than in 2016.[11] Still, the custodial sentence is the most imposed sentence in 2017, followed by community service. The number of community service orders fell by 26% compared to 2007 to 32,000 in 2017.[12]

Moreover, since the nineties there has been a huge increase in the number of cases in which defendants are sentenced to life imprisonment, with a high in 2005 (5 sentences to life imprisonment). In 2017 around 40 people in the Netherlands served a life sentence. The penalty was introduced in 1870 to replace the death penalty that was abolished that year. Recently, after criticism of European Court of Human Rights (ECtHR), a new policy considering life sentences was introduced. Since 2017 every prisoner sentenced for life is entitled to a reassessment of this penalty after 27 years. If the sentence no longer serves a legitimate aim, the prisoner is pardoned.[13]

In their report of 2017 WODC & CBS Statistics Netherlands conclude that the decline in the number of detainees and prisoners in the Netherlands in the period from 2007 to 2017 (rate from 78 to 52) does not occur – or at least to a lesser extent – in other countries. The decline has brought the Netherlands even

---

[9] This definition is reproduced from Walmsley, *World Pre-trial/Remand Imprisonment List (second edition)*, 2014, p. 1.

[10] See *Criminaliteit en rechtshandhaving 2015. Ontwikkelingen en samenhangen*, WODC, CBS & Raad voor de Rechtspraak, The Hague, 2016, p. 39, and *Criminaliteit en rechtshandhaving 2017. Ontwikkelingen en samenhangen*, WODC, CBS & Raad voor de Rechtspraak, The Hague, 2018, p. 63.

[11] *Criminaliteit en rechtshandhaving 2017. Ontwikkelingen en samenhangen*, WODC, CBS & Raad voor de Rechtspraak, The Hague, 2018, p. 63.

[12] Idem.

[13] https://www.rechtspraak.nl.

below the level of its neighboring countries. Since 2015 the number of detainees per 100,000 persons is the lowest of all European countries. Only in Denmark, Finland, the Netherlands and Sweden the number is 60 or below.

Table 3.1. Characteristics of criminal detainees and prisoners (counted on 30 September of each year) (source: WODC & CBS Statistics Netherlands, 2017)

Year	2005	2010	2011	2012	2013	2014	2015	2016	2017
Total	15,206	11,736	11,545	11,160	10,544	9,909	8,976	8,806	9,138
Sex									
Male	14,338	11,002	10,882	10,562	9,983	9,349	8,487	8,329	8,642
Female	868	734	663	598	561	560	489	477	496
Age									
18–19	555	479	451	412	316	216	158	143	143
20–22	1,589	1,299	1,282	1,174	1,038	895	681	592	632
23–29	3,660	2,875	2,817	2,818	2,650	2,534	2,214	2,162	2,133
30–39	5,108	3,318	3,234	3,128	2,968	2,803	2,601	2,595	2,810
40–49	3,121	2,563	2,536	2,428	2,302	2,170	1,990	1,988	2,033
50 and over	1,173	1,190	1,225	1,193	1,269	1,291	1,332	1,326	1,386
unknown	0	12	11	7	1	0	0	0	1
Important categories of offences									
Property crimes without violence	–	2,104	2,107	2,029	1,966	1,904	1,850	1,762	1,907
Property crimes with violence	–	1,861	1,999	1,966	1,771	1,550	1,230	1,183	1,124
Violence (excl. sex offences)	–	2,809	2,770	2,755	2,537	2,335	2,219	2,147	2,147
Sex offences	–	430	431	442	379	393	364	393	376
Vandalism and public order offenses	–	441	394	416	332	328	342	367	389
Traffic offences	–	340	324	339	422	408	169	120	124
Drug crimes	–	2,107	1,855	1,666	1,600	1,397	1,362	1,311	1,404
Weapon crimes	–	117	89	92	79	108	97	108	104
Title of detention									
Pre-trial detention	6,194	5,623	5,643	5,453	4,911	4,251	3,874	3,840	3,874
Prison sentence	6,910	4,206	4,039	3,969	3,879	3,994	3,739	3,552	3,718
ISD measure for persistent offenders	327	492	500	478	409	393	451	555	611

Year	2005	2010	2011	2012	2013	2014	2015	2016	2017
Total	15,206	11,736	11,545	11,160	10,544	9,909	8,976	8,806	9,138
Detention (as a penalty)	160	134	152	104	87	89	55	45	63
Substitute detention for task penalty	602	435	342	333	362	297	325	327	320
Substitute detention for fine	310	183	201	178	141	109	88	83	85
Committal for non-paid traffic fines	56	185	188	223	310	279	66	18	1
Committal for non-paid damages	137	147	154	171	186	164	131	117	119
Committal for confiscation of illegally obtained profits	21	48	61	43	24	25	18	25	22
Committal for violating penal order						95	22	5	1
Entrustment order	245	32	17	20	11	37	16	12	20
Psychiatric hospital order	29	31	19	20	23	25	14	18	15
Detention for extradition etc.	49	80	80	65	77	68	60	54	76
Miscellaneous	166	140	149	103	124	83	117	155	213
Duration	8,309	5,450	5,234	5,062	4,878	4,882	4,658	4,671	4,890
Less than 1 month	884	591	580	500	511	549	456	529	491
1 to 3 months	1,017	575	486	449	480	460	480	466	544
3 to 6 months	885	399	427	380	388	407	371	372	419
6 months to 1 year	971	790	709	679	591	612	537	522	574
1 to 2 years	1,027	678	616	621	522	535	493	476	457
2 to 3 years	1,019	871	831	783	698	695	710	758	859
3 to 4 years	593	300	330	339	305	287	264	257	299
4 to 6 years	775	352	362	393	444	412	400	396	412
6 to 8 years	425	260	239	261	265	236	249	244	213
8 to 12 years	411	288	275	290	300	307	296	282	258
12 years or over	292	294	310	318	340	348	362	369	364
Unknown	10	52	69	49	34	34	40	0	0

Between 1980 and 2005, the total prison capacity increased from almost 3,300 cells to more than eighteen thousand prison places, and even to over twenty-one thousand in 2008. In the early 1990s, the policy had been to extend the total prison capacity by building new prisons. In recent years, the extension of prison capacity has been reached by abolishing the rule of one cell per prisoner. Prison cells have been adapted to accommodate two prisoners, and in recently constructed prisons multi-person cells have been established. The core of the present criminal policy remains to slow down the pressure on the prison capacity by extending the options for the judiciary to impose non-custodial sentences. Since 2008 the government has been decreasing the capacity: from 21,640 places in 2008 to 18,759 places in 2012.[14]

The stereotype of the Netherlands as a country with exceedingly mild penal policies has become – like most stereotypes – greatly oversimplified. Nonetheless, in comparison to many European countries, and the United States, the Dutch penal policy is clearly still less centerd on incarceration. Penal policies since the 1980s have been characterized by a strong tendency to reduce the use of short-term imprisonment and to increase the use of non-custodial sanctions. During the same period, in which prison sentences became longer and the number of prison cells rose sharply, the use of short-term imprisonment fell. Fines became the preferred sanction, prosecutorial diversion (such as out of court settlement or suspended prosecution) grew rapidly, community sentences came into use, and new non-custodial sentences were developed.

3.3 CRIME STATISTICS AND LAW ENFORCEMENT POLICY

In the Netherlands, as in many countries, incarceration rates (see above) and crime rates are not fully in line with each other. For example, between 1990 and 2017 the prison population rose with 33% (from 6,890 to 9,138 detainees and prisoners), while recorded crime in that same period decreased with 13% (from 1.15 million to less than 1 million crimes); the drop of crime since 2005 (when crime came to a high: 1.35 million crimes) is even higher: 38% in twelve years. This is mainly due to the fall of property crimes: from 792,350 in 2005 to 502,840 in 2017 (which is a decrease of around 37%). In addition, violent and sexual crimes have been decreasing, from 2005 (122,470) to 2015 (85.120). See further Table 4.2 below.

In their report of 2017, WODC & CBS Statistics Netherlands conclude that the Netherlands joins the downward trend in recorded crime in Northern and Western European countries in the period 2002–2011.[15] They find that

---

14 Ministry of Justice and Security, *Masterplan DJI 2013–2018*, 22 March 2013, p. 11.
15 See *Criminaliteit en rechtshandhaving 2017. Ontwikkelingen en samenhangen*, WODC, CBS & Raad voor de Rechtspraak, The Hague, 2018, p. 103.

the proportion of underage suspects is high in comparison to many European countries. Another interesting finding in the report is that, due to the frequent use of transactions and penalty decisions by the police and the Public Prosecution, the Netherlands has relatively few suspects who are convicted in court. However, the chance of imprisonment in case one is convicted by a court is relatively high compared to other countries.

The Netherlands have a low average police presence when compared with American and European countries. In 2011, the Netherlands had 38,300 FTE police officers or a rate of 230 police personnel per 100,000 inhabitants according to the *European Source Book* (5th edition), while the Police Annual Report 2014[16] establishes a number of 51,442 FTE police offers (excluding civilians) for that same year, which entails a rate of 304. The Police Annual Report of 2017 establishes a number of 60,920 FTE police officers[17], which entails a rate of 357. Since 2010 the number of police personnel has slightly increased. In 1970, 40% of all registered crimes were solved by the police. In absolute figures the number of cases resolved grew until 1984, but in later years the average clearance rate has dropped to around 14.3% in 2000. After that the clearance rate has grown. Since 2005 it has been fluctuating around 26%. With 27% the percentage of solved cases was in 2017 a bit better than in the two previous years. In 2015 some 25.4% of the crimes were solved and in 2016 25.6%.[18]

A remarkable feature of present-day criminal law enforcement in the Netherlands is that only a small percentage of all crimes that are registered by the police are actually processed through the system. This happens for less than 25% of all registered crimes. Only a little over 10% of all these crimes go through the courts, which is less than half of the crimes that are processed. Whereas there were 830,780 registered crimes (and 245,010 registered suspects) in 2017, that year the police transacted about 19,000 crimes, while the prosecution rendered a prosecutorial decision for some 173,500 crimes: for over 49,000 crimes a (conditional) non-prosecution decision; a transaction for 8,800 crimes; a penal order for 31,700 crimes, while 8,700 crimes where finalized in yet a different way. About 97,000 crimes were brought to court through a writ of summons. That year the courts rendered a final judgment in 93,000 cases, 89% of which entailed a guilty verdict. For a long time, the number of cases tried by criminal courts had substantially increased. In 2007 this reached a high of 131,000 but has been decreasing since then to 95,000 in 2016 and the just mentioned number of 93,000 in 2017. Of all tried persons in 2015, 86% was male, 13% female and 1% a legal person (companies etc.).[19]

---

[16]   Jaarverslag Politie 2014.
[17]   Jaarverslag Politie 2017.
[18]   See *Criminaliteit en rechtshandhaving 2017. Ontwikkelingen en samenhangen*, WODC, CBS & Raad voor de Rechtspraak, The Hague, 2018, p. 51.
[19]   See idem, p. 64.

Table 3.2. Recorded crimes and suspects, inflows and sanctions (source: WODC & CBS Statistics Netherlands, 2017)

Year	2005	2010	2011	2012	2013	2014	2015	2016	2017
Registered crimes	1,348,280	1,200,830	1,206,560	1,139,760	1,105,560	1,025,630	978,950	930,300	830,780
Registered suspects	513,450	406,510	397,790	373,480	350,400	327,320	301,560	278,690	245,010
Stop measure (Halt) referral by police	14,384	8,409	7,166	7,411	7,441	7,643	7,496	7,522	7,409
Police transaction	35,639	7,733	4,204	79	57	1	0	0	0
Police penal order		20,423	22,338	23,274	24,916	22,762	16,382	14,228	11,554
Sanctions police total	50,023	36,565	33,708	30,764	32,414	30,406	23,878	21,750	18,963
Intake public prosecution (PP)	264,310	210,975	229,990	224,155	208,730	210,825	189,825	189,410	173,530
Sanctions by PP: transactions	73,825	44,240	34,700	23,615	17,530	15,300	12,155	7,910	8,835
Sanctions by PP: penal order		11,845	25,050	45,265	42,360	38,905	30,730	33,285	31,700
Conditional dismissal on policy grounds by PP	4,575	5,875	6,540	8,585	9,325	10,500	8,695	8,115	8,715
Sanctions PP: total	78,400	61,960	66,290	77,465	69,215	64,705	51,580	49,310	49,250
Court Judgements: total	133,000	106,000	102,000	96,000	93,000	98,000	102,000[20]	95,000	93,000
Courts: finding of guilt	128,180	102,685	98,125	92,835	92,860	89,805	92,255	83,080	82,835
– with a penalty	127,250	101,255	96,395	90,995	90,790	87,365	89,025	80,665	80,640
Courts: (fully or partly) unconditional principal penalties	123,220	93,145	87,845	82,860	81,940	78,155	78,550	71,920	72,160

[20] The figures from before 2016 were missing in the 2017 report, but can be found in reports from previous years. See: https://www.wodc.nl/cijfers-en-prognoses/Criminaliteit-en-rechtshandhaving/.

Year	2005	2010	2011	2012	2013	2014	2015	2016	2017
– Incl. (fully or partly) unconditional fine	51,090	36,390	32,035	25,515	25,030	22,375	22,775	18,850	19,235
– Incl. (fully or partly) unconditional task penalty	40,415	34,110	32,015	32,300	30,910	30,385	30,380	28,445	28,130
– Incl. (fully or partly) unconditional prison sentence	31,715	22,645	23,795	25,045	26,000	25,395	25,395	24,625	24,795
Courts: (fully or partly) conditional principal penalties	42,985	38,705	37,505	37,605	37,600	37,975	39,380	37,190	36,900
Sanctions PP + Courts	205,650	163,215	162,685	168,460	160,005	152,070	140,605	129,975	129,890
Sanctions Police + PP + Courts	255,673	199,780	196,393	199,224	192,419	182,476	164,483	151,725	148,853
– Incl. (partly) conditional (%)	19	22	22	23	24	27	29	30	31

These figures show that a custodial sentence is still rather considered a last resort, and that, despite the increased length of prison sentences, elements of relative mildness, such as the expediency principle, the lack of mandatory sentences and wide sentencing discretion for the judiciary, are built into the system itself as a core element of Dutch criminal policy. Meanwhile, particularly the last two decades, proper law enforcement and administration of criminal justice have become issues of growing public concern.

3.4 TOLERANCE IN CRIMINAL POLICIES

An important characteristic of Dutch society and of the criminal justice system of the Netherlands is its tolerance towards societal and morally controversial issues such as pornography, drugs, induced abortion, prostitution and euthanasia.[21] Despite the fact that all these phenomena may fall within statutory definitions of criminal offences and may result in prosecution and punishment, policies have been developed to regulate legal tolerance towards those phenomena. Legal tolerance does not mean that the criminal justice system is indifferent towards these phenomena, but rather that no criminal investigation takes place when they occur, provided that policy instructions which define the borders of legal tolerance are complied with.

This may be better understood by considering the development of the policies on abortion, euthanasia and drugs in more detail. Although induced abortion, termination of life on request (euthanasia) as well as possession and trafficking of drugs (including cannabis) still all constitute a crime, special grounds of exemption from criminal liability have been defined in law in order to regulate tolerance for medical doctors who act in conformity with medical ethics, relevant procedure and/or other requirements. The present policy of tolerance in relation to induced abortion, euthanasia and drugs is the result of long and sometimes heated discussions by professionals, by the public at large and, eventually, by Parliament. Some of these discussions are still on-going as will become clear hereafter.

3.5 CRIMINAL POLICY RE INDUCED ABORTION

Termination of pregnancy (*Abortus arte provocatus*) is criminalized in Article 296 CC. According to the first section of this provision, "Any person who gives a woman treatment, when he knows or has reasonable cause to suspect that this treatment may terminate the pregnancy, shall be liable to a term of

---

[21]   On legal tolerance see Y. Buruma, 'Dutch Tolerance: On Drugs, Prostitution, and Euthanasia', *Crime and Justice* 2007, vol. 35, no. 1, pp. 73–113.

imprisonment not exceeding four years and six months or a fine of the fourth category." If the offence results in the death of the woman and/or is committed without the woman's consent, higher maximum terms of imprisonment apply up to a maximum of fifteen years of imprisonment. However, the offence of termination of pregnancy is not punishable "if the treatment is performed by a medical doctor in a hospital or clinic in which such treatment may be performed under the Termination of Pregnancy Act[22]", according to the fifth section of the provision. This exception manifests legal tolerance on induced abortion in the Netherlands.

3.5.1 SOCIETAL DEVELOPMENT

The prohibition of induced abortion has been debated in the Netherlands ever since the enactment of the provisions on abortion in the 1886 Criminal Code but a more tolerant social attitude towards induced abortion stems from the 1960s, when the opinion on abortion and contraceptives changed very quickly. More liberal ideas emerged about social and cultural issues, especially in the field of morals. This happened for a number of reasons:

- first, contraceptives were perfected and became more widespread;
- second, medical-technical developments regarding artificial insemination and sterilization resulted in a discussion on the beginning of human life;
- finally, discussions and law reform abroad regarding abortion, such as in England in 1967, also stimulated discussion in the Netherlands. A sizeable number of Dutch women at that time had an abortion abroad.

Consequently, traditional opinions in Dutch society about topics such as sexuality, marriage, pregnancy and family planning began to shift and conservatism lost ground. Higher demands were placed on the quality (the physical and psychological quality of the individual and the quality of society as a whole) of each individual human's existence. In addition, the demand to be able to arrange one's life according to one's own philosophy or insights and to take one's own responsibility increased. As a corollary, this required that unwanted pregnancies were to be prevented as much as possible but, where an unwanted pregnancy does occur induced abortion should offer a way out.

The widespread availability of contraceptives, and especially the introduction of the birth control pill in 1962, allowed an enormous revolution in sexual norms, as sexuality and reproduction were no longer linked. Moreover, it contributed to the emancipation process of women. In this atmosphere of change, the issue of abortion could once again become an important subject of public discussion.

---

22   Official name: Wet Afbreking Zwangerschap.

For those in religious circles, the protection of unborn human life took center stage. In socialist and liberal circles, the right of self-determination of women was emphasized. The emergence of the Women's Liberation Movement around 1970, which regarded a woman's right to abort as a fundamental part of female emancipation, played an important role in the discussions.

3.5.2 LEGAL VACUUM IN THE 1970s

Until 1970, the discussion on abortion took place outside the political arena and had a strong medical and ethical tone. There was a tendency in medical circles to take up a more liberal position in relation to abortion than laid down in the Penal Code. In fact, a legal vacuum emerged at this time and within that legal vacuum there was room for the establishment of abortion clinics and thus an ability to perform abortions. Around 1970 the first abortion clinics appeared, established by the Foundation for Medically Safe Termination of Pregnancy (STIMEZO), where pregnancies of less than twelve weeks were terminated on non-medical indication. STIMEZO clinics committed criminal offences, for abortion at the request of women without medical need was not legitimized by statute or by case law.

By the end of 1971, this legal vacuum led the prosecution service to state publicly that a prosecution for abortion would only be started after consultation with the State Inspectorate of Public Health, which was in charge of the supervision of health care at large. The supervision of the Inspections of Public Health concerning abortion was reduced from an integral review of the validity of the medical or social indication to a merely technical supervision. This was related to the fact that there existed no unanimity among physicians about the cases in which induced abortion was permissible, or even necessary. As such, there was no control of the ground for termination, merely supervision of the technique, hygiene and possible aftercare in relation to an abortion performed.

Since there was no review of the validity of the reason, the prosecution service had to give physicians the benefit of the doubt. Hence, the prosecution service abstained from prosecuting in these cases. As a result, the courts were not able to clarify the question as to whether induced abortion for social reasons was punishable or not. Moreover, the Minister of Justice and Security had made prosecution in criminal cases regarding abortion clinics dependent on his prior consent, suggesting that the prosecution service could not prosecute without the Minister of Justice and Security's consent. At the time, the prosecution service only rarely took action against a physician. Where they did so, the outcome was often a dismissal rather than a conviction.

3.5.3 THE 1981 TERMINATION OF PREGNANCY ACT

After seven bills on the exemption of punishment for induced abortion were submitted to Parliament between 1970 and 1979, the 1981 Termination of Pregnancy Act finally entered into force in 1984. Under this Act, induced abortion is not punishable if it is performed in compliance with the requirements of the Act (see also Article 296(5) CC, quoted in the introduction of this paragraph). These requirements are the following:

– abortion may only be performed by a physician in a hospital or in an abortion clinic, which has a permit from the Ministry of Public Health for that purpose;
– prior to the performance of an abortion, a period of five days for reflection must be observed. This means that the physician may not terminate a pregnancy other than on the sixth day after the woman has consulted the physician and at that occasion discussed her intention with him.

The total number of abortions had been around 33,000 per year since 2000.[23] As of 2008 a slight downward trend is noticeable. In 2016, 30,144 abortions were performed in the Netherlands. The abortion rate for the Netherlands is 8.5 (number of terminations per 1000 women aged 15 to 45). Around 12% of the patients are from abroad; they came to the Netherlands for abortion. More than half of all abortions took place in the first seven weeks of pregnancy, while just over 19% took place during the second trimester (13 to 24 weeks). The number of teenage patients undergoing a termination was 2,941, nearly 4.5% fewer than in 2015, with 65 procedures performed on girls aged 15 or under. Most abortion procedures are carried out in licensed abortion clinic (91.4%), although the percentage of terminations performed in a hospital is slowly increasing. In the Netherlands the abortion rate is amongst the lowest in the world. This is mainly due to the quality of information and a supply of a wide range of contraceptive methods.

3.6 CRIMINAL POLICY RE EUTHANASIA

Euthanasia is a criminal offence under Article 293 §1 CC, which states: "Any person who terminates the life of another person at that other person's express and earnest request, shall be liable to a term of imprisonment not exceeding twelve years or a fine of the fifth category." However, Article (2) 293 CC makes

---

[23] The numbers presented here are derived from the annual report of the Dutch Health Care Inspectorate (Inspectie voor de Gezondheidszorg, IGZ): *Jaarrapportage 2016 van de Wet afbreking zwangerschap*, Utrecht: 2018 (with summary in English).

an important exception to this. It holds that the offence of euthanasia is not punishable "if it is committed by a medical doctor who meets the requirements of due care referred to in Article 2 of the Termination of Life on Request and Assisted Suicide (Review Procedures) Act[24] and who informs the municipal forensic pathologist in accordance with Article 7(2) of the Burial and Cremation Act[25]".[26]

3.6.1 SOCIETAL DEVELOPMENT

The means by which a policy of tolerance towards induced abortion was established has been more or less model for the policy of tolerance towards euthanasia. The cultural change and the change in medical technology in the 1960s and 1970s led to a number of scientific publications and public discussions on end of life decisions (intervention or non-intervention) taken by doctors. The issue of euthanasia gradually became the focus of a number of empirical medical and legal studies. In the 1980s, the prosecutorial policy and a number of criminal court decisions fueled the discussions and led to the establishment of various advisory committees and eventually to a solid basis of codification.

In 2002, the Termination of Life on Request and Assistance in Suicide (Review Procedures) Act came into force after thirty years of societal discussions and parliamentary debates on the question of whether a termination of someone's life on request under all circumstances and without any differentiation constitutes the crime of euthanasia. The Act included in Article 293(2) CC a special ground of exemption from criminal liability in case of termination of someone's life on request, provided that the physician complies with statutory standards of due care (see above).

3.6.2 MAJOR RULINGS ON DUE CARE STANDARDS

The statutory standards of due care are not included in Article 293 CC but are laid down in the Termination of Life on Request Act. This Act in fact codified a series of lower and Supreme Court decisions with regard to euthanasia. Five court decisions are of particular importance.

---

24   Official name: Wet Toetsing Levensbeëindiging op Verzoek en Hulp bij Zelfdoding.
25   Official name: Wet op de Lijkbezorging.
26   On euthanasia in the Netherlands, see also Y. Buruma, 'Dutch Tolerance: On Drugs, Prostitution, and Euthanasia', *Crime and Justice* 2007, vol. 35, no. 1, pp. 73–113; P. Mevis, L. Postma, M. Habets, J. Rietjens & A. van der Heide, 'Advance directives requesting euthanasia in the Netherlands: do they enable euthanasia for patients who lack mental capacity?', *Journal of Medical Law and Ethics* 2016, vol. 4, no. 2, pp. 127–140.

The first court decision was that of the Leeuwarden district court in the *Postma case*, in which a female physician stood trial for terminating her mother's life on request.[27] The mother was old and suffering unbearable physical pain as a result of a cerebral hemorrhage. The Court formulated three conditions for impunity. These conditions are:

- the patient is considered by medical opinion to be incurably ill;
- the patient is, either physically or psychologically, suffering to an unbearable or severe extent;
- the patient has previously, in writing or orally, expressed his explicit will that his life will be terminated in order to be free from his suffering.

Some nine years later, the Rotterdam District Court in the *Wertheim case* refined these conditions.[28] In this case, a friend who was not a physician, assisted in the suicide of a 67-year-old woman who assumed she suffered from cancer. The court formulated two additional requirements for due care to be met in order to achieve impunity:

- termination of life on request may only be performed by a physician; and
- the physician must inform his patient thoroughly on his health prospects and on viable alternatives to termination of life on request.[29]

In 1984 in the *Schoonheim case*, the Supreme Court ruled that the termination of life performed by a physician according to objective medical insights may be considered as an act of necessity due to a conflict of duties, and therefore may be justified.[30] When performing euthanasia, the physician is confronted with conflicting obligations: the professional obligation to act in conformity with objective medical insights, the norms of medical ethics, and his medical expertise on the one hand, and the obligation as a civilian to obey criminal law, on the other hand. In the assessment as to whether the defense of necessity is applicable, the Supreme Court considers the following questions of importance:

---

[27] Leeuwarden District Court 21 February 1973, ECLI:NL:RBLEE:1973:AB5464, *NJ* 1973/183 (*Postma case*).

[28] Rotterdam District Court, 1 December 1981, ECLI:NL:RBROT:1981:AB7817, NJ 1982/63 (*Wertheim case*).

[29] A more recent case involving assistance to suicide by a non-physician is Supreme Court, 14 March 2017, ECLI:NL:HR:2017:418, NJ 2017/269 (*Heringa case*). Heringa assisted his 99-year-old stepmother with committing suicide. He claimed necessity which was accepted by the Court of Appeal. This decision, however, was subsequently quashed by the Supreme Court. The final decision in the case is Supreme Court, 16 April 2019, ECLI:NL:HR:2019:598.

[30] Supreme Court, 27 November 1984, ECLI:NL:HR:1984:AC8615, *NJ* 1985/106 (*Schoonheim case*).

1. should, according to professional medical insight, an ever-increasing deterioration and further aggravation of unbearable suffering be feared?
2. does the possibility exist that the patient will soon no longer be able to die in a dignified way?
3. were (other) means left to relieve the suffering?

If questions 1 and 3 are expressly answered negatively, and question 2 motivated affirmative, this implies that the euthanasia performed by the physician, according to objective medical insights, can be considered as an act of necessity.

In the *Chabot case*, the Supreme Court stipulates that, for a doctor who terminates the life of a patient who is not suffering physically but mentally and who is not in a terminal phase, a defense to necessity is not *per se* excluded.[31] However, the court has to proceed with extreme caution when assessing whether there is a viable defense of necessity in case a patient's suffering does not follow demonstrably from a physical disease or disorder, and may in fact only consist of a perception of pain and the loss of bodily functions. Furthermore, the Supreme Court confirms that in such a case there has to be an unbearable and incurable mental suffering. In general, there is no incurable psychiatric suffering if a realistic alternative to relieve that suffering has been turned down by the patient in full freedom. As the court has to show extremely great caution in assessing whether the defense of necessity has to be recognized, it must also involve the opinion of an independent expert who has seen and examined the patient. If that second opinion of an independent expert is not available, the defense to necessity cannot be admitted.

Finally, the *Brongersma* judgment.[32] This is on first sight a rather atypical case because it concerns euthanasia performed on somebody who was suffering neither physical nor psychological unbearable suffering pain. Brongersma was 86 years old, had lived his life and wanted to cease the continuation of his life because he considered it as senseless. He was afraid of becoming very lonely, dependent upon others, and of deteriorating physically to the point where he was in a bad physical state. After a number of talks with his patient, and after consulting two independent doctors, the physician assisted in suicide. Brongersma was suffering the continuation of his life, he was tired of life and, as such, his suffering was existential. According to the Supreme Court, this type of suffering falls outside the scope of the medical domain of euthanasia. Only suffering that is in a substantial sense caused by a medically classifiable somatic or psychiatric disease can legitimate an intentional termination of life (the classification prerequisite).

---

[31]   Supreme Court, 21 June 1994, ECLI:NL:HR:1994:AD2122, *NJ* 1994/656 (*Chabot case*).
[32]   Supreme Court, 24 December 2002, ECLI:NL:HR:2002:AE8772, *NJ* 2003/167 (*Brongersma judgment*).

3.6.3 THE 2001 ACT

The 2001 Termination of Life on Request and Assistance in Suicide (Review Procedures) Act formulates six statutory due care criteria to be met by a physician in order to guarantee him impunity (Article 293(2) CC):

–   the physician must be satisfied that the patient's request is made voluntarily and is well-considered;
–   the physician must be satisfied that the patient's suffering was unbearable and that there was no prospect of improvement of the situation;
–   the physician must have thoroughly informed his patient about his situation, the prospects and the expected course of his illness;
–   the physician, together with his patient, must have come to the conclusion that there is no viable alternative in the patient's situation;
–   the physician must have consulted at least one other independent physician, who must have seen the patient, and who must have given a written opinion on the compliance with the due care criteria referred to under a-d; and
–   the physician must have terminated the life of his patient with due medical care and attention.

Physicians are required to disclose their life terminating acts in a notification procedure for which the Burial Act provides the statutory basis. Five regional (euthanasia) review committees[33], established in 1998, assess whether the physician, in case of termination of life, has acted with due care. They consist of three members: one legal expert, one physician and one expert on ethical issues. The number of notifications on euthanasia or assisted suicide that is reviewed by the five regional review committees annually has been increasing. The committee reviewed 6,585 such notifications in 2017 (against 6091 in 2016). This comes down to 4.4% of the total of persons that died in the Netherlands in 2017 (150,027). In 2016 the Regional Euthanasia Review Committees (RTEs) received 6,091 notifications, which is 4% of the total number of deaths (148,973). The number of reports of euthanasia has thus grown in 2017 but remains relatively small compared to the total number of deaths in the Netherlands.[34] In 83 cases of euthanasia a psychiatric disorder was the basis of the suffering of the patient. Only in twelve cases, less than 0.18% of the total number of notifications, the RTEs came to the conclusion that the doctor had not fully complied with all due care criteria.

---

[33]   On their tasks and operations, see *Euthanasiecode 2018 of the Regional Euthanasia Review Committees (RTEs)*, 2018.
[34]   For the numbers presented here, see the annual report of the Regional Euthanasia Review Committees (RTEs): Regionale toetsingscommissies euthanasia RTE, *Jaarverslag 2017*, Den Haag, 2018.

In cases of non-compliance with the standards of due care, a report is sent to the Board of Prosecutors General, which will take a decision on whether or not to prosecute based on prosecutorial directives in relation to euthanasia and assisted suicide. The existence of only a small number of cases in which a committee concludes that the physician did not comply with the standards of due care is a strong indication that the physician's knowledge on how to act in cases of request for euthanasia over the years has substantially improved. The Act, the prosecutorial directives and the published assessments of the regional review committees have had the result that in virtually all cases a physician facing a request for euthanasia knows how to act and have improved the legal certainty of the physicians in the performance of euthanasia.

In 2017, the Third Evaluation of the Law on the Review of Termination of Life on Request and Assisted Suicide (Euthanasia Act) was published. This study provides insight in the development of reasons for not notifying the regional review committee. In 2005 very few physicians did not notify because of doubts as to whether they met all the criteria of due care or because they feared prosecution. In 2017 the only reason mentioned for non-notification was the opinion of the physician that the act preformed was not a "life terminating act".[35]

3.6.4 PALLIATIVE CARE

In the majority of the cases, the request for termination of life is expressed at the moment that no further medical treatment is feasible for a patient, as a curative effect can no longer be hoped for. Such a situation primarily concerns patients with terminal cancer and with acute short syndromes or with chronic diseases such as dementia, stroke, pulmonary emphysema, heart and vascular diseases, and Parkinson disease. When further medical treatment becomes useless, all that is left is to wait for death. In as far as the patient is hospitalized, a further stay in hospital is no longer necessary after this medical conclusion. The patient is sent back home to await death, supported and looked after by family, relatives and additional professional home care such as district nurses, home health aides and other care providers.

There is a wide range of palliative care services available in the Netherlands. There are opportunities to receive palliative care at home, in nursing homes, care homes, hospitals, independent professionally staffed hospices and volunteer-run hospices. A striking feature of the situation in the Netherlands is that special facilities for terminally ill patients, such as hospices, only began to appear since the beginning of the 1990s, whereas neighboring countries had established such facilities much sooner. This is probably explained by the fact that, in the

---

[35]   Derde evaluatie Wet toetsing levensbeëindiging op verzoek en hulp bij zelfdoding, 2017, pp. 185–186.

Netherlands, general practitioners, nursing home doctors, home care workers and others have always given high priority to caring for the dying in addition to providing care for other patients. In the Netherlands, there is therefore a relatively large number of possibilities for nursing and care at home, and staff in nursing homes and care homes are becoming progressively better equipped to care for the dying.

As part of the palliative care for terminally ill patients, palliative sedations have been applied in cases where one or more medically incurable or intractable symptoms of a disease – the so-called refractory symptoms – exist and which leads to unbearable suffering. In such a case, on the basis of informed consent by the patient, he is sedated so as to mitigate his suffering. Part of the palliative sedation is that hydration and nutrition is ceased. Palliative sedation happens rather frequently. Annually, approximately 146,500 people die in the Netherlands, according to CBS Statistics Netherlands. Approximately 22.2% of all deaths are the result of terminal sedation (2016). This constitutes an increase of 14,000 people compared to five years before.[36] Palliative sedation was considered to be a form of euthanasia and therefore fell under the legal regime of the 2001 Act up till 2005. After the publication in December 2005 by the Royal Dutch Medical Association of its guidelines for palliative sedation, the Board of Prosecutors General decided in 2006 that palliative sedation is a professional treatment and therefore does not fall within the scope of the 2001 Act.

3.6.5 FURTHER DISCUSSION: COMPLETED LIFE

In 2014, the Minister of Public Health and the Minister of Justice and Security appointed the Committee on Assisted Suicide for people who consider their lives completed (Committee Schnabel). Two years later the Committee published their report, in which it is concluded that the current legislation on euthanasia functions well for people who fall within its scope and that there is no reason to broaden it.[37] The committee does not consider it desirable to amend the law in such way that it would also legalize assisted suicide in cases where people have a wish to die but whose suffering does not have a medical dimension.

According to the government, however, "this conclusion does not do justice to the wishes of people who regard their life as completed and request help in ending it. The government takes the view that such a request for help made by a person who is suffering unbearably and with no prospect of improvement, but whose suffering does not have a medical dimension, can be legitimate."

---

[36] See Stichting Farmaceutische Kengetallen, 'Palliatieve sedatie vaker ingezet bij levenseinde', *Pharmaceutisch Weekblad*, 16 februari 2017, vol. 152, no. 7.

[37] Adviescommissie voltooid leven, *Voltooid leven. Over hulp bij zelfdoding aan mensen die hun leven voltooid achten*, Den Haag, 2016, pp. 11–16.

According to the government, "People who have come to a well-considered decision that their life is completed must be allowed, under strict and carefully identified criteria, to end their life with dignity. In consultation with various care organizations, the government intends to develop new legislation based on this principle. The system would exist alongside and separately from the current legislation on euthanasia." The government furthermore stresses that it "is firmly committed to protecting human life. This means that the preconditions under which people would be allowed to exercise their freedom to choose how their life ends will be an essential component of the solution the government seeks."[38]

3.7 DRUG POLICY

The Netherlands has an internationally well-known and long-standing liberal reputation relative to narcotic drugs.[39] Nevertheless, contrary to what is often thought, the production, possession, distribution, purchase and sale (but not use) of all generally recognized narcotic substances is long since criminally prohibited under the Opium Act. This thus not only applies to, for example, heroin, cocaine, methamphetamine, GBH, ecstasy and LSD, but also to the possession etcetera of cannabis products (hashish and marijuana/weed) in even very small amounts which is still an offence under Dutch criminal law. The well-deserved liberal reputation of the Netherlands rests not so much on its legislation but rather on its law enforcement policy. Although Dutch drug policy has slowly but surely shifted from a primarily public health focus to also include an increasing focus on law enforcement in recent years[40], it is still rather pragmatic and lenient and rooted in a generally tolerant attitude towards drug use. There are still a number of unique elements in the present Dutch drug policy:

- a distinction is made between substances with acceptable health risks for the user, such as marihuana or weed, and drugs with unacceptable health risks such as heroin, cocaine, XTC or other synthetic drugs. Substances with acceptable health risks are called soft drugs; the other hard drugs;
- the market for soft drugs (coffee shops) is strictly separated from the market for hard drugs;

---

38 See: Letter of 12 October 2016 from the Minister of Health, Welfare and Sport and the Minister of Security and Justice to the House of Representatives on the government position on 'completed life'.

39 On drug policy in the Netherlands, see also M. van Ooyen-Houben & E. Kleemans, 'Drug Policy: The "Dutch Model"', *Crime & Justice* 2015, vol. 44, pp. 165–226; Y. Buruma, 'Dutch Tolerance: On Drugs, Prostitution, and Euthanasia', *Crime and Justice* 2007, vol. 35, no. 1, pp. 73–113.

40 See M. van Ooyen-Houben & E. Kleemans, 'Drug Policy: The "Dutch Model"', *Crime & Justice* 2015, vol. 44, pp. 165–226 at 165.

- drug users are in principle not treated as criminal offenders but as medical patients who might need help to improve their physical and mental health;
- the main feature of the Dutch drug policy is harm reduction and its objectives are to prevent the use of (hard) drugs and to limit the risks and harm to the drug user;
- law enforcement is concentrated on the production, possession, selling, import and export of drugs. The maximum statutory sentences for these offences differ considerably dependent on the type of drug involved.

The policy to separate the markets of hard and soft drugs was a response to the social crisis of widespread heroin use in the 1970s. In the 1970s, a drug policy was adopted that was seen as rather tolerant towards the use of cannabis. The theory behind this policy was that if one makes small amounts of less harmful substances available for sale in a controlled setting (coffee shop), this will prevent users from buying less harmful substances from an illegal dealer who may subsequently persuade them to try and buy hard drugs.

Hashish and marijuana – which are considered soft drugs – can be bought in a coffee shop. To run a coffee shop, one needs a license from the municipality. Municipalities will attach conditions to this license. The main additional conditions concern the prohibition of sale of alcohol, the minimum distance between the coffee shop and schools, and opening hours. Coffee shop owners/operators are not prosecuted for selling or possessing soft drugs provided that they comply with the criteria laid down in the so-called AHOJ-GI guidelines; these include:

- no advertising (A);
- no hard drugs sale (H);
- no nuisance (O);
- no sale to juveniles (J);
- no sale in large quantities (max. 5 grams per purchase) (G);
- no sale to international consumers (resident criterion: only selling to people who live in the Netherlands) (I).

Coffee shop owners who comply with these criteria may stock up to a maximum of 500 grams of cannabis.

Although the selling and possession of soft drugs constitutes a crime, the application of the expediency principle by the prosecution service results in non-prosecution of this crime. Since 1999, the mayor of a given municipality has been empowered to close a coffee shop when the above conditions are not respected. Furthermore, municipalities can regulate the number of coffee shops, and in a not insignificant number of municipalities (around 80%), coffee shops are simply not tolerated at all. The decision not to allow a coffee shop has to be taken in consultation with neighboring municipalities in order to avoid a too heavy burden falling upon municipalities that do tolerate them. A restriction of the number of coffee shops has to be reasoned, because the decision can be appealed to an administrative court. One important reason often given is that additional coffee shops would have a negative effect on the quality of life in the area. These new powers have resulted in a serious reduction of the number of coffee shops from around 1,179 in 1997, to 729 in 2005, and 573 in 2016.[41] By the end of March 2017, there were 567 coffee shops.[42] Meanwhile, the number of municipalities with coffee shops is rather stable: 103 in 2016 and 2017, and the fifteen years before never more than 107 (2002) and never fewer than 101 (2009, 2010). In 272 municipalities it is stated in local policy that coffee shops are not allowed to settle within the municipality borders: these apply a so-called zero tolerance policy. The number of coffee shops in smaller and medium-sized municipalities is fairly stable since many years. Particularly larger municipalities with more than 200,000 inhabitants are responsible for the decrease in the number of coffee shops the last years.

Tolerance has never been extended towards the drug trade, production or large-scale supply, regardless of whether it concerned soft drugs (such as (hashish and marijuana/weed) or hard drugs (such as heroin, cocaine, methamphetamine). However, the rather tolerant approach towards possession and supply of small amounts of soft drugs has, in recent years, become less so. The increase in the number of plants for home grown weed and of the number and size of professional cannabis nurseries to respond to the demand from coffee shops has led to drug-related criminality and, furthermore, caused serious societal problems. With the same drug policy aims in mind, recent measures have been taken to reduce street dealing, drug tourism, cannabis cultivation, sales of tools and resources to grow cannabis, and the number of coffee shops. Stricter rules for the establishment of coffee shops have been issued, municipalities have been empowered to combat undesirable side effects, and measures to counter drug tourism have been taken by authorizing municipalities to refuse or withdraw a coffee shop's operating license on grounds of unacceptable effects on the quality of life.[43] Tougher action against cannabis cultivation in residential areas is intended to make cultivation of home grown weed as unattractive as possible; and educational programs have been developed for schools in order to discourage the use of (soft) drugs. This all constitutes a far less tolerant policy towards soft drugs.

---

[41]   See B. Bieleman & R. Mennes, 'Steeds minder coffeeshops in Nederland', Secondant, Platform voor maatschappelijke veiligheid, 2016, at: www.ccv-secondant.nl/platform/article/steeds-minder-coffeeshops-in-nederland/.

[42]   B. Bieleman, R. Mennes & M. Sijtstra, *Coffeeshops in Nederland 2016*, Groningen-Rotterdam, 2017, p. 1 (Summary in English).

[43]   An important case in this respect is the *Checkpoint case*: Supreme Court, 2 July 2013, ECLI:NL:HR:2013:7, *NJ* 2013/563 with case note by P.H.P.H.M.C. van Kempen; Supreme Court, 26 April 2016, ECLI:NL:HR:2016:742, *NJ* 2016/388 with case note by B.F. Keulen.

The tolerance towards the sale of soft drugs in coffee shops on the one hand and the repression against the cultivation of cannabis on the other has also become increasingly problematic from a legal point of view. This contradictory system has brought courts to render prosecutions for the large scale cultivation of cannabis inadmissible (dismissal) in some cases, while in other cases to abstain from imposing a penalty although the charges were proven and the accused was criminally liable for the offence.[44] It has also lead to a nationwide discussion on whether the cultivation of and trade of cannabis for recreational use should be regulated and legalized. Such regulated legalizations are not permitted under international law, considered strictly from the internal perspective of the relevant UN Narcotic Drugs Conventions (the UN 1961 Single Convention and the UN 1988 Illicit Traffic Convention).[45] However, the answer is different when considered from the external perspective of international human rights conventions. From this external perspective there is a possibility to regulate, even by legalization, the cultivation of and trade in cannabis for the recreational user market if five primary conditions are met.[46] The conditions for regulated legalization are:

1. This must be in the interest of the protection of human rights.
2. The state must demonstrate that the regulated legalization of the cultivation and trade of cannabis will result in the more effective protection of human rights.
3. The decision regarding such regulation must have public support and must be decided through the nationwide democratic process.
4. There must be a closed system so that foreign countries are not disadvantaged in any way by this measure.
5. The state is required to actively discourage cannabis use.

If a state can meet these conditions, under current international law it is permissible to give priority to human rights obligations over the obligations of the UN drug conventions, according to the analysis of Van Kempen & Fedorova.

In 2015 a bill has been introduced by two parliamentarians to amend the Opium Act with a view to tolerate the cultivation and sale of cannabis (hashish

---

[44] See, for example, M. Fedorova, 'De "achterdeur-problematiek" van de coffeeshop in de rechtspraak: wetgever help de strafrechter uit de spagaat', *Delikt en Delinkwent* 2016, vol. 46, no. 7, pp. 568–594 (title in English: The 'back door problem' of the coffee shop in the case law: legislator, please help the criminal courts from the quandary).

[45] See P.H.P.H.M.C. van Kempen & M.I. Fedorova, *International Law and Cannabis I. Regulation of Cannabis Cultivation for Recreational Use under the UN Narcotic Drugs Conventions and the EU Legal Instruments in Anti-Drugs Policy*, Cambridge/Antwerp/Portland: Intersentia 2019.

[46] P.H.P.H.M.C. van Kempen & M.I. Fedorova, *International Law and Cannabis II. Regulation of Cannabis Cultivation and Trade for Recreational Use: Positive Human Rights Obligations versus UN Narcotic Drugs Conventions*, Cambridge/Antwerp/Portland: Intersentia 2019.

and marijuana) through a closed system (Act on closed coffee shop chain).[47] The bill intends to put an end to the paradoxical policy for coffee shops, which presently leaves the so-called backdoor (i.e. the supply of cannabis to coffee shops) unregulated. In the bill the cultivation, distribution and wholesale of cannabis in order to supply coffee shops is regulated through a closed coffee shop chain where criminals are kept out and where coffeeshops have to pay taxes. In the meantime, in 2018 the Government sent a Bill to parliament that makes it possible to start an experiment with a closed coffee shop chain.[48] The Bill has passed the Lower House early 2019 and will soon be discussed in the Senate.[49]

The foregoing shows two different approaches within the Netherlands relative to soft drugs and the problems it causes in society: whereas the law and the enforcement thereof have become more repressive against particularly cannabis cultivation and wholesale, at the same time there is are bills in parliament that intend to legally regulate all of this.

3.8 CULTURAL TOLERANCE

The Netherlands has also been famous for its cultural tolerance, even as far back as the 17th century, when religions others than Calvinism and Catholicism could be practiced peacefully. The Netherlands was a refuge for French Huguenots, as well as Portuguese and Spanish Jews in a period of European history in which religious intolerance was the norm. In present times, however, tolerance towards new foreign immigrants and towards other religions and non-Western cultures is declining.

In the wake of 11 September 2001 and other similar attacks, the cultural tolerance, in particular tolerance towards immigrants who bring their own culture and religion with them, is increasingly under pressure. In public debates, voices proclaiming the belief that cultural tolerance is responsible for the uncertainty in Dutch society and that it has thus gone too far can be heard loud and clear. Dutch tolerance began in a society that was fairly homogenous, with more or less common values and norms. The differences in then existing values and norms, mainly based on religion, could be bridged by the exchange of views and opinions, and tolerance was never considered to have been applied beyond acceptable and understandable limits. Furthermore, this model of tolerance was the result of a process of public debate, during which extreme views and

---

[47] See *Kamerstukken II* 2014–2015, 34165, no. 2 (Voorstel van wet van de leden Berndsen-Jansen en Bergkamp tot wijziging van de Opiumwet in verband met de regulering van de teelt en verkoop van hennep en hasjiesj via een gesloten coffeeshopketen).

[48] See *Kamerstukken II* 2017–2018, 34997 (Wet experiment gesloten coffeeshopketen).

[49] For up-to-date information on the Bill, see: https://www.eerstekamer.nl/wetsvoorstel/34997_wet_experiment_gesloten.

standpoints were reconciled. In a relatively short period of time, the Netherlands has become a multi-ethnic and multicultural melting pot in which values and norms are no longer based on common religious, social and political views.

Exponents of tolerance had been gradually extending the limits of tolerance without a careful process of debates and exchange of views. The murder of provocative exponents against cultural tolerance – such as Pim Fortuyn (2002) and Theo van Gogh (2004) – sent a serious shockwave through Dutch society. It also revealed that large groups within society, both with and without a migration background, were either not yet ready or no longer ready to apply tolerance towards their neighbors on all matters where tolerance had previously held sway, such as on sexuality, foreign immigrants, foreign religions, non-conformist ways of life, freedom of speech, etcetera. One is therefore left to wonder whether what went before was really tolerance or rather simply disinterest. In any case, tolerance towards Islam and Muslims has collapsed following those murders. In the present climate there is mistrust and mutual fear between Muslims and non-Muslims.[50] This mistrust and fear is very detrimental for a tolerant Dutch culture.

A relevant criminal offence in this respect is "group insult" in Article 137c CC. The first section of this provision holds that any person "who in public, either verbally or in writing or through images, intentionally makes an insulting statement about a group of persons because of their race, religion or beliefs, their hetero- or homosexual orientation or their physical, mental or intellectual disability" shall be liable to a term of imprisonment of a maximum of one year or a fine. Furthermore, for example, inciting hatred, discrimination and violence, is an offence under Article 137d CC. The first section thereof states that any person "who publicly, either verbally or in writing or through images, incites hatred of or discrimination against persons or violence against their person or property because of their race, religion or beliefs, their sex, their hetero- or homosexual orientation or their physical, mental or intellectual disability" shall be liable to a term of imprisonment of a maximum of also one year or a fine.

Important recent criminal cases in this regard are the criminal prosecutions of Mr. Geert Wilders, a member of the House of Representatives of the Netherlands and the leader of the Party for Freedom (*Partij voor de Vrijheid*, PVV), which is a nationalist and right-wing populist political party. Mr. Wilders was first (2010) prosecuted on the basis of Articles 137c and 137d CC for statements made in an article with the title "Enough is enough: ban the Koran" in the newspaper *the Volkskrant* (2007), in which Mr. Wilders describes the Islam as a fascist ideology and argues in favor of banning the Koran, and in his film *Fitna* that speaks of "the fascist Islam, the sick ideology of Muhammad" and of the increasing influence that

---

50   See the report by the Netherlands Institute for Social Research (SCP): I. Andriessen, H. Fernee & K. Wittebrood, *Ervaren discriminatie in Nederland*, Den Haag: Sociaal en Cultureel Planbureau, 2013.

it has or will have on the Netherlands, according to Mr. Wilders. The District Court found that the statements did not constitute offences under the criminal law and Mr. Wilders was acquitted.[51]

In 2016 a second criminal trial was initiated against Mr. Wilders for new statements he had made in 2014. When the results of the municipal elections came out in March that year, Mr. Wilders was at the PVV party meeting in a Hague café. Mr. Wilders asked the public: "I'm asking you, do you want more or fewer Moroccans in this city and in the Netherlands?" The public responded to this by chanting around 16 times: "Fewer, fewer!" Mr. Wilders responded by saying: "Well, we'll arrange that then". A week before that meeting, Mr. Wilders remarked in an interview with a national news service when speaking about the inhabitants of The Hague: "Those are the people we are doing it for. They vote for a safer and more social city and in any event a city with fewer burdens and also, if possible, fewer Moroccans."[52] More than 6,400 people reported the statements to the police, which was one of the reasons why the Public Prosecution Service decided to prosecute Mr. Wilders for his statements. Again, the prosecution of Mr. Wilders for these statements is based on Articles 137c and 137d CC. In its judgment of 9 December 2016, the District Court of The Hague found Mr. Wilders guilty of group insult and inciting discrimination, but acquitted him of incitement to hatred.[53] The court decided not to impose a punishment. Both Mr. Wilders and the prosecution office have appealed against the judgment. The appeal was still pending when this book went to print.

---

51 Amsterdam District Court, 23 June 2011, ECLI:NL:RBAMS:2011:BQ9001, *NJ* 2012/370 with case note by P.A.M. Mevis.
52 See also about the Wilders Case the website of the Public Prosecution, at: https://www.om.nl/vaste-onderdelen/zoeken/@93631/ten-questions-about/.
53 The Hague District Court, 9 December 2016, ECLI:NL:RBDHA:2016:15014.

PART II
SUBSTANTIVE CRIMINAL LAW

4. SUBSTANTIVE CRIMINAL LAW

Maartje KRABBE, Roel KLAAR,
Sjarai LESTRADE & Mikhel TIMMERMAN*

4.1 INTRODUCTION

The present chapter addresses the major doctrines of substantive criminal law in the Netherlands. First the backgrounds of the Dutch Criminal Code (*Wetboek van Strafrecht*) – such as its history and specific characteristics – are discussed (section 4.2). Criminal offenses are the topic of section 4.3: how are criminal offenses governed by the legality principle and what are the general conditions of criminal offenses? Section 4.4 discusses 'complete defenses', a legal argument brought up in situations where the defendant has committed a crime, but did this for an acceptable reason. From complete defenses we move on the offenses that have not been completed, the so-called inchoate offenses (section 4.5). In this context the legal definitions of preparation and attempt are discussed. The final section of this chapter (section 4.6) is devoted to the doctrine of participation (committing crimes with multiple perpetrators). This section ends with an a few words on corporate criminal liability.

4.2 THE CRIMINAL CODE

4.2.1 HISTORY

The history of the present Dutch Criminal Code starts in 1810, when the Kingdom of Holland under Louis Napoleon Bonaparte was annexed to the French Empire. After this annexation, the Penal Code for the Kingdom of Holland, in force since 1809, was replaced by the French Napoleonic *Code Pénal*.

---

* M.J.M. Krabbe (Ph.D.) is assistant professor at the department of jurisprudence of Radboud University in Nijmegen and a judge *ad litem* at the District Court of Gelderland. R.J.A. Klaar is law clerk at the district court of 's-Hertogenbosch. S.M.A. Lestrade (Ph.D.) is assistant professor at the department of Criminal Law and Criminology of Radboud University, and a judge *ad litem* at the District Court of Gelderland. M.A.P. Timmerman (Ph.D.) is law clerk at the Supreme Court of the Netherlands, and research fellow at Radboud University.

When the Kingdom of the Netherlands was established in 1815, the French code was kept in force provisionally. Important changes were nevertheless made. The penalty system was reformed considerably, for instance by abolishing deportation and lifelong forced labor. The Dutch Constitution of 1813 stipulated that the main body of substantive and procedural criminal law be regulated in codes. During the nineteenth century, a number of draft criminal codes were proposed, but the lack of parliamentary unanimity on both the penalty system and the prison system prevented adoption of any of these drafts. However, important revisions of the criminal code did take place, in particular regarding sanctions. The range of sentences was reduced to various forms of imprisonment, fines, suspension of certain rights and forfeiture of certain goods. Corporal punishment was abolished in 1856, and life imprisonment replaced the death penalty in 1870. In 1870, a penal law reform committee was established that drafted a criminal code which, accompanied by an extensive explanatory memorandum, was submitted to Parliament in 1879 by Minister of Justice Anthony Modderman. The Criminal Code (CC) was adopted in 1881. Its entry into force was delayed until 1886, because a number of Acts had to be reformed and the cellular prison system required the construction of new prisons.[1]

4.2.2 MAJOR CRIMINAL CODE REFORMS

Since 1886, the Criminal Code has undergone considerable reform. New criminal provisions have been added, for example on discrimination, intrusion of privacy, environmental pollution, illegal computer activities, commercial surrogate motherhood, stalking, and virtual child porn. Other offenses, such as adultery or homosexual acts between adults and juveniles over sixteen, have been decriminalized. Termination of pregnancy (induced abortion), termination of life on request and assistance to suicide (euthanasia) are no longer punishable, if certain legal requirements are met. Major criminal law reforms took place in juvenile criminal law (1965 and 1995), on sentencing, the extension of suspended sentences (1987), the introduction of early release (1987), the reform of fines (1983), the introduction of community sentences and so called task penalties (1989–2001), on corporate criminal liability (1976) and on serious offenses against public morals (1986–2002). With the 1989 Administration of Road-Traffic Offenses Act (*Wet administratiefrechtelijke handhaving verkeersvoorschriften*), minor traffic offenses were classified as administrative offenses instead of criminal offenses. Furthermore, the code has been reformed by the introduction of the crime of conspiracy (1994), the introduction of new criminal law measures such as the Confiscation and Compensation Order, the Detention of Persistent Offenders Order (1993–2004), and by legislation related to terrorism (2004).

---

[1]   J. de Hullu, Materieel strafrecht, Deventer: Wolters Kluwer, pp. 61–63.

Finally, the implementation of EU law has resulted in criminal law reforms such as legislation on money laundering, the fight against terrorism, and on mutual recognition of decisions to confiscate.

On the occasion of the 100th anniversary of the Criminal Code in 1986, the question was raised as to whether a full re-codification of criminal law was necessary. There was no great enthusiasm for this idea, however.[2] Instead, a preference was expressed for ongoing partial criminal law reforms, and for a gradual modernization of the present Criminal Code. New criminal law legislation is published at www.overheid.nl.

4.2.3 CHARACTERISTICS OF THE CRIMINAL CODE

The Dutch Criminal Code is characterized by its simplicity, practicality, its faith in the judiciary, and its absence of specific religious influences. Its simplicity, for instance, is illustrated by the legal definitions of criminal offenses, the division of criminal offenses into either crimes or infractions, and its penal system containing only four principal sentences: imprisonment, detention, community service (*taakstraf*), and fines. The Code contains definitions neither on culpability nor on causation. The Criminal Code is a very practical one, leaving the development of criminal law doctrine in general to the courts and to the Supreme Court in particular. Its faith in the judiciary is also evident from the absence of lay judges or mandatory sentences for serious offenses[3] and the discretionary power in sentencing. The Dutch Criminal Code does not contain distinctions and definitions of a dogmatic nature.

The Criminal Code consists of three books. The first book (Articles 1–91) is a general part concerning the scope of application of the code, sanctions and measures, defenses, attempt and conspiracy, the extension of criminal liability through participation, the reduction of sentences in case of concurrence, the statute of limitations, and the *non bis in idem* principle. The second (Articles 92–421) and third (Articles 424–479) book define the offenses and infractions.

4.2.4 OTHER MAIN CRIMINAL LAW STATUTES

The Dutch Criminal Code does not define all criminal offenses. Numerous other statutes complement it and contain rules of substantive criminal law. Main examples are the 1950 Economic Offenses Act (*Wet op de economische delicten*), the 1994 Road Traffic Act (*Wegenverkeerstwet*), the 1928 Narcotic Drug Offenses

---

2   See for an overview of the debate about an integral revision or re-codification of the Dutch Criminal Code, De Hullu 2018, pp. 570–579.

3   There is, however, a general prohibition on community service in case of serious offenses (Article 22b CC).

Act (*Opiumwet*), and the 1989 Arms and Munitions Act (*Wet wapens en munitie*). Violation of these Acts (e.g. drunk driving, hit-and-run, drug trafficking, illegal possession of firearms) constitutes a crime. Military criminal law is found in the 1991 Military Criminal Code (*Wetboek van Militair Strafrecht*). The Code contains criminal law provisions supplementary to the provisions in the Criminal Code. Furthermore, hundreds of by-laws contain criminal provisions for the proper law enforcement of administrative legislation. The general part of the Criminal Code is also applicable to other criminal law statutes and criminal by-laws (Article 91 CC).

It is important to note that offenses of terrorism are included in the Criminal Code itself and not, like in many other countries, in a separate statute or act.[4] Article 83 CC enumerates 42 offenses that qualify as a terrorist offense when they are committed with 'terrorist intent'. Article 83a CC defines terrorist intent as the intention of causing fear in the population or a part of the population of a country, or unlawfully compelling a public authority or international organization to act or to refrain from certain acts or to tolerate certain acts, or of seriously disrupting or destroying the fundamental political, constitutional, economic or social structures of a country or an international organization.

There is no special statute on juvenile offenders. The Criminal Code does, however, contain a number of special provisions on juveniles. These primarily concern the applicable sanctions for juvenile offenders (Articles 77a through 77kk CC).

4.3 CRIMINAL OFFENSES IN GENERAL

4.3.1 PRINCIPLE OF LEGALITY

The importance of the legality principle is reflected by its position in the Dutch Criminal Code: it is enshrined in the very first provision, which states:

> "1. No act or omission which did not constitute a criminal offence under the law at the time of its commission shall be punishable by law. 2. Where the statutory provisions in force at the time when the criminal offence was committed are later amended, the provisions most favorable to the suspect or the defendant shall apply.".[5]

The first section of Article 1 CC underlines that the determination of criminal liability is only allowed for acts or omissions that constituted criminal offenses under the law that was applicable at the time of the conduct.[6] The legality

---

4   De Hullu 2018, pp. 82–83. See further: K. Veegens, *A disrupted balance? Prevention of terrorism and compliance with fundamental rights and principles of law – the Dutch anti-terrorism legislation*, Cambridge: Intersentia, 2012.

5   The wording of Article 1 (1) CC is also enshrined in Article 16 of the Dutch Constitution since the constitutional amendment of 1983.

6   See further De Hullu 2018, pp. 84–113.

principle thus requires an existing and applicable statutory definition of offenses and penalties at the time of the accused's conduct. The offenses and penalties also need to be defined in the Dutch language.[7] The legality principle's purpose is to serve as a guarantee against arbitrary administration of criminal justice and to offer a high degree of legal certainty in the field of criminal law.[8]

Unlike Article 7 ECHR – which accepts that offenses and penalties are defined by other sources than mere statutory law[9], most notably case law –[10] the Dutch legality principle demands a statutory basis for offenses and penalties.[11] Therefore, Article 1 CC underlines the primacy of the legislator in the definition of offenses and penalties. The legality principle is generally acknowledged to contain multiple specific secondary principles. These are: the principle of non-retroactivity of offenses and penalties, the principle that offenses and penalties require a clear definition (*lex certa* principle), and the prohibition of overly extensive interpretation.

The principle of non-retroactivity is the only secondary principle that follows explicitly from the wording of Article 1 (1) CC. It requires the legislator to define offenses and penalties that exclusively apply to future acts and omissions. It also merely allows the courts to apply definitions of offenses and penalties to acts that occurred at the time when the definitions had already entered into force. The notable exception to the general prohibition on retroactive application in substantive criminal law is the *lex mitior* principle, which is enshrined in Article 1 (2) CC. The *lex mitior* principle requires the court to retroactively apply criminal law that entered into force after the accused's acts if the new law is more favorable to the accused than the law that was applicable at the time of his acts.[12] Retroactive application of substantive criminal law remains exceptional, however, and retroactivity of offenses and penalties will, in general[13], be precluded by the legality principle.[14]

---

7   See Supreme Court, 24 June 1997, ECLI:NL:HR:1997:ZD0773, *NJ* 1998/70 with case note A.C. 't Hart, par. 5.6.

8   For a historical and theoretical examination of the legality principle, see: M. Timmerman, *Legality in Europe. On the principle* nullem crimen, nulla poena sine lege *in EU law and under the ECHR*, Cambridge: Intersentia 2018, pp. 15–52.

9   By virtue of the broad definition of the term 'law' in Article 7 ECHR, see, e.g., European Court of Human Rights (GC), *Del Río Prada v. Spain*, 21 October 2013, appl. no. 42750/09, par. 91, and M. Timmerman, 2018, pp. 70–74.

10   See, e.g., European Court of Human Rights, *Contrada v. Italy (No. 3)*, 14 April 2015, appl. no. 66655/13, par. 66–70 and 74–75.

11   De Hullu 2018, pp. 85–86.

12   See, e.g., Supreme Court, 12 July 2011, ECLI:NL:HR:2011:BP6878, *NJ* 2012/78, par. 3.6.1–3.6.2.

13   A notable exception to the non-retroactivity of offenses and penalties was made in the aftermath of World War II where war criminals were convicted on the basis of offenses that entered into force after the acts occurred. The reasoning that the Dutch Special Supreme Court (*Bijzondere Raad van Cassatie*) employed to uphold the convictions despite problems with retroactivity are largely comparable to the reasons for including an exception to the non-retroactivity principle in Article 7(2) ECHR.

14   Rules on statutory limitation can nevertheless be retroactively amended to the detriment of the accused because they are not, strictly speaking, rules that define offenses and penalties,

The legality principle also requires the legislator to define offenses and penalties with sufficient clarity.[15] The requirement of a clear definition demands that offenses and penalties be published.[16] In addition, legal definitions of substantive criminal law need to be as clear and precise as possible in order to enable individuals to foresee the legal consequences of their acts and omissions. The enforceability of this secondary principle is, however, questionable. Complaints about the violation of the clarity requirement are dismissed by Dutch courts in nearly all cases.[17] The notion that many legal definitions are inevitably couched in indeterminate terms by virtue of the need for them to apply to many different factual situations, certainly plays a role in that regard.[18] The idea that indeterminacy in legal definitions is inevitable is also explicitly accepted by the ECtHR.[19] Dutch case law converges with the Strasbourg jurisprudence on this matter.

In addition to the principles of non-retroactivity and clarity, Article 1(1) CC also limits the room for judicial interpretation of offenses and penalties.[20] Historically, Dutch criminal law doctrine has generally excluded the possibility for the courts to use analogy to the detriment of the accused in their interpretation of a statutory provision. The Strasbourg Court has taken a more encompassing approach and merely considers analogy to be a form of the broader category of extensive interpretation of offenses and penalties. The ECHR's legality principle excludes extensive judicial interpretation to the accused's detriment when it leads to problems with the foreseeability of offenses or penalties, or when that interpretation would diverge from the essence of the offense.[21] As a result of the influence of the Strasbourg jurisprudence, the Dutch legality principle presently

---

see, e.g., Supreme Court, 17 December 2013, ECLI:NL:HR:2013:2013, *NJ* 2014/204, par. 4.2.

[15] Although the principle that offenses and penalties require a clear definition is not explicitly enshrined in Article 1(1) CC, the Dutch Supreme Court has accepted it to be a secondary principle enshrined in the Dutch legality principle, see, e.g., Supreme Court, 31 October 2000, ECLI:NL:HR:2000:AA7954, *NJ* 2001/14, par. 3.3–3.4.

[16] The ECtHR requires the publication of offenses and penalties under the legality principle of Article 7 ECHR by virtue of the accessibility requirement, see, e.g., European Court of Human Rights (GC), *Korbely v. Hungary*, 19 September 2008, appl. no. 9174/02, par. 74–75 and further P.H.P.H.M.C. van Kempen & M.I. Fedorova, 'Foreign terrorist fighters': *strafbaarstelling van verblijf op een terroristisch grondgebied? Een toetsing aan materieel strafrechtelijke, mensenrechtelijke en volkenrechtelijke parameters*, Deventer: Kluwer 2015 (with summary in English), p. 21, and M. Timmerman, 2018, pp. 82–101.

[17] See further about the meaning of this secondary principle under Dutch criminal law: J.S. Nan, *Het lex certa-beginsel*, Den Haag: Sdu Uitgevers 2011 (with summary in English), and P.H.P.H.M.C. van Kempen & M.I. Fedorova (2015), pp. 15–18.

[18] See, e.g., C. Peristeridou, The principle of *lex certa* in national law and European perspectives, in: *Substantive Criminal Law of the European Union*, A. Klip (ed.), Antwerp [etc]: Maklu 2011, pp. 69–95, p. 77.

[19] See, e.g., European Court of Human Rights (GC), *Rohlena v. The Czech Republic*, 27 January 2015, appl. no. 59552/08, par. 50, and M. Timmerman, 2018, pp. 72–75.

[20] This is a clear consequence of the primacy of the legislator in the field of substantive criminal law.

[21] See, e.g., European Court of Human Rights (GC), *Del Río Prada v. Spain*, 21 October 2013, appl. no. 42750/09, par. 93, and further M. Timmerman, 2018, pp. 102–115.

precludes certain forms of (overly) extensive interpretations of offenses and penalties and not just analogical interpretations.

4.3.2 CLASSIFICATION OF OFFENSES

Offenses are categorized as either crimes or infractions.[22] This division is used in all Dutch criminal law statutes. The categorization of a crime may have several implications for both criminal procedure and substantive criminal law. In criminal procedure, the categorization of a crime may limit the ability of prosecuting authorities to use coercive measures (*dwangmiddelen*) and limit the ability of the accused to use legal remedies (*rechtsmiddelen*). Furthermore, the categorization of offenses determines the competent tribunal. As a rule, crimes are tried by the district court (by one or three judges), whereas infractions are tried by a cantonal judge (Article 382 CCP). In substantive criminal law, attempting, participating and aiding and abetting an infraction does not trigger criminal liability. The provisions on concurrence (*samenloop*) and statute of limitations (*verjaring*) also distinguish between crimes and infractions.

No clear criterion exists for the distinction between crimes and infractions. There are, however, some elementary differences. First, serious offenses, which are sanctioned with imprisonment or detention, are generally qualified as a crime. Less serious offenses, sanctioned with fines, are generally qualified as infractions. Secondly, crimes contain a mental element (*subjectief bestanddeel*) as a precondition for criminal liability: intent or negligence. Infractions lack these components. The mental element is discussed below, in the section 4.3.4.

In the last decades, the legislature increasingly decriminalized relatively minor offenses. More and more crimes are converted to administrative offenses and enforced through administrative law. For example, through adoption of the 1989 Administration of Road Traffic Offenses Act, minor traffic offenses were converted to administrative offenses.

4.3.3 CONDITIONS FOR CRIMINAL LIABILITY

The Dutch Criminal Code does not offer a definition of the concept 'criminal offense', it merely provides the statutory definitions of punishable conduct. In light of the legality principle, the statutory definition of the offense is the obvious starting point for the determination of criminal liability. The statutory preconditions for criminal responsibility are generally referred to as elements (*bestanddelen*) and differ from offense to offense.

---

22   De Hullu 2018, pp. 72–73.

If we take the straightforward statutory definition of manslaughter in Article 287 CC as an example[23], we find that it requires causality between the prohibited consequence (*i.e.* death) and the acts of the defendant.[24] It also requires that the defendant caused the death of the victim intentionally.[25] As a result, the statutory definition of Article 287 CC includes both objective components (*i.e.* a prohibited consequence and causality) that set requirements for the prohibited act (*actus reus*) and a subjective component (*i.e.* intent) that requires the defendant to have acted with a certain state of mind (*mens rea*). The public prosecutor is required to incorporate the *actus reus* and the *mens rea* in the indictment (*tenlastelegging*) and prove their presence by presenting the facts in court. Where a component is missing in the charge *ontslag van rechtsvervolging* must follow. If the public prosecutor cannot prove by evidence that all the charged components are matched by the facts, *vrijspraak* must follow (Article 352 CCP). Both verdicts are modalities of acquittal.

Contrary to the components that differ from offense to offense, two additional, non-statutory, preconditions for criminal liability are deemed to apply to all offenses: the behavior of the defendant must have been wrongful (*wederrechtelijk*) and blameworthy (*verwijtbaar*). When a person has violated a statutory definition of an offense his conduct will, as a rule, have been wrongful and blameworthy. Therefore, the point of departure is that these two conditions are assumed to be satisfied when the specific requirements set by statutory definition of the offense (*i.e.* the elements) are fulfilled. If we return to the example of Article 287 CC it is easy to see why the non-statutory conditions for criminal liability are, *generally*, not hard to satisfy. When it is established that the defendant violated the statutory components of manslaughter by having intentionally caused the death of the victim, it will indeed be hard to argue that his conduct was not wrongful, because it is explicitly prohibited by the Criminal Code. It will also be difficult to argue that the defendant's conduct was not blameworthy, because the violation of Article 287 CC implies that the defendant's intention was to cause the death of the victim.[26] There are nevertheless exceptional cases wherein a violation of a statutory definition fails to give rise to criminal responsibility as a result of a problem with the non-statutory preconditions of wrongfulness and blameworthiness. These cases mostly concern complete defenses.[27]

---

[23] Article 287 CC states: 'any person who intentionally takes the life of another person shall be guilty of manslaughter and shall be liable to a term of imprisonment not exceeding fifteen years or a fine of the fifth category'.

[24] This follows from the wording 'takes the life of another person'.

[25] This follows from the term 'intentionally'.

[26] De Hullu 2018, pp. 68–69.

[27] See section 4.4 below on complete defenses.

4.3.4 MENTAL ELEMENT

As stated above, the *mens rea* or mental element is a precondition for criminal liability. In Dutch criminal law, two species of mental elements can be distinguished: intent (*opzet*) and negligence (*culpa*). Strict liability does not exist in Dutch criminal law.[28]

The general meaning of intent is to act willingly and knowingly.[29] However, the legislator has included different degrees of intent in the statutory definitions of crimes. The highest degree of intent, intent as a purpose (*opzet als bedoeling*), is reflected in the element of *oogmerk*. *Oogmerk* requires that the offender acted purposefully in order to reach a certain goal. For example, the defendant wants to smash up a bus shelter, he picks up a large piece of wood and smashes up the bus shelter. However, most crimes that entail the mental element of intent, require at least the presence of conditional intent. Conditional intent or *dolus eventualis* (*voorwaardelijk opzet*) represents the state of mind where the offender consciously accepts a considerable risk that the prohibited result may occur. Since conditional intent is the lowest degree of intent, it is the most relevant in practice. In order to establish the presence of intent, the prosecution has to prove the criminal act was *at least* performed with conditional intent. Because of its relevance in practice, conditional intent is discussed more extensively now.

The first requirement for conditional intent is the presence of a considerable risk (*aanmerkelijke kans*) that a certain result will occur. For example, if you drive with a speed of 100 kms per hour in an urban area, there is a considerable risk that you will cause an accident. The second requirement for conditional intent is the consciousness of this considerable risk (*bewust*). This means, referring back to the previous example, that the defendant has to know that speeding in an urban area may cause an accident. Third, the defendant has to accept the considerable risk (*aanvaarden*). He must accept that his behavior may cause an accident. In case of mere indifference of the offender as to the prohibited result, the court may reason that the conduct of the offender is to such an extent directed at a certain result, that he consciously *accepted* the considerable risk that the result would occur.[30]

Negligence[31] includes both conscious and unconscious negligence. Conscious negligence is present when the offender is aware of a considerable and

---

28 Nevertheless, the legislator exerts considerable pressure on the fault principle by increasingly using duties of care to criminalize conduct. See for extensive discussions on this topic M.J. Borgers, I.M. Koopmans & F.G.H. Kristen (red.), *Verwijtbare uitholling van schuld?*, Nijmegen: Ars Aequi Libri 1998.

29 De Hullu 2018, pp. 220–264.

30 Supreme Court, 25 March 2003, ECLI:NL:HR:2003:AE9049, *NJ* 2003/552 (*HIV-I*). For recent important case law on conditional intent, see e.g. Supreme Court, 29 May 2018, ECLI:NL:HR:2018:718, *NJ* 2019/103 with case note H.D. Wolswijk.

31 De Hullu 2018, pp. 264–282.

unjustifiable risk that a certain result will occur, but unreasonably thinks that the risk will not materialize. The difference between conscious negligence and conditional intent (discussed above) lies thus with the absence of acceptance of the prohibited result in case of conscious negligence. Conscious negligence may, for example, be present when the defendant caused an accident, while speeding on a highway. The defendant knows that speeding is dangerous, but thinks the risk of an accident will not materialize.

Unconscious negligence is present when the offender was not aware of the risk, but should have been. For example, when the defendant is a pharmacist and caused injuries by preparing the wrong prescription drug. In this case the pharmacist did not know he was selling the wrong medicine, but he should have been aware of this, considering his background and responsibilities. Consequently, his negligence in unconscious.

Both forms of negligence require three – identical – conditions. The defendant must have acted with substantial inattentiveness or carelessness (*aanmerkelijke onvoorzichtigheid of grove schuld*)[32], his behavior must have been wrongful (*wederrechtelijk*) and blameworthy (*verwijtbaar*). Mere slight inattentiveness or carelessness is not sufficient for negligence. For example, the Supreme Court has considered that it cannot generally be held that one traffic offense is sufficient for substantial inattentiveness or carelessness. The nature and gravity of the whole set of acts of the offender and other relevant circumstances of the specific case must be taken into account as well.[33] As to the second condition for negligence, wrongfulness, it has to be established whether the offender diverged from the required standard of conduct. The court has to identify the applicable standard of conduct by verifying how a person with average knowledge and capabilities (*criteriumfiguur*) would have acted in the same situation. In order to recognize the applicable standard of conduct, several factors may be important. First, it may be relevant whether the offender has a duty of care (*Garantenstellung*)[34] to prevent the manifestation of certain harmful consequences. If a breach of a duty of care can be established, courts will apply a lower standard for judging that the offender acted unlawfully. Equally important may be whether the offender has violated certain safety norms. Finally, it may be relevant whether the offender had a duty of investigation (*onderzoeksplicht*) in order to prevent committing a criminal offense. Considering the third requirements for negligence, it has to be established that the offender's act is blameworthy (*verwijtbaar*). The offender's act is blameworthy when he had a choice to act differently. The blameworthiness of

---

[32] See for a detailed analysis of substantial inattentiveness with regard to traffic offenses P.H.P.H.M.C. van Kempen, 'De ondergrens van culpa. Opmerkingen over de eis van 'grove schuld' bij artikel 6 WvW 1994 mede in relatie tot de wederrechtelijkheid en de verwijtbaarheid', *Delikt en Delinkwent*, 2004, pp. 996–1014.

[33] Supreme Court, 1 June 2004, ECLI:NL:HR:2004:AO5822, *NJ* 2005/252 (*Blackout*).

[34] The concept of *Garantenstellung* is more elaborately discussed in section 4.4 (Common features of complete defenses).

negligence may be negated due to the lack of foreseeability of the result, personal circumstances of the offender, and external circumstances.[35]

4.3.5 OBJECTIVE ELEMENT: CAUSATION

Causation is a necessary condition for establishing criminal liability in two types of offenses.[36] The causing of harm of a particular kind may be the key component of an offense (*materiële delicten*), but it may also be a ground for imposing a more serious sanction (*door het gevolg gekwalificeerde delicten*).[37] The Criminal Code does not define the circumstances under which an act may be perceived as the legally relevant cause of a result. The criteria for causation are developed in the Supreme Court's case law. The establishment of causation requires a two-pronged test.

The first part of the test consists of a 'but for' or *conditio sine qua non* test.[38] The *conditio sine qua non* test requires that the court verifies whether the conduct of the accused was an indispensable cause for the occurrence of the result. This can be done by testing whether the result would still occur, if the accused had not acted like he did. If the answer is negative (the result would not have occurred), the behavior of the defendant was a necessary condition and the *condition sine qua non* criterion has been met. In some cases, the application of the *conditio sine qua non* test may prove to be difficult or even impossible, for example in case of multiple causes or omissions.

The second part of the test consists of the doctrine of reasonable imputation (*redelijke toerekening*). This doctrine requires that the result may reasonably be imputed to the conduct of the accused. Reasonable imputation can be inferred from several specific theories on causation. The foreseeability of the result is an important factor. The theory of relevance focusses on the most relevant cause, in the view of the legislature. For example, in case of assault resulting in death (Article 300(3) CC) the injuries of the victim would be a relevant cause of death and not a fire in the hospital where the assault victim was treated. Another theory, *causa proxima*, holds that the latest event in the causal chain of events anticipating the result is legally relevant. In addition, a breach of a duty of care by the defendant may be an argument for the presence of causation. Finally, the Supreme Court considers relevant for reasonable imputation that no other act has predominantly influenced the occurrence of the result.[39]

---

[35]   See A.A. van Dijk, *Strafrechtelijke aansprakelijkheid heroverwogen*, Antwerp: Maklu 2008, pp. 191–192.

[36]   De Hullu 2018, pp. 178–190.

[37]   See for a typology of different ways of framing statutory definitions of criminal offences De Hullu 2018, pp. 73–84.

[38]   The importance of the '*conditio sine qua non* test' was emphasized by the Supreme Court in Supreme Court, 11 October 2005, ECLI:NL:HR:2005:AT5772, *NJ* 2006/548 (*Trunk*).

[39]   See for an extensive overview E.M. Witjens, *Strafrechtelijke causaliteit*, Deventer: Kluwer 2011.

4.3.6 OBJECTIVE ELEMENT: DEFINITIONS OF SOME MAJOR CRIMES

Murder (Article 289 CC). Any person who intentionally and with premeditation takes the life of another person shall be guilty of murder and liable to life imprisonment or a determinate term of imprisonment not exceeding thirty years or a fine of the fifth category.

Intentional homicide (Article 287 CC). Any person who intentionally takes the life of another person shall be guilty of manslaughter and shall be liable to a term of imprisonment not exceeding fifteen years or a fine of the fifth category.

Assault (Article 300(1) CC). Assault shall be liable to a term of imprisonment not exceeding three years or a fine of the forth category.[40]

Theft (Article 310 CC). Any person who takes any property belonging in whole or in part to another person, with the intention of unlawfully appropriating it, shall be guilty of theft and shall be liable to a term of imprisonment not exceeding four years or a fine of the fourth category.[41]

Robbery (Article 312(1) CC). Theft preceded, accompanied or followed by an act of violence or threat of violence against persons, committed with the intention of preparing or facilitating the theft or in the event of being caught in the commission of the serious offense to secure for himself or the other participants in that offense either escape or possession of the stolen property, shall be liable to a term of imprisonment not exceeding nine years or a fine of the fifth category.[42]

Human trafficking (Article 273f CC). This is a complex and lengthy provision which aims to cover a broad range of activities related to human trafficking.[43]

4.4 COMPLETE DEFENSES

4.4.1 INTRODUCTION

Complete defenses[44] are arguments by which a defendant admits to committing a crime, while – at the same time – asserting that this crime was committed for

---

[40] For important recent case law, see Supreme Court, 3 July 2018, ECLI:NL:HR:2018:1051.

[41] For important recent case law on theft and the demarcation between the property crimes of theft (Article 310 CC), embezzlement (Article 321 CC), fraud (Article 326 CC) and deception (Article 326a CC), see Supreme Court, 20 March 2018, ECLI:NL:HR:2018:367, *NJ* 2018/326 with case note N. Rozemond.

[42] The categories of fines can be found in Article 23(4) CC.

[43] More information about the content and meaning of Article 273f CC can be found in: S. Lestrade, *De strafbaarstelling van arbeidsuitbuiting in Nederland*, Deventer: Wolters Kluwer 2018, chapter 3 (with summary in English).

[44] De Hullu 2018, pp. 295–389.

an acceptable reason. For example: a defendant admits to committing murder. However, he claims he did so because he had to defend himself against an unlawful attack. If a court accepts this argument, the defendant is completely absolved from criminal responsibility (hence the expression *complete* defense). A successful appeal to a complete defense thus leads to acquittal.[45] This section is restricted to a discussion of the *general* complete defenses applicable in the Netherlands. General complete defenses may be raised against *any* criminal offense. The counterparts of general defenses are so-called specific defenses. Specific defenses can only be invoked against a particular crime.[46]

4.4.2 JUSTIFICATIONS AND EXCUSES

In Dutch criminal law complete defenses generally consist of two subcategories: justifications and excuses.[47] In case of a justification, the violation of the law is not wrongful, because the defendant made the right choice in a difficult situation. If a defendant, for example, has broken down a door in order to save a person in a burning house, this destruction of property is not wrongful, for it was necessary to save the life of another person. Therefore, the criminal responsibility of the defendant is negated.

In case of an excuse, the violation of the law is wrongful, but the offender is not blameworthy. If, for example, a defendant was forced at gunpoint to shoot another person, this shooting would be wrongful. There is no justification for taking an innocent life. Still, the defendant could lack blameworthiness if he had no reasonable choice to behave differently. Consequently, also in case of an excuse, the criminal responsibility of the defendant is negated.

4.4.3 COMPLETE DEFENSES IN DUTCH CRIMINAL LAW

The Criminal Code contains a number of provisions establishing complete defenses (Articles 39–43 CC). Statutory grounds for justifications are: necessity

---

45   M. Krabbe, *Complete defenses in international criminal law*, Cambridge: Intersentia, 2014, pp. 5–6. However, when a complete defense is rejected by the court, the defense can still have a mitigating effect on the sentence. See: De Hullu 2018, p. 295. Please take note that the Dutch Criminal Code distinguishes two types of acquittal: *ontslag van alle rechtsvervolging* and *vrijspraak* (Article 352 CCP). Depending on the definition of the crime charged, a successful appeal to a complete defense can result in either of these two options. See section 4.4.7, below.

46   For example, under Dutch law a medical doctor preforming an abortion cannot be held responsible for the crime of abortion under Article 296 of the Criminal Code.

47   The distinction between justifications and excuses is not explicit in the Dutch Criminal Code, is not airtight (see: K. Greenawalt, 'The perplexing borders of justification and excuse', 8 *Columbia Law Review*, 1984, pp. 1897–1927) and is criticized in Dutch legal doctrine (De Hullu 2018, pp. 297–299). Nevertheless, the distinction is often referred to in textbooks and has relevance in practice, for example when determining the type of verdict (See section 4.4.7).

(Article 40 CC), self-defense (Article 41 CC), statutory requirement (Article 42 CC) and official orders (Article 43 CC). Statutory grounds for excuses are: insanity (Article 39 CC), duress (Article 40 CC), excessive self-defense (Article 41(2) CC) and obeying an unlawful order (Article 43(2) CC). In addition to these statutory grounds, two complete defenses have been developed in the case law of the Supreme Court. The first, the absence of substantive wrongfulness, is a justification; the second, the absence of all blameworthiness (a category including defenses such as mistake of fact, mistake of law and intoxication) is an excuse. All these complete defenses are addressed more extensively below.

4.4.4 COMMON FEATURES OF COMPLETE DEFENSES

Proportionality and necessity

The success of an appeal to a complete defense largely depends on the proportionality and necessity[48] of the defendant's behavior when committing the offense. Proportionality refers to the balance between harm avoided and the harm done by the defendant. Necessity refers to the availability of other options to the defendant. As to the proportionality requirement, an appeal to a complete defense will be unsuccessful, for example, when the defendant shot a person who tried to steal his wallet. Shooting to avert theft, namely, is not a *proportionate* reaction. In this very same example, the necessity requirement would not have been met when the defendant used a fair amount of violence while in fact there was enough time to call the police. In such a situation, using violence is not *necessary.*[49]

In general, the requirements of proportionality and necessity are more of a decisive factor with justifications than in case of excuses. The defendant who successfully invokes a justification must have acted in a proportionate and necessary fashion, since his act was not wrongful. The defendant, who successfully invokes an excuse, did commit a wrongful act. Therefore, the requirements of proportionality and necessity are less stringent.

Garantenstellung

A *Garantenstellung* refers to the weight of the societal position of the defendant when determining how he should have behaved in a given situation. From certain people we simply demand a more proportionate reaction, or more of an effort to come up with an alternative solution. For example: a mistake of law may

---

[48] Necessity is referred to in Dutch as *subsidiariteit* (subsidiarity).
[49] The relationship between the concepts of proportionality and subsidiarity is a complicated one. For a quick attempt to unravel this relationship see M. Krabbe, 2014, p. 312.

sooner be an excuse to an illiterate person than to a lawyer. Or: we expect a more proportionate response to an unlawful attack from a trained police officer than from a fashion designer. A *Garantenstellung* may thus influence the assessment of the requirements of proportionality and necessity in a specific case.

Prior fault

A successful appeal to a complete defense can be barred by a prior fault of the defendant. In Dutch doctrine this is referred to as *culpa in causa*. For example: a defendant voluntarily joins a criminal gang. Before joining the gang, he knew that the leader of this gang occasionally forces its members to kill innocent people. This knowledge (which qualifies as the prior fault of the defendant) may bar a successful appeal to an excuse in case the defendant was, for instance, forced to kill an innocent person at gunpoint. The influence of prior fault in Dutch case law is, however, limited. 'Absence of prior fault' is not a cumulative requirement for a successful appeal to a complete defense. Courts tend to focus on the moment the crime was committed, not on earlier decisions made by the defendant. Still, prior fault can influence the outcome of a case.

4.4.5 JUSTIFICATIONS

Necessity (noodtoestand)

Article 40 Criminal Code reads:

> Any person who commits an offense under the compulsion of an irresistible force shall not be criminally liable.

Based on the history of the Dutch Criminal Code, the Supreme Court ruled that this provision includes the defense of necessity.[50] Necessity is a situation in which the defendant has to choose between conflicting duties. If the defendant lets the most important duty prevail and, by doing so, violates criminal law, his act is justified. The example in section 4.4.2 of a justification (defendant destroys property in order to save a person in a burning house) is a typical case of necessity. The defendant is confronted with two conflicting duties: saving the person and not destroying property. If he chooses the most important duty (saving the person) and, by doing so, violates criminal law (by destroying property), a successful appeal to necessity is possible. Conditions for a successful appeal to necessity are the above-mentioned requirements of proportionality and necessity. Before the adoption of specific legislation on euthanasia in 2001, Article 40 of the Criminal Code was often invoked by doctors assisting patients

---

[50] Supreme Court, 15 October 1923, ECLI:NL:HR:1923:243, *NJ* 1923/1329 (*Optician*).

who chose to terminate their life. Lately the article has been invoked in cases of non-medical assistance with suicide.[51]

Self-defense (noodweer)

Article 41 Criminal Code reads:

> Any person who commits an offense where this is necessary in the defense of his or another person's physical or sexual integrity or property against an immediate, unlawful attack shall not be criminally liable.

As a rule, the State has a monopoly on violence. However, an immediate unlawful attack may be lawfully averted by an individual, if he can successfully claim self-defense. Self-defense has several conditions. There must have been no other reasonable mode of escape (necessity requirement). Also, the amount of force used must be *proportionate* to the harm avoided. As to the immediacy of the attack: the attack must be imminent. Preventive self-defense is excluded from Article 41.[52] An attack is unlawful, when a legal ground for the attack is absent. A legal ground for an attack may, for example, be present in case of a lawful arrest by a police officer. Defensible interests under Article 41 CC are limited to the defendant's or another's physical integrity, sexual integrity or property. Consequently, self-defense cannot be invoked in case of, for example, insult. Whether the Supreme Court of the Netherlands requires the defendant to act with the intent to act in self-defense (mental element requirement) is debatable.[53]

Statutory requirement (wettelijk voorschrift)

Article 42 Criminal Code reads:

> Any person who commits an offense in carrying out a statutory requirement shall not be criminally liable.

Article 42 CC guarantees impunity in case the defendant acted in accordance with a statutory requirement. The provision covers situations in which acting

---

[51]   A well-known case in this respect is the *Heringa case*: Supreme Court, 14 March 2017, ECLI:NL:HR:2017:418, *NJ* 2017/269. Heringa assisted his 99-year-old stepmother with committing suicide. He claimed necessity which was accepted by the Court of Appeal. This decision, however, was subsequently quashed by the Supreme Court. On euthanasia cases, see chapter 3, para. 3.6.

[52]   Supreme Court, 8 February 1932, ECLI:NL:HR:1932:BG9439, *NJ* 1932/617 (*Fear judgement*).

[53]   Supreme Court, 22 March 2016, ECLI:NL:HR:2016:456, *NJ* 2016/316 with case note by N. Rozemond (*Overview judgment on self-defense*). For an interpretation of this judgement considering the mental element in the context of self-defense, see A. van Verseveld, 'Noodweer: de Hoge Raad geeft een overzicht', *Delikt en Delinkwent*, 2016, 5, p. 34.

in accordance with the law coincides with breaking another law. For example: police officers, when preforming their duties, often fulfill the elements of crimes such as trespassing, destruction and the deprivation of freedom. As to the conditions of Article 42 CC: the statutory requirement acted upon has to be compulsory, and the behavior of the defendant has to be in accordance with the principles of proportionality and necessity. In that sense, Article 42 can be considered a *lex specialis* Article 40 CC (necessity) in case the two conflicting duties arise from legal provisions.

Official orders (ambtelijk bevel)

Article 43 (1) Criminal Code reads:

> Any person who commits an offense in carrying out an official order issued by the proper authority shall not be criminally liable.

In case of Article 43(1) impunity is guaranteed because the defendant acted in accordance with an official order. The provision covers situations in which acting in accordance with an official order coincides with breaking the law. The defense is thus very similar to the defense of statutory requirement – the difference being the source of the obligation –, has similar requirements and can also be considered a *lex specialis* of necessity. Appeals to statutory requirement and official orders are rare in published case law. They may be more frequently employed as a ground to drop the prosecution of a case.

Absence of substantive wrongfulness

The defense of absence of substantive wrongfulness (*afwezigheid van materiële wederrechtelijkheid*) was developed in the case law of the Supreme Court. In 1933, the Court ruled that, even though wrongfulness is not an element in the statutory definition of the offense, the offender cannot be convicted when his act does not result in a substantive wrongfulness. In this case the substantive unlawfulness was absent because the act (that was in conflict with the law) served the same interest as was guaranteed by the law.[54] The legal impact of this non-codified justification is limited. After 1933, the Court did not repeat its ruling. This may be explained by the fact that the distinction between the defense of absence of substantive wrongfulness and the defense of necessity is not clear. The concepts seem to overlap.[55]

---

[54] Supreme Court, 20 February 1933, *NJ* 1933/918 (*Veterinarian*).
[55] De Hullu 2018, pp. 364–365.

Another non-codified defense that may negate the wrongfulness of a crime is the consent of the victim.[56] However, consent is not considered a justification when the act consented to violates a general interest.[57]

4.4.6 EXCUSES

Insanity (ontoerekenbaarheid)

Article 39 Criminal Code reads:

> Any person who commits an offense for which he cannot be held responsible by reason of mental disease or defect shall not be criminally liable.

The insanity defense provides the defendant with an excuse in case he committed the crime while he was suffering from a mental disorder. The insanity defense consists of three requirements. First, a mental disease or defect had to be present at the time the crime was committed. This can be any mental disorder. A personality disorder, for example, but also mental illnesses, such as depression or schizophrenia. Physical diseases and mere emotions (fever, fear, lust) are excluded from the defense. Second, the mental condition of the defendant must have *caused* the commission of the crime. If the defendant suffered from pyromania and he has robbed a bank, there is no causal relation between mental disease and crime committed. Consequently, an appeal to insanity will fail. Third, the defendant must not be accountable for the crime committed. If the defendant suffered from a mental illness at the time he committed the crime (first requirement) and this illness caused him to commit a crime (second requirement), the defendant could still be held accountable for the crime if the court holds that despite the influence of his illness he was capable to refrain from committing a crime. For example, if the schizophrenic condition of the defendant caused him to shoot eight persons, the court may still find that – despite the illness influencing the defendant's behavior – the defendant had the ability to realize the wrongfulness of his act and the capacity to make a different decision.

When assessing the mental condition of the defendant, the court is advised by experts (a psychiatrist, among others). These experts may conclude that the defendant is accountable (*toerekeningsvatbaar*) – in which case he is criminally responsible for his act – or completely unaccountable – in which case an appeal to insanity may[58] be successful. However, these experts may also conclude that the

---

[56]   De Hullu 2018, p. 362.
[57]   J.M. ten Voorde, *Tekst & Commentaar Strafrecht*, commentaar op titel III Sr, Inleidende opmerkingen, par. 11 sub (e), 2018 (online on Kluwer Navigator).
[58]   Ultimately, the court decides on the accountability of the defendant.

defendant's accountability is only diminished[59], in which case the defendant is still criminally responsible but can also be committed to a mental hospital or an outpatient program.

Duress (overmacht)

Article 40 Criminal Code includes not only necessity (cited and discussed above under justifications) but also duress. The defense of duress offers an excuse to the defendant who acted under the pressure of an external force he could reasonably not resist. For example: the defendant has committed a crime because he was threatened at gunpoint. The external force may be an unlawful threat originating from another person or from a natural force. If the defendant was forced by his moral conscience – e.g. his religion or vegan principles – the defense of duress will fail. The defendant must have been unable to resist the external force (subjective criterion) and the defendant can *reasonably* not be blamed for his inability to resist (objective criterion). The reasonability of the defendant's reaction is determined by the proportionality and necessity of his behavior, which in turn, may be colored by a *Garantenstellung* (see above under 'Common features of complete defenses'). Continued external pressure, such as in case of battered women syndrome, is generally rejected as a duress defense, since the defendant had the opportunity to explore other options (i.e. the necessity requirement has not been met).

Excessive self-defense (noodweerexces)

Article 41(2) Criminal Code reads:

> Any person who exceeds the bounds of necessary defense, if the excess force is the direct result of a violent emotion caused by the attack, shall not be criminally liable.

When self-defense – Article 41(1) CC, discussed above under justifications – causes strong emotions such as rage, anger, fear or desperation, the defendant may exceed the limits of proportionality. For example, a woman is mugged, panics, and stabs her attacker. Stabbing to avert theft is disproportionate. An appeal to self-defense will therefore fail. Excessive self-defense (Article 41(2) CC), a defense offered in situations of disproportionate self-defense, may however be available. For a successful appeal to excessive self-defense, several conditions have to be met. First of all, a 'self-defense situation' must have existed. This means that some of the conditions for self-defense must have been present. There

---

[59]   Three different levels of diminished accountability are employed in Dutch legal practice: somewhat diminished accountability (*enigszins verminderd toerekenbaar*), diminished accountability (*verminderd toerekenbaar*) and severely diminished accountability (*sterk verminderd toerekenbaar*).

must have been an *immediate unlawful attack* to a *defensible interest*. In addition, no alternative course of action must have been available to the defendant (i.e. the *necessity requirement* must be met). Second, this self-defense situation must have *caused* a violent emotion in the defendant. Third, this violent emotion, in turn, must have *caused* the defendant to exceed the bounds of necessary defense. Consequently, if the woman in the previous example was struck by a violent emotion *due to* an immediate and unlawful attack on her property and this violent emotion *caused* her to exceed the limits of a proportionate defense, she may successfully appeal to excessive self-defense.[60] Still, if the limits of proportionality are excessively exceeded, even an appeal to excessive self-defense may be fruitless. The court may then argue that the emotions of the defendant could not have triggered such a disproportionate reaction.[61]

Obeying an unlawful order (onbevoegd gegeven ambtelijk bevel)

Article 43(2) Criminal Code reads:

> Any person who carries out an official order issued without proper authority shall not be exempted from criminal liability, unless, acting as a subordinate, he believed in good faith that the order was issued by the proper authority and he complied with it in his capacity as subordinate.

Article 43(2) CC offers a defense to the subordinate who acted in good faith when obeying an unlawful superior order. Nevertheless, clarity lacks as to the exact interpretation of this good faith. Good faith may be subjective (did the defendant *sincerely* belief he executed a lawful order?) or objective/normative (did the defendant *reasonably* belief he executed a lawful order?). In the latter case, there is still a responsibility on the subordinate to be prudent, and in case of doubt to refrain from obeying the order.[62]

Absence of all blameworthiness (afwezigheid van alle schuld)

In line with the principle 'no criminal liability without blameworthiness' the excuse of absence of all blameworthiness has been developed in the Supreme Court's case law. 'Absence of all blameworthiness' can thus be best described

---

[60] Supreme Court, 22 March 2016, ECLI:NL:HR:2016:456, NJ 2016/316 with case note by N. Rozemond (*Overview judgment on self-defense*) also contains information on the requirements for excessive self-defense.

[61] As was held in Supreme Court, 8 April 2008, ECLI:NLHR:2008:BC4459, NJ 2008/312 (*Testicle squeezer*). In this case lethally hitting an 86-year-old man on the head with a vase after he – in the context of a sexual encounter – grabbed the 38-year-old defendant by the testicles, was considered too disproportionate for as successful appeal to excessive self-defense.

[62] J.M. ten Voorde, *Tekst & Commentaar Strafrecht*, Commentaar op titel III Sr, Commentaar op artikel 43 Sr, 2018 (online Kluwer Navigator).

as a residual category of non-codified excuses. The category covers four sub-categories of excuses: mistake of fact[63], mistake of law[64], excusable incapacity[65] (which may include cases of intoxication) and the maximum care doctrine.[66] For each of these sub-categories the crucial question is: was, considering the circumstances, the behavior of the defendant excusable? Generally, behavior is excusable when the offender has done everything he can reasonably be expected to do in order to avoid the commission of a crime. If the crime is committed due to indolence, frivolity or indifference, the defense will not be successful. Below, examples of all four sub-categories are briefly addressed.

Mistakes of fact are often brought up in traffic cases, where the defendant argues he did not see the pedestrian/traffic light/oncoming car, for example. In addition, mistakes as to complete defenses may qualify as a mistake of fact. For example, a defendant mistakes a fake weapon for a real one (mistake of fact) and thinks he is threatened. He defends himself by hitting his attacker. This hitting cannot be justified under the heading of self-defense, since the defendant was not responding to an imminent unlawful attack. However, if the defendant reasonably thought he was threatened by a weapon, he may have the excuse of mistake of fact.[67]

Mistake of law can be viewed as a *specialis* of mistake of fact, namely a mistake as to a very specific set of facts: the law. Mistake of law is generally not an excuse ("Yes I did steal that car, but I didn't know I was not allowed to that."), since this would undermine the efficiency law enforcement. However, mistakes as to the applicability of a law, especially when the phrasing of the law is ambiguous, may occasionally offer an excuse. Mistake of law may also excuse the defendant who has actively sought expert legal advice by a person or agency having such an authority, but was misinformed.

Excusable incapacity covers situations where the defendant was incapacitated by a cause he could not control. By an unforeseen effect of prescription drugs (intoxication), for example, or by a sudden epileptic seizure.

Finally, the *maximum care doctrine* is an excuse relevant to defendants in a responsible position.[68] For example, when a manufacturer is prosecuted for selling a defective product (e.g. poisonous food), he may have an excuse if he can establish that he provided the maximum level of care (e.g. he followed the protocols, carried out the necessary checks etcetera) to prevent the defect.

---

[63] *Verontschuldigbare feitelijke dwaling.*
[64] *Verontschuldigbare rechtsdwaling.*
[65] *Verontschuldigbare onmacht.*
[66] *Maximaal te vergen zorg.*
[67] Mistakes as to complete defenses may also qualify as a mistake of law when the defendant made a reasonable mistake pertaining to the specific legal conditions of a complete defense.
[68] Although the defense has also been raised in the context of illegal aliens. See, for example: Supreme Court, 28 October 2008, ECLI:NL:HR:2008:BE9611, *NJ* 2008/570.

4.4.7 PROCEDURAL CONSEQUENCES OF COMPLETE DEFENSES

A successful appeal to a complete defense leads to acquittal. The Dutch Criminal Code distinguishes two types of acquittal: *ontslag van alle rechtsvervolging* and *vrijspraak* (Article 352 CCP). In case the indictment cannot be proved, the verdict is *vrijspraak*. In case of another ground for acquittal the verdict is *ontslag van alle rechtsvervolging*. In case of a successful appeal to a complete defense the verdict is usually *ontslag van alle rechtsvervolging*: the indictment can be proved, but there are valid reasons not to convict the defendant. However, when wrongfulness – which is negated by a justification – and/or blameworthiness – negated by an excuse – are part of the definition of the offence and therefor part of the indictment, a successful appeal to a complete defense leads to *vrijspraak*. Wrongfulness is part of the indictment when the words *wederrechtelijk* (wrongfully) and/or *schuld* (culpably) appear in the indictment. Blameworthiness is an element of the indictment through the word *schuld*. So if the indictment reads *Henry stole Bob's bike intentionally and wrongfully* and Henry successfully appeals to a justification, the verdict in this case will be *vrijspraak*, because, due to the successful appeal to a justification the element 'wrongfully' cannot be proved.

4.5 INCHOATE OFFENSES

4.5.1 INTRODUCTION

Dutch criminal law distinguishes between three inchoate offenses: attempt, preparation and conspiracy.[69] A general feature of these crimes is that they are committed even though the substantive offense is not completed. The rationale for inchoate offenses lies in the danger for society posed by an individual who has started committing an offense. Criminalization of these offenses provides judicial authorities procedural powers to prevent risk and safeguard prosecution at an earlier stage. Recent developments show that – in addition to the common inchoate offenses which refer to classic substantive crimes (such as murder and assault) – the Dutch legislator has increasingly phrased statutory offenses in an 'inchoate manner'. For example, substantive crimes in which a certain act is committed with an intent to cause harm, or offenses that encourage or assist other crimes (e.g. terrorist acts). In these situations, the investigative and prosecutorial authorities have instruments to act at an early stage without using the classic modalities described below. Below the following inchoate offenses are discussed: attempt, preparation and conspiracy.

---

[69]   De Hullu 2018, pp. 391–436.

4.5.2 ATTEMPT

An attempt to commit a crime is punishable when the offender manifests his intention by initiating the crime (Article 45 CC). In case of attempt, the statutory principal penalty for the crime is reduced by one third. The rationale of this reduction is twofold: first, non-completion of a crime imposes less danger to society than a completed crime. Second, the sentence reduction may be an incentive for the offender to cease the commission of a crime.

Intent is an important element of attempt. It must be proved that the defendant has acted at least with conditional intent. The Dutch Criminal Code does not define where the preparation of a crime starts and its execution ends. The Dutch Supreme Court's holds that an act, which in its outward appearance must be regarded as being directed at the completion of the crime, is an act initiating the crime.[70] For example, when a group of robbers have entered a bank building with stockings over their heads, carrying firearms, this is an act, which in its outward appearance (carrying masks and arms in a bank building) must be regarded as being directed at completing the crime of bank robbery. However, when the same group of robbers buys stockings at the local supermarket, with the intention to use those stockings when robbing a bank, this is not an act, which in its outward appearance (buying stockings) must be regarded as being directed at the completion of the crime (robbery).

Voluntary withdrawal

Article 46b CC establishes voluntary withdrawal as a ground for excluding criminal liability. The offender cannot be convicted for committing an attempt if the crime is not completed and the non-completion of the crime was a voluntary decision. A decision is voluntary when the defendant was not *forced* to make a choice. Leaving in the midst of a burglary because you hear police cars coming is not a voluntary decision. Leaving, however, before completing the burglary because you feel remorse, is. Furthermore, the accused must have withdrawn from further executing the offense in a timely and effective manner. There are two reasons behind the voluntary withdrawal rule: first, the offender is not as blameworthy as he initially appeared to be. Second, the prospect of impunity may be an incentive not to complete the crime.

4.5.3 PREPARATION

Preparation does not fall within the legal scope of attempt since there is not yet an initiation of the crime. For preventive purposes it was felt to be

---

70   Supreme Court, 24 October 1978, ECLI:NL:HR:1978:AC6373, *NJ* 1979/52 (*Employment agency Cito*).

unsatisfactory that the police could not arrest offenders preparing serious crimes. In 1994, therefore, the preparation of serious crimes – that carry statutory prison sentences of eight years or more – was criminalized (Article 46 CC). Preparation of these crimes is punishable where the offender intentionally obtains, manufactures, imports, transits, exports or has at his disposal, objects, substances, monies or other instruments of payment, information carriers, concealed spaces or means of transport clearly intended for the joint commission of such a crime. The means and the modalities of preparation are so widely interpretable that they have little distinctive ability. The core of liability is thus determined by the intention the suspect has with his means and actions. For instance, if I have a detailed street map and a knife in my house this might be innocent. But if I plan to use this map and knife to carry out a murder, I become subject to punishment. In case of preparation, the statutory maximum penalty for the crime is reduced by one half (with a maximum of fifteen years imprisonment in case of preparation of an offense that carries a life sentence as a maximum penalty). As with attempt, Article 46b CC excludes liability for voluntary withdrawals.

4.5.4 CONSPIRACY

Conspiracy exists as soon as two or more persons agree to commit an offense (Article 80 CC). Conspiracy is only subject to punishment with respect to certain serious offenses such as crimes against the security of the State (Articles 92–95a CC) and crimes with terrorist intent (Articles 114b, 120b, 176b, 289a, 304b, 415b CC). Here, the fact of a specific agreement with others about one of the previously mentioned crimes is regarded as sufficient evidence that the parties will carry out the crime. The reason for criminalization is largely preventive. It enables the police to act at a very early stage, before any real harm has been caused.

4.6 PARTICIPATION

4.6.1 INTRODUCTION

Participation concerns the cooperation of two or more people in the commission of an offense (before and during and sometimes even after the fact).[71] The main question in this doctrine is how much involvement is necessary in the course of carrying out the offense to be held liable. Dutch criminal law distinguishes between principals and accessories. For corporate crimes a separate doctrine has been developed.

---

[71]   De Hullu 2018, pp. 437–525.

4.6.2 PRINCIPALS

Principals are those who commit a criminal offense, either personally (*plegen*) or jointly with another person (*medeplegen*), or who cause an innocent person to commit a criminal offense (*doenplegen*) and those who, by means of gifts, promises, abuse of authority, use of violence, threat or deception or providing the opportunity, means or information, intentionally solicit the commission of a crime (*uitlokken*) (Article 47 CC). The modalities of *doenplegen* and *uitlokken* are of decreasing importance, since the introduction of prosecution based on corporate criminal responsibility (discussed below). According to the Supreme Court's case law a person can only be held liable for 'participation as a principal' if the intellectual and/or material contribution is of sufficient weight. Relevant factors can be the intensity of the cooperation, the division of tasks in the criminal enterprise, the role of the accused in the preparation, the execution, or settlement of the crime and the importance of the role of the accused and his presence at key moments.[72] For example, two persons who agree to commit a robbery – one threatening the security guard while the other grabs the money – are both liable for the robbery since their intellectual and/or material contribution is of equally (or at least sufficient) weight.

4.6.3 ACCESSORIES

Accessories to crimes are those who intentionally assist during the commission of a crime and those who provide the opportunity, means or information to commit the crime (Article 48 CC). This is for instance the case if a person turns off the alarm before a robbery because he is asked to do so by another suspect, and the person has had no other contribution than switching of the alarm. The main reproach to an accessory is the fact that a person promotes and/ or facilitates another person to commit a crime.[73] In case of complicity as an accessory, the statutory maximum of the principal penalty is reduced by one third. In case the offense carries a life sentence, the accessory may be sentenced to an imprisonment of twenty years maximum (Article 49 CC). Being an accessory to an infraction is not punishable.

4.6.4 CORPORATE CRIMINAL LIABILITY

A somewhat separate category of participation is the doctrine of corporate criminal liability. In principle, private corporations are able to commit any type

---

[72]   Supreme Court, 16 December 2014, ECLI:NL:HR:2014:3637, *NJ* 2015/391, par. 3.2.1–3.2.3 (*Overview judgement participation*).

[73]   Supreme Court, 22 March 2011, ECLI:NL:HR:2011:BO2629, *NJ* 2011/341, par. 2.2.

of offense.[74] According to Article 51 CC, offenses can be committed by 'legal persons'. The definition of a 'legal person' is to be found primarily in Dutch private law.[75] However, Article 51 (3) CC broadens this definition by stating that certain entities without legal personality in civil law can nevertheless commit an offense. In order for a corporation to be held criminally liable, two conditions must be fulfilled. First, since a corporation cannot 'act' itself, the conduct of natural persons must be attributed to the corporation. Second, it must be established that the corporation acted with intent (*opzet*) or negligence (*culpa*). Both conditions for criminal liability of private corporations are discussed below.

The legislator did not explicitly state the conditions for attribution of conduct to a corporation. In 2003, the Supreme Court clarified in a general ruling how corporate criminal liability should be established: the attribution of illegal conduct to the corporation may under certain circumstances be reasonable if the illegal conduct took place within the scope of the corporation.[76] The Supreme Court provided four circumstances or factors that may be relevant in determining whether the conduct may be said to be carried out within the scope of a corporation: a) whether the illegal conduct was carried out by someone who works for the corporation, b) whether the conduct fits the everyday 'normal business' of the corporation, c) whether the corporation gained profit from the illegal conduct and d) whether the illegal conduct was accepted (*aanvaarden*) by and at the 'disposal' (*beschikken*) – of the corporation. Acceptance includes the failure to take reasonable care or to prevent the conduct from being performed, but proof of intent is not necessarily required in the context of this condition.

Proof of a mental element (intent or negligence) is, however, a separate requirement to establish corporate criminal responsibility for a crime.[77] As far as infractions are concerned, attribution of conduct suffices for punishment. With regard to the attribution of intent or negligence to corporations in case of crimes, two approaches can be followed. The indirect approach consists in ascribing intent or negligence of a natural person to the corporation. This approach may be particularly suitable in cases of sole proprietorship. The direct approach consists in deriving intent or negligence from other circumstances closely related to the corporation itself, for example corporate policy or decisions from highly placed officials within the corporation (Article 51 (2) CC). This approach is particularly suitable in cases of gross negligence, since gross negligence can be derived from the failure to act according to appropriate standards of conduct.

---

[74] See for an extensive analysis: A.N. Kesteloo, *De rechtspersoon in het strafrecht*, Deventer: Kluwer 2013; De Hullu 2018, pp. 169–179, and B.F. Keulen & E. Gritter, 'Corporate Criminal Liability in the Netherlands', in: M. Pieth & R. Ivory (red.), *Corporate Criminal Liability: Emergence, Convergence, and Risk*, Dordrecht: Springer 2011, pp. 177–191.

[75] Articles 2:1–2:3 of the Dutch Civil Code.

[76] Supreme Court, 21 October 2003, ECLI:NL:HR:2003:AF7938, *NJ* 2006/328 (*Slurry*).

[77] De Hullu 2018, pp. 282–287.

Only when a corporation is found to be liable, the liability of a responsible individual (*feitelijk leidinggever*) may be established. Several conditions must be fulfilled (Article 51(2) sub 2 CC).[78] First, the alleged offense must have been committed by the corporation. Second, the offender must have exercised control over the alleged offense. Third, the offender must have been actively or passively involved in committing the offense. In cases of active involvement, consent or even incitement may be sufficient. In cases of passive involvement it is required that the offender was authorized and reasonably expected to take measures to prevent the illegal conduct, but failed to do so and thereby consciously accepted the considerable chance that the illegal conduct would occur.[79] As a rule, it suffices for conscious acceptance that the offender generally knew that the corporation engaged in illegal conduct. Specific knowledge of the type of offense that was committed is not required.[80] Fourth, a causal relation between the involvement of the offender and the illegal conduct of the corporation must be established. Fifth, double intent must be proven. The offender must have had both intent to become actively involved in committing the offense and at least conditional intent to commit the perpetrated offense.[81]

The State and any province, municipality or district water board are legal persons. Therefore, public law legal persons (*publiekrechtelijke rechtspersonen*) can in principle commit criminal offenses.[82] Such entities can only claim immunity for acts that can, according to the legal system, merely be executed by civil servants acting within the framework of a task assigned to that body.[83] The State as a public corporate body, however, enjoys criminal immunity for all acts. The Supreme Court has ruled that criminal liability of the State is incompatible with the political accountability of Ministers for acts of the State in Parliament.[84]

---

78   De Hullu 2018, pp. 505–515.
79   Supreme Court, 16 December 1987, ECLI:NL:HR:1986:AC9607, *NJ* 1987/321 (*Slavenburg II*).
80   Supreme Court, 26 October 1993, ECLI:NL:HR:1993:ZC9475, *NJ* 1994/51 (*Klaver Fashion*).
81   Supreme Court, 16 December 1987, ECLI:NL:HR:1986:AC9607, *NJ* 1987/321 (*Slavenburg II*).
82   See also: D. Roef, *Strafbare overheden*, Deventer: Kluwer 2001.
83   Supreme Court, 6 January 1998, ECLI:NL:HR:1998:AA9342, *NJ* 1998/367 (*Pikmeer II*).
84   Supreme Court, 25 January 1994, ECLI:NL:HR:1994:ZC9616, *NJ* 1994/598 (*Air base Volkel*).

PART III
CRIMINAL PROCEDURE LAW

5. CRIMINAL PROCEDURE LAW

Sven BRINKHOFF, Joeri BEMELMANS & Maarten KUIPERS[*]

5.1 INTRODUCTION

In this part of the book the Dutch criminal procedure will be discussed. First its history and background will be discussed, with a focus on major developments in the last few decades (section 5.2). Thereafter the expected reform ("modernization)" of the Dutch Code of Criminal Procedure will be discussed. Section 5.3 discusses some key general characteristics of the Dutch criminal procedure. Criminal procedural law will be discussed more in-depth in sections 5.4 and 5.5. These sections distinguish between the pre trail phase (section 5.4) and the trial phase (section 5.5).[1]

5.2 HISTORY AND RECENT DEVELOPMENTS

In 1810 the Netherlands was annexed by France and was therefore absorbed by the French Empire of Napoleon Bonaparte. As a result the *Code d'instruction criminelle* entered into force in the Netherlands in 1811. In 1813 the French occupation of the Netherlands ended. The French jury system was abolished immediately after the defeat of France. Nevertheless, it took until 1838 before the *Code d'instruction criminelle* was replaced by a Dutch Code of Criminal procedure. To a large extent the 1838 *Code* was a translation of the former *Code d'instruction criminelle* and as a result featured strong inquisitorial elements. Just as the French code, the Code of Criminal Procedure focused on truth-finding.[2]

---

[*]   S. Brinkhoff (Ph.D.) is associate professor at the department of criminal law at the Open University of the Netherlands. He is also justice *at litem* at the court of appeal of 's-Hertogenbosch. J.H.B. Bemelmans (Ph.D.) is a law clerk at the Supreme Court of the Netherlands and a judge ad litem at the district court of Gelderland. M. Kuipers is an Amsterdam based attorney at law.

[1]   The Code of criminal procedure has been officially published in Dutch. The only officially published translation in another language is in German: Die niederländische Strafprozessordnung vom 1. Januar 1926, Übersetzung und Einführung von H.-J. Scholten, Freiburg im Breisgau: edition iuscrim 2003.

[2]   See also P.P.J. van der Meij, *De driehoeksverhouding in het strafrechtelijk vooronderzoek. Een onverminderde zoektocht naar evenwicht in de rolverdeling tussen de rechter-commissaris,*

The suspect had the possibility of legal representation at the trial. However, in the preliminary investigation the suspect was the object of a secret and written investigation procedure and did not have any procedural rights. The numerous attempts to reform the Code of 1838 and to restrict the inquisitorial elements failed until the current Code of Criminal Procedure (*Wetboek van Strafvordering*) (hereinafter: CCP) was enacted in 1926.

Throughout the last few decades several law reforms were carried out within the Code. There are various reasons for these reforms, such as: a crisis within the Dutch police system; the impact of international human rights treaties; legislation regarding counterterrorism as well as the implementation of European Union law and the influence of technological progress.

5.2.1 THE CRISIS IN POLICE INVESTIGATION

In 1996 the Parliamentary Enquiry Committee on police investigations, also known as the Van Traa committee, concluded that there was a crisis in police investigation in the Netherlands.[3] This crisis is also referred to as the 'IRT affair' named after the special police unit which was combatting organized crime (*het Interregionaal Recherche Team*). This police unit used rather radical investigation methods, such as the use of criminal informants and criminal civilian infiltrators, to map drug trafficking organizations. Legal standards for these investigative methods didn't exist at that time. The Van Traa committee also discovered that in order to obtain information about criminal organizations and its high-ranking members, this police unit allowed criminal informants and infiltrators to import vast amounts of drugs without these drugs being confiscated. Neither the courts nor the prosecution service performed its role of supervising this police unit sufficiently and conscientiously. As a result, the police could operate outside the authority and control of the prosecutor in charge. The report of the Van Traa committee was profoundly shocking and led to far-ranging legislation on investigative powers and special investigative methods in The Special Police Powers act (*de Wet Bijzondere Opsporingsbevoegdheden*) which is incorporated in the CCP.[4] This Special Police Powers Act has for example provided a legal basis and described the legal conditions for observation and tailing (Article 126o CCP), police infiltration (Article 126p CCP) and infiltration by a person who is not an investigating officer (Article 126w CCP), running informers (Article 126v CCP) and pseudo-purchase (Article 126q CCP).

---

de officier van justitie en de verdediging, Deventer: Kluwer, 2010, p. 34 (with summary in English).

[3] These conclusions were drawn in the research report 'Inzake opsporing', *Kamerstukken II* 1995/96, 24 072, nos. 10–11.

[4] Act of 27 May 1999 (Wet bijzondere opsporingsbevoegdheden), *Kamerstukken* 25403, *Staatsblad* 1999/245. See articles 126g et seq. CCP.

5.2.2 INTERNATIONAL HUMAN RIGHTS INSTRUMENTS: THE IMPACT OF THE EUROPEAN CONVENTION FOR THE PROTECTION OF HUMAN RIGHTS

The Dutch criminal procedure is influenced by several treaties. Whenever the Netherlands is a member state of a treaty and the provisions of this treaty are directly applicable, the Dutch courts are obliged to assess the compatibility of national legislation with that treaty. In this regard Article 94 of the Dutch Constitution states that national law is not applicable if it is in conflict with provisions of a binding and directly applicable treaty.

The European Convention on Human Rights and Fundamental Freedoms (ECHR) is an international treaty to protect human rights and fundamental freedoms in Europe, which particularly governs the Dutch legislation and practice, including criminal proceedings. The European Court of Human Rights (ECtHR) has the task of guaranteeing the rights enshrined in the ECHR. The ECHR had a much bigger impact on the national legislation than was expected by its member states.[5] In the Netherlands the provisions of the ECHR are directly applicable and do not need legislative implementation. Dutch criminal procedure must be in line with the provisions of the Convention as well as the decisions of the ECtHR. A Dutch judge will interpret national in accordance with the rules set out in the ECHR. In this regard, a Dutch judge will not apply a national law if it conflicts with a provision of the ECHR or a decision of the ECtHR. In order to align the Dutch criminal procedure with the ECHR as well as the decisions of the ECtHR, it can be necessary to modify the CCP. ECtHR decisions in cases against other member states can also lead to changes within Dutch criminal proceedings. Some influential decisions of the ECHR are set out hereafter.

The ECtHR's decisions in the *Cubber and Hauschildt* cases resulted in the reform of the criminal procedure for juveniles.[6] The *Kruslin and Huvig* cases necessitated new procedural provisions for the interception of (telephone) communications.[7] The *Kostovski case* led to the introduction of legislation on anonymous witnesses in Article 344a CCP.[8] The *Kamasinski case* formed the reference point for new legislation on interpretation and translation during

---

[5] For example L.F. Zwaak, 'The Netherlands', in: R. Blackburn & J. Polakiewicz (red.), *Fundamental Rights in Europe: The ECHR and its Member States*, 1950–2000, Oxford: Oxford University Press, 2001, pp. 595–624, p. 595.

[6] European Court of Human Rights, *De Cubber v. Belgium*, 26 October 1984, appl. no. 9186/80, *NJ* 2012/649, and European Court of Human Rights, *Hauschildt v. Denmark*, 24 May 1989, appl. no.10486/83, *NJ* 1990/ 627.

[7] European Court of Human Rights, *Kruslin/Huvig v. France*, 24 April 1990, appl. no. 11801/95 and 11105/84, *NJ* 1991/523.

[8] European Court of Human Rights, *Kostovski v. the Netherlands*, 20 November 1989, appl. no. 11454/85, *NJ* 1990/245.

the criminal procedure.[9] While the *Brogan case* has resulted in control by the investigating judge of the lawfulness of the detention within the first period of 72 hours of police custody.[10]

In 2008 the ECtHR's decision in the *Salduz* case was ground-breaking.[11] The ECtHR ruled that, according to Article 6 (3) (c) of the Convention, a suspect must have 'access to a lawyer' as soon as the interrogation by the authorities starts. However, the ECtHR did not explain the exact scope of Article 6 (3) (c). The Dutch Supreme Court therefore initially interpreted Article 6 (3) (c) of the Convention as the right to speak to a lawyer before the first interrogation, but not the right to have a lawyer physically present during the interrogation.[12] The ruling of the ECtHR in the *Salduz* case also led to European Union law regarding the right to a lawyer – which will be discussed further in this chapter – that actually demands modification in the CCP. This modification has been made in 2017 in the Articles 28c – 28e CCP.

5.2.3 THE IMPLEMENTATION OF EU LAW

The EU Council has issued several framework decisions (*kaderbesluiten*)) to harmonise criminal procedural law within the European Union. These framework decisions are binding upon the Member States as to the result to be achieved but leave the choice of form and methods to the national authorities. They do not have direct effect and therefore have to be implemented. Framework decisions have resulted in criminal procedural law reforms. The Council framework decision of 15 March 2001 (2001/220/JHA) for example led to the adoption of new rules strengthening the position of the victim in the criminal procedure.

Framework decisions that have been implemented in Dutch law include: the Council framework decision on mutual recognition of financial penalties (2005/214/JHA); the framework decision on the execution of orders to freeze property or evidence (2003/577/JHA); the Council Framework Decision on simplifying the exchange of information and intelligence between law enforcement authorities of the Member States of the European Union (2006/960/JHA); the Council framework decision on the European evidence warrant for the purpose of obtaining objects, documents and data for use in proceedings in criminal matters (2008/978/JHA); and the Council Framework Decision on

---

[9] European Court of Human Rights, *Kamasinksi v. Austria*, 19 December 1989, appl. no. 9783/82, *NJ* 1994/26.

[10] European Court of Human Rights, *Brogan and others v. United Kingdom*, 29 November 1988, appl. no. 1266/84, 11234/84 and 11209/84, *NJ* 1989/815.

[11] European Court of Human Rights, *Salduz v. Turkey*, 27 November 2008, appl. no. 36391/02, *NJ* 2009/214.

[12] Supreme Court, 30 June 2009, ECLI:NL:HR:2009:BH3079, *NJ* 2009/349, par. 2.

the organization and content of the exchange of information extracted from the criminal record between Member States (2009/315/JHA).

After the entry into force of the Treaty of Lisbon on 1 December 2009, the instrument of the framework decision was replaced by the instrument of the directive (*richtlijn*) as far as cooperation on criminal matters within the EU is concerned, was then. Just as the framework decision, the directive is a legal instrument that harmonizes national laws within the European Union. Member states have the freedom to choose the form and methods to align their national legislation with the directive. In contrast to framework decisions, directives can have direct effect if they are implemented too late or are implemented incorrectly.

Recently the directive on the right to information in criminal proceedings was implemented (2012/13/JHU), as well as the directive on the right to translation and interpretation in criminal proceedings (2010/64/JHA) and the directive establishing minimum standards on the rights, support and protection of victims of crime (2012/29/JHU). The latter directive replaced Council Framework Decision 2001/220/JHA.

The directive on the right of access to a lawyer in criminal proceedings and in European arrest warrant proceedings (2013/48/JHA) resulted in a modification of the CCP. According to the directive a suspect must have physical access to a lawyer during the first interrogation. This meant that the original interpretation of the *Salduz* case by the Dutch Supreme Court did not meet the standards of the directive. The directive had to be implemented in national legislation before 27 November 2016. However, the Dutch Supreme Court ruled that the right to have a lawyer present during interrogation must be respected in the Netherlands as of 22 December 2015.[13] Accordingly, a suspect already had the right to the presence of a lawyer, despite the absence of legislation in the CCP. As mentioned before, a law has been adopted in 2017 concerning the right to the presence of a lawyer during the first police interrogation.[14] This modification has been made in the Articles 28c–28e CCP.

5.2.4 TECHNOLOGICAL PROGRESS

New technological developments have enabled the police to use advanced technical means of coercion to combat crime. Several major changes can be highlighted.

Currently DNA technology is often used to investigate crime. DNA is tested after cell material is collected. There are various methods to use DNA technology

---

[13] Supreme Court, 22 December 2015, ECLI:NL:HR:2015:3608, *NJ* 2016/52, par. 6 and Supreme Court 12 March 2019, ECLI:NL:HR:2019:341.

[14] Act of 17 November 2016 (Wet raadsman bij politieverhoor), *Kamerstukken* 34159, *Staatsblad* 2016/476.

in the investigation of crime. The main method is to compare DNA material with DNA profiles of several suspects. Another form of DNA testing is to establish consanguinity. Since the different methods were gradually introduced in the CCP, the definition of DNA testing in Dutch criminal proceedings, as set out in Article 138a CCP, has been modified several times. The 1993 DNA Act introduced the possibility for the authorities to conduct a DNA test on a suspect without his consent.[15] Since 2001 it is possible for the authorities to take a buccal (mouth) swab for a DNA test from anyone suspected of a crime that carries a statutory imprisonment of four years or more.[16] Since 2006, DNA samples may be taken from all convicts sentenced for crimes that carry a statutory prison sentence of four years or more.[17] The collected DNA data is entered in a DNA database and compared with filed DNA profiles. This method proved to be efficient in so called 'cold cases', when evidence is scarce. Since 2012 it is possible to conduct DNA testing aimed at establishing consanguinity. DNA testing must always be conducted by an expert witness attached to one of the laboratories be designated by Governmental Decree. Articles 151a to 151i CCP grants the public prosecutor the means to conduct DNA testing. Articles 195a to 195g also give the examining judge the means to carry out DNA testing. In principle the DNA from a non-suspect can only be taken on a voluntary basis.[18]

The Computer Crime Acts introduced the possibility for investigators to intercept all forms of telecommunication and the possibility to intercept all forms of communication by means of long-distance target microphones.[19] The interception of communication can be conducted by means of a technical device (for example Articles 126l, 126s, 126zf CCP). Another method is interception by means of computerized devices (for example Articles 126m, 126t, 126zg CCP). Information exchanged on the internet also qualifies as 'communication' and may therefore also be intercepted by the authorities.[20] Apart from the interception of both internet and telephone communication, it is possible for the authorities to conduct research on available information of both internet providers and telephone services. These measures are categorized under the

---

[15]   Act of 8 November 1993 (Wet DNA-onderzoek), *Kamerstukken* 22447, *Staatsblad* 1993/596.

[16]   Act of 5 July 2001 (Wet wijziging DNA-onderzoek in strafzaken), *Kamerstukken* 26271, *Staatsblad* 2001/335.

[17]   Act of 16 September 2004 (Wet DNA-onderzoek bij veroordeelden), *Kamerstukken* 28685, *Staatsblad* 2004/465.

[18]   See extensively on the subject P.H.P.H.M.C. van Kempen & M.G.M. van der Staak, *Een meewerkverplichting bij grootschalig DNA-onderzoek in strafzaken?*, Deventer: Kluwer 2013 (with summary in English).

[19]   Act of 23 December 1992 (Wet computercriminaliteit), *Kamerstukken* 29271, *Staatsblad* 1993/33, and Act of 1 June 2006 (Wet computercriminaliteit II), *Kamerstukken* 26671, *Staatsblad* 2006/300.

[20]   See more extensively on the subject of Dutch legislation regarding cybercrime E.J. Koops, Cybercrime legislation in the Netherlands, in: J.H.M. van Erp & L.P.W. van Vliet (Eds.), *Netherlands Reports to the Eighteenth International Congress on Comparative Law*, Antwerp, Intersentia, 2010, pp. 595–633.

before mentioned special investigation measures. In 2018 a law proposal (*het wetsvoorstel computercriminaliteit III*) that grants the authorities the possibility to hack computerized devices, has been adopted by the Parliament.

5.2.5 THE PREVENTION AND INVESTIGATION OF TERRORISM

In 2007 several Articles were introduced in the CCP to prevent and investigate terrorist offences.[21] In this regard the police was granted several special powers (Article 126za to 126zu CCP). These coercive measures are similar to the ones the police already used to combat serious and organized crime, such as infiltration, observation and the interception of communication. The coercive measures regarding counter terrorism are therefore categorized under the umbrella of the Special Police Powers Act. However, the legislation regarding terrorism enables the use of these coercive measures in an earlier stage of the investigation. Whereas the majority of the coercive measures can be used when a person qualifies as a 'suspect' (*verdachte*) of an offence as described in Article 27 CCP, the counter terrorism measures can already be used if there exists mere indications (*aanwijzingen*) of an offence. The legislation concerning counter terrorism also provides leeway for the ordering of pre-trial detention. Article 67(3) CCP requires 'serious suspicions' (*ernstige bezwaren*) for a remand in custody order. Article 67(4) of the CCP, however, states that serious suspicions shall not be required in the case of suspicion of a terrorist offence. Therefore, in the case of suspicion of a terrorist offence a 'normal' suspicion (*verdenking*) is sufficient for a remand in custody order up to 14 days. Moreover, in case of certain terrorist offences it is possible to further extend deprivation of liberty with a maximum of three times ten days on the basis of normal suspicion. Thereafter, remand detention does require 'serious suspicion', also in terrorism cases.

5.2.6 LEGAL POSITION OF THE VICTIM

The victim (*slachtoffer*) used to play a marginal role in Dutch criminal procedure.[22] The victim had a procedural role only in his capacity as a witness, an informer or injured party claiming damages. He had no right to be informed about the criminal investigation or to be heard on the charges presented by the public prosecutor.

---

[21] Act of 20 November 2006 (Wet opsporing terrorisme), *Kamerstukken* 30164, *Staatsblad* 2006/580.

[22] See also S. van der Aa & M.S. Groenhuijsen, 'Slachtofferrechten in het strafproces: drie stapjes naar voren en een stapje terug?' *Ars Aequi* 2012, pp. 603–609, p. 603.

As a result of the changing attitude towards the weak legal position of the victim, and in line with the United Nations Declaration on Basic Principles of Justice for Victims of Crime and the Abuse of Power (1985) as well as the EU Council framework decision on the standing of victims in criminal proceedings (15 March 2001), a number of guidelines on how to treat victims have been issued by the prosecution service. These guidelines oblige police and prosecutors to inform the victim whether the offender will be prosecuted, and about the possibility of financial compensation by the offender. The directive establishing minimum standards on the rights, support and protection of victims of crime (2012/29/JHU) has now replaced the before mentioned framework decision. This directive has led to national legislation in the CCP that considerably improved and strengthened the position of the victim.

The victim was mentioned in the CCP only since 2011. At that time a new law came into force which strengthened the victim's position within Dutch criminal procedure.[23] Title III A (Article 51a et seq.) of the CCP concerns the legal position of the victim in Dutch criminal proceedings. This title is divided into two separate chapters. The first chapter concerns the rights of the victim and the second chapter concerns compensation for damages suffered as an injured party (*benadeelde partij*).

5.3 MODERNIZATION OF THE CRIMINAL CODE OF PROCEDURE

In recent years the call for a major reform of the CCP has increased. Various arguments were presented for this law reform. The Code dates back to 1926 and is in fact based upon an even older code: the Code d'instruction Criminelle. As a result, the adaptation of certain important changes has been fragmented and incomplete. Due to the many reforms and supplements throughout the years, the Code became less comprehensive. Additionally, some decisions of the Dutch Supreme Court went against the literal meaning of the CCP in order to secure the code's functioning in practice, resulted in the wording of the code not always being in accordance with its current interpretation. One could argue that these matters therefore call for a major law reform to 'modernize' the Dutch Code of Criminal Procedure.

In 1997, a team of researchers from various Dutch Law Faculties started the research project 'Criminal procedure 2001' (*Strafvordering 2001*), which has led to four voluminous reports on the various phases of criminal procedure. According to these reports, the reforms should be guided by three basic ideas:

---

[23]   Act of 17 December 2009 (Wet versterking positie slachtoffer), *Kamerstukken* 30143, *Staatsblad* 2010/1.

- that the purpose of criminal procedure is to provide an appropriate response to criminal behavior; it should focus on the finding of truth and thus be concerned with more than the simple realization of substantive criminal law;
- the re-calibration of the legal position of the various participants in the criminal procedure through:
- the recognition of the witness and the victim as participants in the criminal justice procedure;
- the abolition of the judicial preliminary investigation and confirmation of the public prosecutor as leader of the criminal investigation as well as the confirmation of the examining judge as performer of two main duties: deciding on requests to apply coercive measures and interrogating witnesses on request; and
- the strengthening of the role of the trial judge, as well as of the rights of the defense lawyer;
- the implementation of a multiple tracks model: the procedure for the administration of criminal justice should depend upon the seriousness of the offence and the sanctions or measures that can be imposed.

Since the publication of the reports, a number of reform bills have been discussed by Parliament, but not all reform proposals put forward by the research group have been adopted. Reform proposals that have been adopted by Parliament include the empowerment of the public prosecutor to deal with cases outside the courts[24], to restructure the appeal procedure[25], several laws to strengthen the position of the victim[26], and the law concerning documents in criminal proceedings.[27] The proposal to abolish the judicial preliminary investigation (*gerechtelijk vooronderzoek*) has been adopted. As a result of the law to strengthen the position of the investigative judge, the investigative judge has been repositioned as more of a supervisor to the investigation lead by the public prosecutor.[28]

Despite the mentioned reform proposals that were adopted, the reformation of the CCP did not go as rapid as planned. Therefore in 2014 further reformation was announced by the Minister of Justice and Security. The Minister stated that attention for reformation is required, since the current code is not in harmony with

---

24   Act of 7 July 2006 (Wet OM-afdoening), *Kamerstukken* 29849, *Staatsblad* 2006/330.
25   Act of 5 October 2006 (Wet stroomlijnen hoger beroep) *Kamerstukken* 30320, *Staatsblad* 2006/470.
26   Act of 17 December 2009 (Wet versterking positie slachtoffer) *Kamerstukken* 30143, *Staatsblad* 2010/1.
27   Act of 1 December 2011 (Wet herziening regels betreffende de processtukken in strafzaken), *Kamerstukken* 34090, *Staatsblad* 2011/601.
28   Act of 1 December 2011 (Wet versterking positie rechter-commissaris), *Kamerstukken* 32177, *Staatsblad* 2011/600.

technological developments and contains unnecessary burdens. This project to reform the code is called 'Modernisering Strafvordering'. The purpose is to achieve a future-proof, accessible and workable code that provides a balanced system of safeguards. The relaunch of the reformation is generally based upon the ideas of the before mentioned research group. Prime consideration remains that the principles of the criminal procedure are not abandoned. An argument for reformation concerns the before mentioned discrepancy between legislation in the CCP and important judgments. The CCP needs to be a reflection of current legislation. Important judgments should therefore be enshrined in the CCP. Depending on the type of investigation, a single measure can be found in various Articles and under various titles of the CCP. To strengthen the cooperation between the different authorities within the criminal procedure, the criminal files or documents are digitized. In this regard the current code has insufficient means to keep up with this technology. For example, the code does not yet have a provision for an electronic case file or signature. A reform proposal which will start digitizing the criminal procedure has already been adopted by Parliament and went into force on 1 December 2016.[29] Since 2014, the Ministry of Justice and Security as well as several other parties, lawyers and other relevant parties discuss various options to reform the CCP.[30] In February 2017 the Ministry of Justice and Security gave notice that a concrete law proposal regarding the new books one and two of the CCP has been sent for consultation to several parties.[31] In December 2017, proposals regarding books three through six were also made public for consultation.

5.4 SOME GENERAL CHARACTERISTICS OF THE CRIMINAL PROCEDURE

5.4.1 THE LEGALITY OF CRIMINAL PROCEDURE

An important characteristic of the Dutch Code of Criminal Procedure can be found in Article 1 CCP.[32] This Article contains the principle of legality of criminal procedure (*strafvorderlijk legaliteitsbeginsel*), which is a key element of the Rule of Law. The principle states that criminal proceedings are to be conducted in accordance with the law. Coercive measures therefore need to have a legal basis. The ratio of this principle is to promote legal certainty and to prevent arbitrary use of power by government authorities, such as the police and the Public Prosecution Service. On the basis of Article 1 criminal procedure has

---

[29] Act of 17 February 2016 (Wet digitale processtukken Strafvordering), *Kamerstukken* 34090, *Staatsblad* 2016/90.

[30] Contourennota Wetboek van Strafvordering, *Kamerstukken II* 2015/16, 29279, no. 278.

[31] *Kamerstukken II* 2016/17, 29279, no. 372.

[32] Article 1 CCP states: "Criminal proceedings shall be solely conducted in the manner provided by law."

to be prescribed in a formal act (*Wet in formele zin*) that has been approved by the Government and Parliament, such as the CCP. However, in practice these formal acts can delegate some further rule-making to lower authorities. The interpretation of law by the Dutch Supreme Court in general does not conflict with the principle of legality either.

5.4.2 THE STRUCTURE OF THE CCP

The Code of Criminal Procedure is divided into six books. The first book (Articles 1–138f) contains general provisions on the competence of the police, the public prosecutor and the judiciary, the rights of the defendant and the defense counsel, the victim and the injured party, and coercive measures such as pre-trial detention, seizure or search of premises, interception of communication, and special covert or intrusive investigative powers. The second book (Articles 139–398) gives rules regarding the criminal procedure in first instance. The third book (Articles 404–482i) deals with legal remedies such as appeal and cassation. The fourth book (Articles 483–552hhh) contains special criminal procedure provisions, such as trials against juveniles and corporate bodies and for international co-operation in criminal matters. The fifth book (Articles 5:3:1–5:4:17) contains provisions regarding international and European cooperation in criminal procedures. The sixth and last book (Articles 553–593) contains provisions on the enforcement of judicial decisions and certain costs.

5.4.3 PROCEDURAL CRIMINAL LAW IN OTHER ACTS

The CCP is not applicable for minor road-traffic offences. These are dealt with through administrative procedures without direct access to a criminal court. The 1989 Administration of Road-Traffic Offences Act empowers the police to impose a maximum administrative fine of €340 per offence. The fine becomes final, unless a complaint is lodged with the prosecution service, which acts as an administrative agency. The decision of the prosecution service can be challenged before the cantonal judge of the district court, who may review the decision of the public prosecutor. Ultimately, an appeal may be filed with the court of appeal in Leeuwarden, which in this case functions as the highest (administrative) court.

Some acts concerning criminal law, such as the 1950 Economic Offences Act, the 1928 Narcotic Drug Offences Act and the 1997 Weapons and Ammunition Act, partly deviate from the Code of Criminal Procedure. These acts include coercive measures that are similar to the measures enshrined in the CCP. However, the requirements that enable the use of these measures are often less stringent. This is in particular the case in the issue of searches of premises. For example, Article 49 of the Weapon and Ammunition Act grants police officers the possibility to search a dwelling if they have a reasonable suspicion that weapons or ammunition can be found in that dwelling. Different from the legislation in the CCP, these police officers in principle do not need a judicial warrant from the investigation judge.

The 1991 Military Code of Criminal procedure regulates the organization of the military court system and contains supplementary provisions for the military court trial.

There is no special statute on criminal procedure for juvenile offenders. The Code of Criminal Procedure contains special provisions on juvenile trials (Articles 486 to 505 CCP).

5.5 THE PRE-TRIAL PHASE

5.5.1 ACTORS

The pre-trial investigation is mainly performed by the police. The prosecutor is in charge of the police investigation (Article 132a CCP). He is for instance the one who decides what kind of coercive measures and special police powers have to be used and is also responsible for the case file. In the Dutch criminal justice system, the public prosecutor is ultimately responsible for the criminal investigation and for adherence by police to all statutory rules and procedures. Formally, the public prosecutor is the senior investigator, and although in practice the police deal with most cases without prior consultation with the public prosecutor, the latter will be informed by the police on content and progress of the investigation, in particular in important criminal cases. In more serious cases, the public prosecutor can give detailed instructions to the police, for example to reduce or extend the scope of investigation, or to contact experts in certain types of expert investigation.

In the pre-trial phase the investigative judge (*rechter-commissaris*) may also play a role. His task is to supervise the progress of the ongoing police investigation (Article 180 CCP). He may also hear witnesses (Articles 181–182 CCP) and is involved with the pre-trail detention. After a maximum of three days and fifteen hours of custody (*inverzekeringstelling*, Article 57 CCP) the suspect has to be seen by a judge and this is the investigative judge. He will assess the legality of the custody up to that point and he can order the suspect to remain in custody (*bewaring*, Article 63 CCP) for fourteen days at the request of the public prosecutor.

In the year 2011 an act to strengthen the role of the investigative judge came into force (*Wet versterking positie rechter-commissaris*).[33] This act is incorporated

---

[33] Kamerstukken 32177, *Staatsblad* 2011/600. For further elaboration on the investigative judge, see P.A.M. Verrest, *Raison d'etre. Een onderzoek naar de rol van de rechtercommissaris in ons strafproces*, Den Haag, Boom 2011.

in the CCP. As of this moment the investigative judge is, among other things, burdened with the supervision on the progress of the police investigation. His task is to supervise the progress of the ongoing police investigation (Article 180 CCP). The investigative judge also plays an actual role in the pre-trial investigation. He may for instance, on the request of the prosecutor or the defense counsel, hear witnesses and experts (Articles 181–182 CCP). During the pre-trial investigation, the defense counsel has the right to attend the hearing of witnesses and experts by the investigating judge, unless prohibited by the interests of the investigation. He can suggest questions to be put by the investigating judge. Where the defense counsel is not present at the hearing, he will be informed as soon as possible of the content of the proceedings unless this is in conflict with the interests of the investigation.

The defense lawyers evidently also play a role in the pre-trial phase. A distinction should be made between two types of defense lawyers active during the pre-trial investigations. Some suspects are wealthy enough to choose and pay their own defense lawyers. Those lawyers are paid for the number of hours they spend on assisting their clients, and one may expect that these privately paid defense lawyers will play an active role in carrying out private investigations as far as possible. The vast majority of arrested suspects will receive legal aid, which means that a defense lawyer is assigned to them by a public organization called the Regional Legal Aid Council. Both the privately paid defense counsel and the legal aid defense counsel have the same rights during the pre-trial investigations. Let us therefore look at the most important rights they have during that phase of the criminal procedure. The defense lawyer has the right to be present during the first police interrogation and to consult with his client prior to this interrogation (Articles 28c–28e CCP). The defense counsel has the right to free and unmonitored access to a client who is in custody (Article 50 CCP). Since such access is not allowed to delay the investigation, the counsel is always partly dependent on the criminal justice authorities and on the time and facilities made available for this purpose by the police. The Articles 30–34 CCP give the suspect and the defense council access to the case file. The defense counsel can ask the investigative judge to hear witnesses and experts and to perform other sorts of investigation (Article 182 CCP).

Finally, the victim plays a role in the pre-trial phase. The responsibility to ensure an appropriate treatment of the victim rests with the prosecutor (Article 51a(2) CCP). The victim has the right to be informed about the commencement and progress of the case against the suspect (Article 51a(3) CCP) and to inspect documents of relevance (Article 51b CCP). Furthermore, a victim has the right to legal representation (Article 51c CCP) and the right to make a verbal statement during the court sessions (Article 51e CCP).

5.5.2 POLICE INVESTIGATION

The criminal procedure is initiated by the pre-trial investigation carried out by the police as soon as they are informed of a criminal offence. The police operates in a reactive way. The filing of a police complaint by a civilian or an anonymous tip to the police by a Crime Stopper Program may for example be ways in which the police becomes informed about a criminal offence.[34] It's also possible that the police operates in a more proactive way. Such is done by the Dutch Criminal Intelligence Team (*Team Criminele Inlichtingen*).[35] Each regional police unit has such a team. Under the supervision of a specific public prosecutor, the TCI seeks to obtain information that may be relevant to criminal proceedings by getting into touch with (criminal) informants, in other words running the informants. In general, the focus of the TCI is to obtain information about serious and/ or organized crime (for example drug and weapon trafficking). The tactical criminal investigation department of the police, which is not informed about the identity of the informant, may on the basis of this report and in consultation with the Public Prosecutor decide to start an investigation and subsequently deploy coercive measures.

The purpose of the pre-trial police investigation is to gather information on the offence and the suspect. A suspect is anyone who may reasonably be suspected of having committed the offence. Article 27 CCP states that facts and circumstances can lead to a suspicion. An example thereof is an incriminating witness statement which is filled by the police.

The police have the right to question any person in relation to the offence, whether or not this person is a suspect. However, no one is obliged to answer questions put by the police. The police prepare a written record of the questioning of the suspect and other persons and of other relevant findings of facts. The written records are prepared by the police under oath, and may be used as evidence by the court.

5.5.3 COERCIVE MEASURES

The police are authorized to carry out coercive measures such as an arrest, a bodily search and the access and the search of the premises when the legal prerequisites to do so exist.

As stated earlier under Dutch law, before a criminal investigation may be started and investigative measures applied, there must be a reasonable suspicion

---

[34] See extensively on the subject S. Brinkhoff, *Startinformatie in het strafproces*, Deventer: Kluwer, 2014 (with summary in English).

[35] For the rules of the TCI, see among other sources "Besluit verplichte politiegegevens" (i.e., Decision Required Police Data), *Staatsblad* 2012, p. 465.

that a criminal offence has been committed. In the last decades the police have focused more and more on the collection of information about networks, groups and individuals especially in order to know what criminal activities are being planned, thus before a criminal offence has been committed, so-called proactive policing. Proactive policing methods and covert policing methods like surveillance, infiltration and the handling of informants has been given a statutory basis in the Code of Criminal Procedure by the 2000 Special Police Powers Act (*de Wet Bijzondere Opsporingsbevoegdheden*).[36]

The Special Police Powers Act is incorporated in Article 126g–126ii CCP. In these Articles a legal basis has been given for observation and tailing (Article 126o CCP), police infiltration (Article 126p CCP) and infiltration by a person who is not an investigating officer (Article 126w CCP), running informers (Article 126v CCP) and pseudo-purchase (Article 126q CCP). General rule in this regard is that in the case of a serious crime the prosecutor can give the order to the police to use a special investigative measure. In some cases, additionally, a warrant of an investigative judge is needed. The order to intercept (tele-) communication is an example thereof.

After the Special Police Powers Act came into force in 2000, new investigative methods arose such as Stealth-SMS and data mining. Stealth-SMS is an investigation technique which is used to gather information on a suspect's location. By using Stealth-SMS, the police sends a message to a suspect's mobile phone and is informed that the message has been received by the suspect. However, the suspect is not notified that the message has been delivered on his mobile phone. This way the police can secretly obtain information about a suspect's location.

Datamining is an investigative method in which with the use of a certain criterion data is automatically analysed.[37] The automated data analysis by the police can be used 1) to bring up additional personalized data about an individual or individuals who were already labelled as a suspect of a criminal offence and 2) to gather personalized results about a possible suspect or group of suspects. The legal basis for use of Stealth-SMS and data mining by the Dutch police is found in the general task-setting, and non-specific, Article 3 of the Dutch Police Act (*de Politiewet*). Article 3 states that the Dutch police is, among other things, burdened with the investigation of criminal offences. Case law of the Dutch Supreme Court has shown that in criminal proceedings Article 3 of the Dutch Police Act can be used as a legal basis for investigative methods that are not specifically regulated in the Special Police Powers Act as long as 1) the use of this method only leads to a limited interference with fundamental rights

---

36   Act of 27 May 1999 (Wet bijzondere opsporingsbevoegdheden), *Kamerstukken* 25403, *Staatsblad* 1999/245.

37   A.R. Lodder, N.S. van der Meulen, T.H.A. Wisman, L. Meij & C.M.M. Zwinkels, *Big Data, big consequenses. Een verkenning naar privacy en big data gebruik binnen de opsporing, vervolging en rechtspraak*, The Hague: WODC 2014.

(such as the right to privacy) of civilians and 2) there are no integrity issues at hand when using this methods.[38]

When the police investigation is completed, upon the written records of the questioning of witnesses and suspects, the use and outcome of coercive measures and special police powers, a case file will be composed. Due to Article 149a CCP this case file has to contain all the relevant information for the judge to make a decision in the case. The case is then forwarded to the prosecutor for a decision on prosecution.

5.5.4 PRE-TRIAL DETENTION

Deprivation of liberty before and whilst awaiting trial of a person suspected of having committed a criminal offence can be divided into five phases:

- police arrest in order to be questioned;
- police custody;
- remand in custody;
- remand detention;
- detention pending trial.

The decision of police arrest and police custody rests with the public prosecutor (or a senior police officer if seeking the permission of the prosecutor would cause undue delay). The decision to remand a suspect into custody, remand detention and detention pending trial rests with the judiciary, a single judge or a full bench of the court. The latter three phases form the pre-trial detention (*voorlopige hechtenis*); the first and second phase are not part of the pre-trial detention.

Police arrest (*aanhouding*, Articles 53–54 CCP) is possible for any offence where offenders are caught red-handed, or for crimes which carry a statutory prison sentence of four years or more. Arrests have to be ordered by a public prosecutor or a senior police officer (*hulpofficier van justitie*) where the order of the public prosecutor would cause undue delay, or in urgent cases by any police officer. The aim of an arrest by the police is the interrogation of the suspect by a (senior) police officer in the interest of the investigation of a criminal offence. During the first interrogation, the police officer must ensure that the right person has been arrested, that the arrest was lawful, and that continuation of the arrest seems necessary. The person arrested has the right to be assisted by his defense counsel and also has the right to speak to his lawyer prior to the police interrogation (Articles 28c–28e CCP). The police arrest may last up to nine hours, not including the hours between midnight and nine a.m., during

---

[38]   Supreme Court, 19 December 1995, ECLI:NL:HR:1995:ZD0328, *NJ* 1996/249, and Supreme Court, 1 July 2014, ECLI:NL:HR:2014:1563, *NJ* 2015/114 and 115.

which the detainee can be further interrogated about the crime allegedly committed by him (Article 61 CCP). During the police arrest, an additional term of six hours arrest – not including the hours between midnight and nine a.m. – may be ordered for the identification of offenders caught red-handed during which investigative measures may be taken, such as fingerprints, photographs, observation, haircut and so on.

After the period for police arrest has passed, the suspect has to be either released or be taken into police custody (*inverzekeringstelling*, Article 57 CCP). Police custody is ordered by the public prosecutor or by a senior police officer. Police custody can only be applied in the interest of the investigation of criminal offences for which pre-trial detention is possible. The police custody order contains a description of the criminal offence, the reasons why the order was issued (in the interest of the investigation), and the circumstances which have resulted in the supposition of these reasons (mostly: interrogation of witnesses/confrontation/further interrogation of the suspect is necessary). The police custody order holds good for three days. The order can be extended once for up to three days by the public prosecutor (Article 58 CCP). Ultimately, after three days and fifteen hours, the arrested person has to be brought before the investigating judge (Article 59a CCP) who may only examine the lawfulness of the police custody. The person in custody may be assisted by his defense counsel.

Once the period of the police arrest and police custody has ended, the suspect has to be released or brought before the investigating judge who can order remand in custody (*bewaring*, Article 63 CCP) for fourteen days at the request of the public prosecutor. The remand in custody order can also be issued without preceding police custody. The suspect is heard by the investigating judge. His counsel may be present at this interrogation. The remand in custody is the first phase of the pre-trial detention. Two statutory requirements for the application of pre-trial detention must be met. The first requirement regards the cases (i.e. the level of suspicion and type of offence) for which pre-trial detention may be applied. The second deals with the grounds on which pre-trial detention may be applied.

With regard to the cases in which pre-trial detention may be applied, Article 67 CCP enumerates them exhaustively. Pre-trial detention can be ordered if a grave suspicion (*ernstige bezwaren*) exists that the offender has committed an offence:

– which carries a statutory prison sentence of four years or more; or
– which is specifically designated, e.g. embezzlement, fraudulent misrepresentation and threat; or
– which carries the penalty of imprisonment whilst the suspect does not have a fixed residence or regular place of abode in the Netherlands.

Article 67a CCP specifies the grounds on which pre-trial detention may be applied. According to this section, for the application of pre-trial detention there must be a danger that the suspect will abscond or will pose a serious danger to public safety. A serious danger to public safety exists:

- if the offence carries a maximum statutory sentence of at least twelve years imprisonment and public order has been seriously affected by the offence;
- if there is a serious risk that the offender will commit a crime that carries a maximum statutory sentence of not less than six years of imprisonment; or which may jeopardize the safety of the state or the health or safety of persons; or create a general danger to property;
- if there is a suspicion that the offender has committed specific offences such as property offences, threat, embezzlement or money laundering and will re-offend, while less than five years have passed since he was sentenced to a deprivation or restriction of liberty or a community service order for such an offence;
- if there is a suspicion that the offender has committed specific offences such as assault in a public place, or directed against persons with a public task, as a result of which social unrest arose and the crime will be trialed within a period of 17 days and 15 hours after the offender's arrest;
- if it is necessary to detain the offender in order to establish the truth by methods other than through his own statement.

If the grounds for pre-trial detention are still valid after the remand in custody, the prosecutor can request the full bench of the court to order that the suspect be remanded (*gevangenhouding*, Article 65 CCP). This request may be repeated twice. The maximum period of detention in remand may not exceed ninety days. The requests are dealt with by the court in chambers. The suspect is heard in processing these requests.

Remand in custody is not permitted if it is not likely that the offender will be sentenced to unsuspended imprisonment. Furthermore, pre-trial detention has to end if it is likely that the actual term of imprisonment (taking into consideration the provisions on early release) will be shorter than the period spent in pre-trial detention (*anticipatiegebod*, Article 67a(3) CCP).

If the suspect is still in pre-trial detention after one hundred and four days (the term of the remand in custody plus that of the detention in remand), the public prosecutor has to present the case to the court for trial. However, often a formal presentation of the cases suffices. Unless the case is actually ready for trial, the trial may and usually will be adjourned. In either case, the detention in remand order may remain valid until sixty days after the final court decision, provided that the verdict in the first instance and on appeal results in a prison sentence exceeding the period spent in detention (Article 66(2) CCP).

A statutory provision (Article 27 CC) provides that the full term of arrest and pre-trial detention shall be deducted from the term of imprisonment. Courts do not have any discretion in this regard.

5.5.5 THE RIGHT TO CHALLENGE PRE-TRIAL DETENTION

For police arrest and the first term (3 days) of police custody, the CCP provides no legal remedy to challenge the lawfulness of the detention. If the lawfulness of these phases of detention is doubtful, a solution has to be sought in consultation with the police and the public prosecutor who has issued the order, or with their superior officers. If this fails, it is possible to initiate summary civil proceedings before a civil judge alleging unlawful detention and urgency of the case.

The suspect can make use of the right to request release when he is brought before the investigating judge before the expiry of three days of police custody (Article 59a CCP).

With regard to remand in custody, it is assumed that the suspect has the right to elicit a release order from the investigating judge. If this is issued, the prosecution service has fourteen days to lodge an appeal with the district court (Article 64(3) CCP).

The suspect cannot appeal against the remand in custody order, but he is entitled to request the court in chambers to cancel the remand in custody order (Article 69 CCP). At the occasion of his first request, the suspect has the right to be heard by the court. Should the court refuse to cancel the remand in custody order, an appeal by the suspect can be lodged with the court of appeal (Article 87 CCP). The public prosecutor may lodge an appeal against the decision of the district court to cancel the remand in custody on its own motion or at the request of the suspect.

In case of a detention in remand and detention pending trial order, the suspect can appeal against this order to the court of appeal within three days (Article 71(1) CCP). The suspect can, however, only lodge one appeal against the decision of the District court to order or to continue the pre-trial detention. The public prosecutor can lodge an appeal within two weeks against a decision to lift a detention in remand or a detention pending trial order (Article 71(3) CCP).

5.5.6 PROSECUTORIAL DECISIONS

When the pre-trial investigation is ended, the files are forwarded to the prosecutor for a decision. He can decide:

– to drop the case;
– to settle the case by means of a penal order;

- to settle the case by means of a transaction (in extraordinary cases); or
- to issue a writ of summons for the offender.

Non-prosecution

The power to prosecute resides exclusively with the prosecution service. No prosecutorial power is granted to private persons or bodies, not even when the prosecution service declines to prosecute. This prosecution monopoly does not require the prosecution service to prosecute every crime brought to its notice.

The prosecution service may decide not to prosecute in cases where a prosecution would probably not lead to a conviction due to lack of evidence.

The prosecution may also decide not to prosecute under the expediency principle. The expediency principle laid down in Article 167 CCP authorizes the prosecution service to waive (further) prosecution 'for reasons of public interest'.

Prior to the late 1960s, the discretionary power to waive (further) prosecution was exercised on a very restricted scale. Thereafter, however, a remarkable change in prosecution policy took place. Research on the effects of law enforcement coupled with the limited resources of law enforcement agencies revealed that it was impossible, undesirable, and in some circumstances even counter-productive to prosecute all offences investigated.

Gradually, the discretionary power not to prosecute for policy considerations began to be exercised more widely. To harmonize the utilization of this discretionary power, the head of the prosecution service, the Board of Prosecutors General, regularly issues national prosecution guidelines. Public prosecutors are directed to follow these guidelines except where there are special circumstances in an individual case.

This freedom to decide to end the prosecution can, in appropriate cases, also be used conditionally. The second section of Article 167 CCP constitutes a legal basis for a suspended prosecution legal basis. That section states: "A decision not to prosecute may be taken on grounds of public interest. The Public Prosecution Service may, subject to specific conditions to be set, postpone the decision on prosecution for a period of time to be set in said decision."

The main reasons to apply the expediency principle are:

- measures other than penal sanctions are preferable (mainly disciplinary sanctions or administrative or private law measures); and
- prosecution will be disproportionate, unjust or ineffective because
- the crime is of a minor nature;
- the suspect's contribution to the crime was minor;
- the crime has a low degree of punishability;
- the crime is old;
- the suspect is too young or too old;
- the suspect has recently been sentenced for another crime;

- the crime has negatively affected the suspect himself (victim of his own crime);
- the health conditions of the suspect;
- rehabilitation prospects of the suspect;
- change of circumstances in the life of the suspect;
- suspect cannot be traced;
- corporate criminal liability;
- the person in control of the unlawful behavior is prosecuted, not the perpetrator;
- the suspect has paid compensation;
- the victim has contributed to the crime; and
- a close relation between the victim and the suspect, and prosecution would be contrary to the interest of the victim.

The grounds for non-prosecution due to technicalities can be:

- erroneously registered as suspect by the police;
- insufficient legal evidence for a prosecution;
- inadmissibility of a prosecution because of the expiry of the time limit, the decease of the suspect, the absence of a complaint in cases of private complaint offences, the non-observance of undue delay (Article 6 ECHR) or suspect not yet criminally liable (< 12 years of age);
- the court does not have a legal competence over the case;
- the act does not constitute a criminal offence;
- the offender is not criminally liable due to a justification or excuse defense; and
- the evidence has been illegally obtained.

Public prosecutors are not obliged to motivate their decisions not to prosecute due to technicalities or due to policy considerations. They are, however, obliged to categorize their decisions under one of the reasons or grounds for non-prosecution previously mentioned. This categorization is no guarantee for a uniform application of the reasons for non-prosecution. However, it provides information on the prosecution policy pursued in each of the nineteen prosecutorial jurisdictions, and provides insight into the difference in these prosecution policies. It is one of the means to harmonize these prosecution policies.

Complaints by the victim against non-prosecution

As said, the Dutch CCP grants the right of prosecution exclusively to the prosecution service. The State thus has a full monopoly on prosecution without any restriction. The victim does not have the right to private prosecution. Nevertheless, a victim can influence the decision whether prosecution is started.

An individual with an interest in the prosecution (e.g. the victim) can request a public prosecutor to review a prosecution decision or, should he refuse to do so, write a letter to a higher official in the hierarchy of the prosecution authority, requesting that the decision of the subordinate prosecutor be reviewed

Anybody with an interest in the prosecution of an offence can file a protest against a decision to waive a case by lodging a complaint with a Court of Appeal (Article 12 CCP). The court examines the manner in which the discretionary power was utilized by the public prosecutor. This examination concerns the legality of the decision (to determine if the law was properly applied) and the use of discretion (to determine if the decision is in line with the general prosecution policy). The complainant has the right to be heard by the court, and may be assisted by his counsel. The court of appeal may order the public prosecutor to initiate a prosecution if it finds that the prosecutor has misused his discretionary power. However, in practice the Court of Appeal rarely orders prosecution.

The penal order

Since the year 2008 the prosecution service statutorily was vested with the power to impose sentences and orders without intervention by the court (Articles 257a–257h CCP). The main purpose for this law reform was to extend the capacity of the criminal justice system by increasing the prosecutorial power to divert cases and to settle cases out of court.

The penal order (*strafbeschikking*) may be imposed for infractions and for crimes which carry a statutory prison sentence of six years or less (Article 257a CCP). In a so-called penal order the prosecution service may impose:

– a community service to perform non-remunerated work lasting 180 hours;
– a fine;
– a withdrawal from circulation of seized objects;
– an order to pay to the treasury a sum of money to benefit the victim;
– the withdrawal of a driving license for a period of up to six months.

Furthermore, the order may consist of instructions to be complied with by the offender. Those instructions may not restrict the offender's freedom of religion or his civil liberties. The instructions may consist of:

– the surrendering of objects that may be eligible for forfeiture or confiscation;
– the payment to the treasury of a sum of money that is equal to the profit of the crime;
– the payment of an amount of money to a public fund the aim of which is to support victims of crimes. The amount of money may not be higher than the maximum statutory fine set for the offence; or

– compliance with specifically designed instructions during a probationary term of one year maximum.

In some cases before the public prosecutor may impose a sentence he has to hear the offender in person or by telephone. For instance, when the sentence consists of a task penalty to perform non-remunerated work (Article 257c CCP). In cases where the public prosecutor intends to impose a fine or compensation order of more than € 2,000, the offender is assigned a defense counsel for the hearing (Article 257c, second paragraph CCP). For the imposition of orders, the offender does not have the right to be heard by the public prosecutor. The sentence or order becomes final unless the offender objects either in person at the public prosecutor's office or by letter. In such cases, a court trial will take place (Article 257e CCP).

Transaction

Before 2008 the prosecution service used the transaction (*transactie*) as a way of settling criminal cases outside of the court. A transaction can be considered as a form of diversion in which the offender voluntarily pays a sum of money to the Treasury, or fulfills one or more (financial) conditions laid down by the prosecution service in order to avoid further criminal prosecution and a public trial (Article 74 CC). A weak point of the transaction is that non-compliance automatically leads to the issuing of a writ of summons and a trial. This automatism creates a lot of work for the prosecution service and the court. Amongst other things this was a reason why the penal order was created. Since the year 2008 the penal order was gradually implemented. The transaction and the penal order have thus co-existed next to each other. The transaction in present time is only used in special cases. For instance in cases in which a large company agrees to pay a significant amount of money to avoid further criminal prosecution.

The writ of summons

When a criminal case has not been settled out of court, the prosecutor will summon the suspect to appear in court. The summons comprises the charge (*tenlastelegging*). The trial stage begins as soon as the prosecutor has issued his summons.

5.6 THE TRIAL PHASE

5.6.1 GENERAL PRINCIPLES GOVERNING THE TRIAL PHASE: PUBLIC TRIAL, ADVERSARIAL TRIAL AND THE DEFENDANTS' RIGHT TO BE PRESENT

After the pre-trial investigation is concluded, the public prosecutor decides whether there will be a writ of summons and a trial against the suspect.[39] In the trial phase of the investigation, the scenery changes quite a bit. Different principles govern the trial phase.

First of all, whereas the pre-trial investigation is a rather undisclosed affair, almost all criminal trials are public. The exceptions being cases in which the court deems it necessary in the interest of public order to hear the case behind closed doors (Article 269 CCP) and cases in which the suspect is underage (Article 495b CCP).

Secondly, the trial phase is of a more accusatorial nature. To a large extent there is equality of arms between the public prosecutor and the defense. At the trial, the evidence is presented in such a way that both the prosecutor and the defense can challenge it. In this sense, the trial is adversarial. Quite different from adversarial trials in the United Kingdom or the United States however, this does not mean that the court leaves the collection of evidence to the prosecutor and the defense. On the contrary, the court takes an active role in the fact-finding process. It has an independent responsibility to find the truth. Therefore, it is primarily the court that questions the defendant, witnesses, experts and such. The judge can also use his own observations during the trial as a means of evidence. In addition, the public prosecutor should not one-sidedly search for a conviction, but has to keep an eye on all interests at stake.

Strictly speaking, only the evidence presented and challenged at the trial can be used to come to a verdict.[40] This is what we call the principle of immediacy which follows from Articles 348 and 350 CCP.[41] The ratio behind it is that the more often information is transferred, the more distorted it can become. Therefore, the fact-finder, i.e. the judge, ultimately needs to see the evidence himself if he is to make an accurate assessment on the merits of the case.

---

[39] If the public prosecutor decides to drop the charges, the victim or his next of kin can file a complaint at the Court of Appeal. The Court of appeal can then, order the public prosecutor to charge the defendant (see Article 12 CCP).

[40] Article 338 CCP explicitly states this for the evidence of the charge, but the Supreme Court has ruled that this also goes for other decisions in the verdict, like the chosen penalty, see Supreme Court, 26 May 1998, ECLI:NL:HR:1998:ZD1050, *NJ* 1998/713; Supreme Court, 24 January 2012 ECLI:NL:HR:2012:BT1856, *NJ* 2012/82.

[41] See extensively on the subject D.M.H.R. Garé, *Het onmiddellijkheidsbeginsel in het Nederlandse strafproces*, Arnhem: Gouda Quint 1994 (with summary in English); M.S. Groenhuijsen & H. Selçuk, 'The principle of immediacy in Dutch criminal procedure in the perspective of European Human Rights Law', *ZSTW* 2014, 126, pp. 248–276.

This principle of immediacy would suggest that the core of the criminal investigation is the trial phase. As a rule, however, this assumption is false. Under Dutch criminal procedural law the main truth finding phase is normally not the court session but the pre-trial investigation by the public prosecutor and sometimes the investigative judge. The task of the court during the trial phase is mainly restricted to an assessment of the legality and reliability of the evidence gathered during that investigation. And, of course, to present the evidence against the defendant in order to give him the chance to defend himself and come up with an alternative to the scenario in which he is guilty.

Although the CCP embodies the immediacy principle requiring the direct presentation of evidence by witnesses and by experts during the court trial, witnesses are as a rule not questioned in court. This has been the case since the Supreme Court famously ruled that hearsay evidence can be used instead.[42] Because of this, the immediacy principle as laid down in the CCP has been seriously watered down. In fact, criminal court sessions to a large extent concern the written statements of witnesses filed by the police or the investigating judge. These written statements may be used as evidence provided that these have been discussed in court.[43] Under the influence of recent case law of the European Court of Human Rights (ECtHR), the adversarial principle receives presently somewhat more emphasis through the more regular summoning of crucial witnesses.[44] However, in general a trial still does not have to take long, especially if the accused confesses and does not contradict the written statements of the witnesses. Even in serious cases a trial usually does not last more than a couple of days.

The roles of the suspect and his defense counsel also change in the trial phase. The defendant is the center of attention at the trial. Although the defendant has the right to be present at his trial, he is usually not obliged to appear unless the court orders so, which is rarely the case (Article 278 CCP). A case may be tried in the absence of the accused (*bij verstek*), unless he was improperly summoned. However, this last condition does not prevent that defendants may be tried and convicted without having any knowledge of the pending trial. Although in general a summons must be served to the accused in person, or to his representative, the summons can also be posted to the official address of the defendant. Prior to 1998, the accused lost the right to be defended by his defense counsel if he himself was not present during court session. The European Court

---

[42]   Supreme Court, 20 December 1926, ECLI:NL:HR:1926:BG9435, *NJ* 1927/85.

[43]   But to be considered 'discussed' it is enough if the court gives a very short summary of the contents. See Article 301 CCP.

[44]   See e.g. European Court of Human Rights, *Vidgen v. the Netherlands*, 10 July 2012, appl. no. 29353/06, *NJ* 2012/649; Supreme Court, 29 January 2013, ECLI:NL:HR:2013:BX5539, *NJ* 2013/145 (*post-Vidgen*). See on this subject: B. de Wilde, *Stille getuigen: het recht belastende getuigen in strafzaken te ondervragen (artikel 6 lid 3 sub d EVRM)*, Deventer: Wolters Kluwer 2015 (with English summary).

of Human Rights decided in the *Lala* and *Pelladoah* judgments that this was in conflict with Article 6 of the European Human Rights Convention.[45] Since then, an absent defendant may be represented by his counsel where the latter is explicitly empowered by the accused to do so. In such cases, the trial is considered to take place in the presence of the accused (Article 279 CCP).

If the defendant is present, he will be interrogated by the judges, who – of course – will inform him that he is not obliged to answer any questions (Article 271 CCP). The defendant can choose to have a defense attorney to plead his case, or he can decide to defend himself. Not only the judge will ask questions, the prosecutor and the defendant's attorney will also be allowed to question the defendant. If all is said and done, the defendant strictly has the right to make the last statement (Article 311(4) CCP).

At the trial stage the defense counsel's role is somewhat limited. He gives guidance to his client when being questioned by the court and public prosecutor. He makes, where relevant, critical remarks regarding the police files and he addresses the court in an oral pleading. And, as said, he can question the defendant and witnesses, insofar as the judge has not yet asked these questions. The possibilities for the defense lawyer to ask for additional evidence or for a rehearing of witnesses or experts during the trial phase, are limited. Cross examination in a true sense is unknown in Dutch criminal procedure. However, in recent years there has been a development in which more is required from the defense counsel and lapses on his side can cost the defendant some serious opportunities to challenge the case against him.

5.6.2 SUMMONS AND INDICTMENT

As mentioned before, the pre-trial phase ends and the trial phase begins with the decision to write a summons. If the public prosecutor decides to prosecute, he then summons the suspect to appear in court. The formal and substantive requirements for a valid summons (*dagvaarding*) are given by Articles 258 to 261 CCP. If an accused wants to, he can file a notice of objection against the summons (Article 262 CCP). In this way, rash prosecutorial decisions that can have a lasting impact on the reputation of the accused, can be remedied by the court in a closed court session. In practice, however, this opportunity is rarely used and hardly ever leads to a discontinuation of the prosecution.

The most important and substantive aspect of the summons is the indictment (*tenlastelegging*). The indictment is a description of the offence or the offences with which the defendant will be charged. This indictment is of great

---

[45] European Court of Human Rights, *Lala v. the Netherlands,* 22 September 1994, appl. no. 14861/89, *NJ* 1994/733, and European Court of Human Rights, *Pelladoah v. the Netherlands,* 22 September 1994, appl. no. 16737/90.

importance in Dutch criminal procedure. It is formulated by the prosecutor and describes with what charges the defendant is charged. It is the basis of the court session. It follows from Articles 348 and 350 CCP that the court can only base its investigation and decisions on this indictment and cannot modify it, even if it deems this necessary for a conviction. This is very strict. If the defendant has not been charged with a certain aspect of a statutory offence, the court cannot consider it proven. So, if the indictment claims the defendant murdered a victim in Amsterdam, and the court finds at trial that it happened in Rotterdam, the defendant must, in principle, be acquitted. This is often characterized as the tyranny of the indictment (*tirannieke werking van de tenlastelegging*), i.e. that the court may only convict on the basis of the charge.[46]

There are ways to mitigate these effects however. For one, the court is allowed to score out words in the indictment and pronounce less proven than was charged, as long as by doing this the court does not alter the meaning of the charge. As a result, indictments are often long and hard to read with a lot of alternative charges ('and/or'). The court also has the possibility to repair obvious errors in the indictment. A third important remedy is the right for the public prosecutor to adjust the indictment during the criminal process (Article 313 CCP). This is also allowed during an appeal, although the act charged has to remain the same at all times.

5.6.3 THE COURT HEARING

After a court clerk has called out the case, a court hearing (*het onderzoek ter terechtzitting*) commences with the identification of the accused by the presiding judge of the court and the reading of the charge (*tenlastelegging*) by the public prosecutor. The accused is explicitly reminded by the court of his right to remain silent and urged to pay close attention.

After this, the court will start its investigation. The presiding judge leads this investigation and will start off by presenting the defendant the documents that are in the case file. By doing this, the presiding judge makes those documents eligible for use as evidence. The presiding judge will also question the defendant. After that, the other judges, the prosecutor and the defense counsel are also allowed to ask questions. The defendant may not be questioned under oath. Not even if he wants to. He has the right to remain silent, and cannot be obliged to tell the truth and nothing but the truth. Lying will therefore not result in perjury and does not constitute a criminal offence.

---

[46]   See on this subject most extensively J. Boksem, *Op den grondslag der telastelegging. Beschouwingen naar aanleiding van het Nederlandse grondslagstelsel*, Nijmegen: Ars Aequi Libri 1996.

Thereafter, if witnesses and/or experts have appeared, the court will proceed by hearing them.[47] There are three ways in which witnesses and experts appear: the public prosecutor calls them, which can be either because the prosecutor deems this appropriate or on request of the defense, the court calls them, or the defendant brings them himself. Typically, if the defense wants to hear witnesses or experts, they will have to request the public prosecutor to call them.[48] The prosecutor can refuse on the grounds laid down in Article 264 CCP. If the defense persists, they can request the court to call the witness or expert anyway (Articles 287 and 288 CCP). In general, the defense has to file its requests early, because a failure to put in a request before the trial starts leads to a stricter criterion for the granting of the request (Article 315 CCP).[49]

Unlike the accused, witnesses and experts are obliged to answer the questions put by the court, the prosecutor and the defense counsel. The examination of the witnesses by the court is usually combined with the reading by the presiding judge of their statements made to the police or the investigating judge. Witnesses are examined under oath. Lying leads to perjury, which is a felony (Article 207 CC).

After the evidence has been presented and discussed, the investigative stage of the trial ends. Now a more evaluative stage commences. The public prosecutor shall address the court with a speech (*requisitoir*) (Article 311 CCP). In his speech, he gives a summary of the evidence, recommends what offence the defendant is to be sentenced for and requests a particular sentence. The Board of Prosecutors General has issued a considerable number of directives on what sentences are appropriate in individual cases. There are all kinds of sentencing suggestion guidelines for the most prevalent types of crime like theft, drug possession, insult and such. The public prosecutor is obliged to follow these guidelines, unless exceptional circumstances occur. Of course, the judge is not bound by this sentence request, although it can be considered an important benchmark in standard cases.

After that, the defendant may respond (*pleidooi*). He usually does so through his counsel. Thereafter, the public prosecutor gets another opportunity to react to what the defense brought forward (*repliek*). If the public prosecutor seizes this opportunity, the defense will get the chance to reply again as well (*dupliek*). Finally, the defendant himself gets the final say.

---

[47] See on experts in particular P.T.C. van Kampen, *Expert evidence compared. Rules and practices in the Dutch and American criminal justice system,* Antwerpen: Intersentia 1998. Although a lot has changed since 1998 (e.g. a register with all experts of the Dutch courts was founded), the book still gives good insight in the basics of expert evidence in the Netherlands.

[48] In the plans to thoroughly modernize Dutch criminal procedural law, this typical peculiar aspect of the Dutch criminal procedure may change.

[49] See extensively on these rules: D.M.H.R. Garé & P.A.M. Mevis, *Over het oproepen van getuigen ter terechtzitting en getuigenbewijs in strafzaken,* Nijmegen: Ars Aequi Libri 2000; G.J.M Corstens, M.J. Borgers & T. Kooijmans, *Het Nederlands strafprocesrecht,* Deventer: Kluwer, 2014, par. 15.12; and the overview ruling in Supreme Court, 1 July 2014, ECLI:NL:HR:2014:1496, *NJ* 2014/441.

Hereafter, the presiding judge closes the court hearing. If it's a hearing by the single-judge division (see Articles 368 CCP and following), the judge will immediately come to a verdict. In complex or severe cases with a three-headed bench, the court deliberates in chambers on the verdict and the sentence. The verdict must be available within two weeks. The verdict is read in a public court session and does not contain concurring or dissenting opinions. As a rule, it takes more than two weeks to actually write the verdict in full and to give a full summing-up of the evidence used to reason the decision. These extensions of the verdict on a later date are allowed. Such extended verdicts are normally only prepared when an appeal or appeal in cassation is lodged.

5.6.4 THE VICTIM AND THE INJURED PARTY

Already since 2005 the victim has a restricted right to give a verbal statement during court trial, the so-called victim impact statement (Article 302 CCP). Article 51e(2) of the CCP also enables certain relatives and caretakers of the victim to make a verbal statement concerning the impact of the crime. In 2012, the number of surviving relatives who can make a verbal statement was extended.[50] Instead of a maximum of one surviving relative, now three surviving relatives can exercise the right to make a verbal statement (Article 51e(4)(b)). The circle of persons who qualify as 'surviving relatives' was also expanded and now includes: the spouse or partner; the relatives by consanguinity in the direct line and the relatives up to and including the fourth degree of the collateral line (Article 51e(4) CCP). A victim or relative can only exercise the right of a verbal statement if certain conditions are met. In this regard Article 51e(1) CCP requires that the committed crime carries a statutory term of imprisonment of at least eight years, or that the committed crime is one of the crimes mentioned in Article 51e CCP. In accordance with Article 51e(2) CCP a verbal statement is restricted to the impact of a crime. However, in 2016 a law has entered into force that grants victims and relatives the possibility to speak without such restrictions.[51] This law embodies the idea that victims and relatives should not be constrained if they want to exercise the right to make a verbal statement. As a result, the victim and his relatives can also speak about the decisions the court should make with regard to – for example – whether the offence can be proven and the penalty that should be imposed.

Since the 1993 Criminal Injuries Compensation Act, the victim can join the proceedings in the pre-trial or trial phase in his capacity as injured party and can claim full financial compensation from the offender to be decided on by the

---

[50]   Act of 12 July 2012 (Wet uitbreiding spreekrecht), *Kamerstukken* 33176, *Staatsblad* 2012/345.
[51]   Act of 14 April 2016 (Wet aanvulling spreekrecht), Kamerstukken 34082, *Staatsblad* 2016/160.

criminal Court.[52] By allowing a victim to claim compensation in the criminal procedure, there is no need for a separate civil procedure.[53] The claim may comprise material and immaterial damages. There is no statutory maximum amount that can be claimed when joining the proceedings.

To qualify as an injured party and thus be able to claim compensation, it is required that a person has incurred direct damage as a result of the criminal offence (Article 51f (1) CCP). The heirs of a victim who died as a result of the criminal offence may join the proceedings as well (Article 51f (2) CCP).

The joiner as a rule is effected by a form in the pre-trial phase to be handed to the public prosecutor, and in the trial phase to be handed to the Court containing personal data of the injured party and information on what the grounds for the claim are and the content of the claim. For the proper preparation of the claim, the injured party has access to the police files of the case. In claiming compensation from the offender, the victim is not assisted by the State, but may be assisted by a lawyer or proxy.

Article 361(3) CCP concerns the admissibility of the claim of the injured party. A claim can be determined as inadmissible when it imposes a disproportionate burden on the criminal proceedings. According to the old legal criterion, a claim had to be clear and not too complex to be dealt with by the criminal court. The renewed criterion broadens the admissibility of the claim and therefore strengthens the position of the victim in his capacity as injured party.

To avoid the situation that recovery of the claim is impossible due to the unwillingness of the offender, the court can either impose a partly suspended sentence under the condition that the offender pays compensation (Article 14c CC (2)) or can impose a compensation order (Article 36f CC). Compensation orders are enforced by the State. As of 2016, the State will pay the victim the remaining amount if the offender convicted of a serious crime does not fulfill his obligation regarding the compensation order within eight months (Article 36f(7) CC) and will later recover the amount from the convict. The State will pay a maximum of €5000, unless it concerns victims of violent and sexual offences. The amount to be paid to victims of those offences is not bound to a maximum.

5.6.5 COURT DECISIONS AND REASONING

Before a Dutch criminal court comes to a verdict, it asks itself a framework of eight questions. The courts always consider these in the same, pre-set, order. The first four of those are formal questions and can lead to procedural end decisions

---

[52]   Act of 23 December 1992 (Wet Terwee), *Kamerstukken* 21345, *Staatsblad* 1993/29.
[53]   S.G.C. van Wingerden, M. Moerings & J. van Wilsem, *De praktijk van schadevergoeding voor slachtoffers van misdrijven*, Den Haag: Boom Juridische uitgevers 2007, p. 43.

(Article 348 CCP). The next four are of a more substantive nature (Article 350 CCP).

Article 348 CCP states: "The District Court shall investigate, on the basis of the indictment and the hearing at the court session, the validity of the summons, its jurisdiction to try the offence as charged in the indictment and the right of the public prosecutor to institute criminal proceedings and whether there are reasons to suspend the prosecution."

This results in the first part of the framework:

1) The court first asks itself whether the summons is valid, or if it has to declare it null and void. A summons is null and void when it has not been served properly, or for instance when the charge is not properly formulated or not comprehensible.

2) Next, the court considers its own competence. The court can declare itself not competent to try the case when the offence charged has not been committed within its geographical jurisdiction (relative competence), or when the offence belongs to the jurisdiction of another specialized court, e.g. the civil court, the juvenile court, the military court or an economic police court (absolute competence).

3) Thirdly, the court decides whether the public prosecutor had the right to institute criminal proceedings. If not, he will be rejected in his prosecution (*niet-ontvankelijk verklaard in zijn vervolging*). This can be the case for several reasons. For instance, the statutory limitation period, the death of the defendant or the double jeopardy rule might bar the prosecution. A more procedural reason to bar the prosecution can be found in the protection of the fairness and integrity of the criminal process when the prosecutor or his subordinates have not complied with procedural requirements which obstruct the fairness of the defendant's trial.

4) The final procedural question is whether there are reasons to suspend the trial against the accused. For instance, if the defendant is unfit to stand, the case should be suspended.[54]

If the court decides that the summons is valid, that the court is competent to try the case, that the prosecution is not to be rejected and that further prosecution does not need to be suspended, the court has to make four substantive decisions, which are all essential to the substantive appreciation of the case. These follow from Article 350 CCP.

Article 350 CCP states: "If the investigation, referred to in section 348, does not result in application of section 349(1), the District Court shall, on the basis of the indictment and the hearing at the court session, deliberate on the question

---

[54] See on Dutch practice: L. van den Akker, L. Dalhuisen & M. Stokkel, 'Fitness to stand trial: A general principle of European criminal law?', *Utrecht Law Review* 2011, pp. 120–136.

whether it has been proven that the defendant committed the criminal offence, and, if so, which criminal offence the judicial finding of fact constitutes under the law; if it is found that the offence is proven and punishable, then the District Court shall deliberate on the criminal liability of the defendant and on the imposition of the punishment or measure, prescribed by law."

This results in the second set of questions of the framework:

5) The first of those is whether the facts as stated in the indictment are proven. This is the question that concerns the evidence, which will be discussed more in depth in the next section. If the case cannot be proven, the court's verdict will be an acquittal (*vrijspraak.*)

6) The second substantive question is whether the facts charged which have been proven constitute a valid, statutory criminal offence. In the Netherlands, the principle of legality demands a statutory basis for all criminal offences. First of all, all elements of the statute should be in the indictment and proven. Otherwise, the proven facts cannot be qualified as an offence. The tyranny of the indictment forbids the court from looking past the indictment even if other facts can be proven. So if one of the elements of the offence is not charged, the proven facts cannot be qualified as the offence and the defendant must be discharged (*ontslagen van alle rechtsvervolging*). Another reason for this could be that the statutory offence is not valid, because it conflicts with higher law (e.g. the ECHR, or – in case of a statute of a municipality or province – the CC) or was not yet or no longer in force.

7) The third question concerns the liability of the defendant for the offence. This question primarily concerns the various defenses available in substantive law. If the court finds that the offence was justified given the circumstances, or that the defendant cannot be held accountable, it discharges him as well.

8) Finally, if the court considers the charge proven, the proven facts a criminal offence and the defendant liable, he will have to decide whether to sanction the defendant. Here it is important to note that the court cannot only impose punishment, but can also apply other measures (*maatregelen*) to – for example – prevent future offending. The court can also convict the defendant without imposing any sanction (Article 9a CC).

Article 121 of the Dutch Constitution stipulates that any court judgment should contain the grounds that it is based on. For a criminal verdict this is prescribed in more detail in Articles 358 and 359 of the CCP.[55] In general, the court not only

---

[55] See extensively on the general obligation to give a reasoned verdict: B.M. Kortenhorst, *De motiveringsverplichting in strafzaken. Een analyse van de artikelen 358 en 359 van het Wetboek van Strafvordering,* Arnhem: Gouda Quint 1990 (with summary in French), and on the obligation to give a reasoned decision that the facts as charged are proven in particular

has to decide on the eight issues described above, but also has to elaborate on the reasoning behind these decisions. Furthermore, the court has long been obliged to reason why it rejects certain defenses raised by the defense. Since 2005 this obligation to respond to viewpoints has been extended: the court has to respond to any position it rejects, as long as this position is expressly substantiated by either the prosecutor or the defense (Article 359 (2) second sentence CCP).

5.6.6 RULES OF EVIDENCE

The finding of facts with regard to questions one through four and six to eight is hardly regulated by Dutch procedural law. The fifth question – can the facts as charged be proven – however, is described comprehensively in Articles 338 through 344a CCP.[56]

It has already been stated above, that the court takes an active role in finding the relevant facts to the case and that the public prosecutors efforts cannot be solely directed at finding evidence against the defendant. Because of this, there is no 'burden of proof' in Dutch criminal procedure, in a strict sense. This does not mean however, that the truth-finding process is not governed by the presumption of innocence. It in fact is fundamental to Dutch criminal procedure. In practice, it is primarily the prosecutor that gathers the evidence and the one on whom the burden of proof rests. An offender can be convicted only when the Court is convinced by the evidence presented at the trial that the offender has committed the offence charged (Article 338 CCP). This requirement of judicial conviction is generally believed to be rather comparable to the standard of proof beyond reasonable doubt.

The conviction requirement that the judge has to be absolutely convinced of the defendant's guilt is applicable to both defendants denying guilt and defendants confessing guilt. A guilty plea is an unknown phenomenon in Dutch criminal procedures.

Article 338 CCP further describes the sources from which the judges' conviction may originate. It stipulates that the judicial conviction must be reached at the trial hearing through legal means of evidence. The first requirement ('at the trial hearing') is the (watered-down) principle of immediacy. The second one ("legal means of evidence") refers to the five – exclusive – means of evidence defined by statute (Article 339 CCP). These are:

W.H.B. Dreissen, *Bewijsmotivering in strafzaken*, Den Haag: Boom Juridische uitgevers, 2007 (with summary in English).

56   See on the subject of evidence J. Simmelink, 'The law of evidence and substantiation of evidence', in: M.S. Groenhuijsen & T. Kooijmans, *The reform of the Dutch code of criminal procedure in comparative perspective*, Leiden: Nijhoff, 2012, pp. 129–154.

1) the court's own observations during the court hearing (e.g. photos or audio/video-recording, but also the appearance of the defendant). This is a safety net for all types of evidence that cannot be qualified under any of the other categories.

2) the statement of the accused made in court. A statement of the accused is his statement during court trial about facts and circumstances he knows from his own knowledge. A refusal to make a statement may in principle not lead to adverse inferences.[57] An obvious lie may be used, as long as the falsehood of the statement follows from other legal means of evidence.

3) the statement of a witness made in court, i.e. the information he gives in court on facts and circumstances he personally perceived and experienced. Personal opinions, guesses and conclusions are excluded as evidence. Hearsay testimony falls within the definition of a witness' statement, which has as effect that a police officer can make a statement about a statement of a witness without the latter appearing in court.[58]

4) The statement of an expert made in court, i.e. an opinion based on his knowledge concerning the subject on which his opinion is sought.[59]

5) Any written materials. This category is crucial to the common trial practice of basing a conviction in large part on the case file drafted by the prosecution. The Code distinguishes five categories of written materials (Article 344 CCP):

   a. written decisions by members of the judiciary;

   b. reports by members of competent agencies, e.g. police reports on facts or circumstances personally perceived or experienced by them;

   c. documents of public agencies concerning subjects related to their competence containing the communication of facts and circumstances perceived or experienced by these agencies;

   d. reports of experts; and

   e. all other written materials. This last category may only be used in relation with the content of other means of evidence.

As long as every fact charged is in some way deducible from the legal means of evidence that are included in the verdict, the court is in principle free to decide whether the evidence is enough to convince it of the defendant's guilt. However, there are some exceptions to this freedom. The statutory provisions on evidence contain a few lower limits. These are evidential minimum rules which

---

[57] There are exceptions however, see Supreme Court, 3 June 1997, ECLI:NL:HR:1997:ZD0733, *NJ* 1997/584; Supreme Court, 15 June 2004, ECLI:NL:HR:2004:AO9639, *NJ* 2004/464.

[58] See on the use of witness statements M.J. Dubelaar, *Betrouwbaar getuigenbewijs. Totstandkoming en waardering van strafrechtelijke getuigenverklaringen in perspectief*, Deventer: Kluwer 2014 (with English summary).

[59] See P.T.C. van Kampen, *Expert evidence compared. Rules and practices in the Dutch and American criminal justice system*, Antwerpen: Intersentia 1998.

limit the freedom of the court in order to prevent careless convictions. The most important are that a conviction may never be based solely on the statement of the accused (Article 341(4) CCP) and that – in principle[60] – a finding of guilt may not rest upon the testimony of a single witness (*unus testis nullus testis*) (Article 342(2) CCP). In practice, it is usually this second restriction that comes into play, but the following is most likely also applicable to a second means of evidence supporting a confession. The rule that there have to be at least two witnesses does not mean that every fact in the indictment has to be supported by at least two means of evidence. It is enough that two means of evidence both support some part of the indictment as long as all facts proven are at least supported by one. In recent years, however, the Supreme Court has added a requirement: the second means of evidence has to 'sufficiently support' the primary means of evidence.[61] Other evidential minimum rules are laid down in Articles 344a and concern more typical witnesses like an anonymous witness or a witness who has made a deal with the prosecutor to testify in exchange for a reduced sentence. A conviction cannot be solely or decisively be grounded on such a witness statement.

5.6.7 PROCEDURAL CONSEQUENCES OF ILLEGAL GATHERING OF EVIDENCE AND OTHER PROCEDURAL IRREGULARITIES

Quite typically, in Dutch criminal procedure, the court assessing the value of the evidence, is also the authority which has to decide whether said evidence is admissible. The same court thus not only has to deal with the matter of reliability, but also with the question of legality of the evidence.[62]

The rules on the consequences of illegal gathering of evidence and other procedural irregularities are outlined in Article 359a CCP. This provision first of all describes some threshold requirements which need to be fulfilled in order to attack any consequences to irregularities. There has to be some violation of Dutch or international law (1), which is irreparable (2), has happened in the pre-trial phase of the criminal charge in question (3), and the consequences of a violation of which are not separately prescribed by law (4) or the assessment of which falls within the jurisdiction of the judge ruling on pre-trial detention (5).

The Article gives the court four options to respond to irreparable irregularities in the pre-trial phase:

---

60 Article 344 CCP makes an important exception to his rule. The conviction can be solely based on the official report of a police officer.

61 See for example Supreme Court, 30 June 2009, ECLI:NL:HR:2009:BG7746, *NJ* 2009/496.

62 The distinction between reliability and legality is important. The exclusion of unreliable evidence is not based on article 359a CCP, but directly on the desire to find the truth.

1) The court may mitigate the sentence in proportion with the seriousness of the irregularity.
2) The court may exclude the evidence.
3) The prosecutor may be rejected in his prosecution.
4) The court can establish the irregularity without any sanction.

Which consequence the court chooses, depends on the gravity of the procedural error, the interest protected by the violated rule and the harm or prejudice caused by the error. The Supreme Court has developed guidelines in its case-law.[63] In summary: barring the prosecution is only allowed when the justice authorities intentionally or with gross negligence have done injustice to the defendant's right to a fair trial (e.g. torture, incitement).

Exclusion of evidence requires that the procedural irregularity relates to the gathering of said evidence. It concerns a substantial violation of an important procedural requirement. The Supreme Court distinguishes three types of reasons for exclusion of evidence.[64] First of all, in light of the right to a fair trial the exclusion of evidence may be necessary, unavoidable even. For instance, when a defendant was not instructed on his right to remain silent and/or his right to consult with an attorney, a confession usually cannot be used without violating the right to a fair trial. A second category is the gross violation of another very important procedural requirement. These are the types of irregularities which must be excluded in order to prevent the investigative authorities from ever committing these types of errors again. Examples are the violation of doctor-client privilege and the internal inspection of the human body without a legal basis. The third and final category concerns irregularities of – in itself – a lower level of gravity. This category can only lead to the exclusion of evidence if it is proven that the irregularities happen so frequently that they are structural and exemplary of the functioning of the investigative authorities. This will most likely be hard to prove.

In other cases, and these are the most common, the court can compensate the harm done by reducing the sentence but may also choose to withhold from any sanctions.[65]

---

[63] See most notably Supreme Court, 30 March 2004, ECLI:NL:HR:2004:AM2533, *NJ* 2004/376 (*Drainage pipe*), and Supreme Court, 19 February 2013, ECLI:NL:HR:2013:BY5321, *NJ* 2013/308 (*Unauthorized auxiliary prosecutor*).

[64] Supreme Court, 19 February 2013, ECLI:NL:HR:2013:BY5321, *NJ* 2013/308 (*Unauthorized auxiliary prosecutor*).

[65] See more extensively on this subject: M.J. Borgers & L. Stevens, 'The use of illegally gathered evidence in the Dutch criminal trial', *Electronic Journal of comparative law*, 2010, vol. 14.3.

5.6.8 VARIOUS FORMS OF APPEAL AGAINST COURT DECISIONS

The CCP provides various forms of appeal against court decisions. Against some of them, like decisions on pre-trial decision, a separate remedy is available. In general, however, all court decisions can only be contested together at once after the verdict. This is the so-called concentration principle (Article 406 CCP). There are two 'normal' remedies against a verdict: appeal and appeal in cassation.[66]

The general legal remedy against a decision by the court of first instance is appeal. An appeal may be filed by both the public prosecutor and the accused. The appeal must be filed in due time, as a rule, within fourteen days (Article 408 CCP). No appeal is allowed in cases of only minor offences where the maximum fine imposed is less than €50 (Article 404 CCP). No appeal against an acquittal is possible for the defense. If the offence carries a statutory term of imprisonment of four years or less and the actual punishment does not exceed a fine of €500, leave to appeal is required. The presiding judge of the Court of Appeal decides whether an appeal is permissible, i.e. whether an appeal decision is necessary in the interest of a proper administration of justice (Article 410a CCP). Leave to appeal was introduced in 2007 in order to reduce the case-load of the appeal courts, but was not a success. It did not have the desired effects and drew critical attention from both the UN human rights committee and the ECtHR.[67] The system of leave to appeal may be abolished if the plans on the modernization of criminal procedure will actually take effect.

The appeal involves a complete reassessment of the case. The Appeal Court has to take its own decision on all points. This does not mean an appeal always involves a complete rehearing of the case. The appeal case is often concentrated on the grounds for appeal cited by the prosecution or the accused, and which are discussed in a memorandum of appeal (see Article 416 CCP). Evidence that has been discussed in first instance, can be used in appeal without discussing it again.

Appeal in cassation may be lodged at the Supreme Court against Court of Appeal decisions. An appeal in cassation may be lodged by both the public prosecutor and the accused, but not if it concerns a minor offence for which a fine of less than €250 is imposed (Article 427 CCP).

Appeal in cassation is not a rehearing of the case, since the Supreme Court is does decide on the facts, but will merely assess the proper application of law by the lower courts. In general, the Supreme Court will not decide on other issues

---

[66]   See also J.W. Fokkens & N. Kirkels-Vrijman, 'The Dutch system of legal remedies', in: M.S. Groenhuijsen & T. Kooijmans, *The reform of the Dutch code of criminal procedure in comparative perspective*, Leiden: Nijhoff 2012, pp. 17–30.

[67]   European Court of Human Rights, *Lalmahomed v. the Netherlands* 22 February 2011, no. 26036/08, *NJ* 2012/306; UN Human Rights Committee, *Mennen v. the Netherlands*, 27 July 2010, no. 1797/2008, *NJ* 2012/305.

than the ones brought forward by the party lodging the appeal in cassation. Where the Supreme Court rules that substantive or procedural law has not been properly applied, the verdict of the lower court will be quashed and the case will usually be referred back to the same or another Court of Appeal. That court has to render a new decision, and is – in practice – bound by the decision of the Supreme Court concerning the proper application of law in that case. Since 2012 there is a simplified procedure to dismiss an appeal in cassation. If there is little at stake or if the appeal in cassation will fail evidently, the Supreme Court will not seek the advice of the procurator general, as it normally does, and dismiss the case without an explanation (Article 80a Judicial Organization act).

Beside the normal legal remedies, there are two extraordinary legal remedies. These are available when a judgement is irrevocable and has obtained *res judicata*, either because the time to appeal has expired or because all normal remedies have been exhausted. The first is appeal in cassation 'in the interest of the law' (Article 456 CCP, *cassatie in het belang der wet*). This is an appeal in cassation lodged by the procurator general. His appeal in cassation has the goal to clear up an issue of law that arose in the case against which he appeals. The difference with normal cassation is that the judgment of the Supreme Court will not have any effect on the people concerned in the case. The second extraordinary legal remedy is review (Article 457 CCP, *herziening*). Review has long been used to remedy miscarriages of justice. In recent years review has also been made available to the detriment of the defendant. Now, acquitted defendants can also be convicted through review if new evidence is found or it turns out that a witness or judge was bribed or threatened to obtain an acquittal (Article 482a CCP).

PART IV
SANCTIONS

6. SENTENCING

Geert PESSELSE[*]

6.1 STATUTORY FRAMEWORK

The Dutch judiciary is vested with its widest discretionary power when sentencing. The very few statutory rules that guide the court in this process are general and do not specifically prescribe the nature and severity of the sanctions in individual cases. The statutory framework of sanctions is set very broadly.[1] The statutory minimum term of imprisonment is one day, and is the same for all crimes, regardless of the generic seriousness of the offence. Moreover, according to Article 9a CC a court may determine that no punishment or measure shall be imposed, even if the defendant is considered criminally liable. On the other hand, maximum terms of imprisonment are specified and reflect the gravity of the worst possible case. Few crimes are subject to life imprisonment, but instead of life imprisonment a fixed term prison sentence of up to thirty years or a fine can in some cases be imposed.

Until recently, mandatory minimum sentences are unknown in Dutch penal law. As of 2012 the sentence of community service (taakstraf) cannot be imposed under circumstances specified in Article 22b CC, for example in the case of conviction for a serious offence which carries, according to the statutory definition, a term of imprisonment of six years or more and has grossly violated the physical integrity of the victim. However, this exceptional provision proves the rule.

Aggravating and mitigating circumstances

The Criminal Code provides a rather restricted set of rules for aggravating and mitigating circumstances. Three general circumstances may result in a more severe sentence: recidivism, the committal of an offence in the capacity as a public official and concurrent offences (Articles 43a; 44 and 57 etc. CC). In case of aggravating

---

[*]   G. Pesselse (Ph.D.) is a member of the scientific staff of the Court of Appeal in 's-Hertogenbosch. He is also a judge *ad litem* at the District Court of Gelderland.

[1]   See extensively on this statutory framework F.W. Bleichrodt & P.C. Vegter, *Sanctierecht*, Deventer: Kluwer 2013, pp. 25–68.

circumstances, the statutory maximum sentence may be increased by one third. In addition, the Criminal Code specifies special aggravating circumstances for a number of criminal offences, which may result in a more severe sentence. This is, for example, the case with offences that are qualified in terms of their consequences (e.g. assault resulting in the death of the injured person).

The Criminal Code contains one general mitigating circumstance, namely the involvement of youth. Young offenders, in principle persons under 18, fall within the limit of juvenile criminal law with a much lighter sanction system (Article 77a etc. CC). Apart from this general mitigating circumstance the criminal Code contains special mitigating circumstances, which are related to specific offences.[2]

Concurrent sentences

Concurrent prison sentences cannot be imposed. When a suspect stands trial for concurrent offences or for multiple offences, the court cannot impose prison sentences simultaneously and cumulatively. In that case, the court can impose a joint sentence, the maximum term of which may be one-third higher than the highest statutory maximum prison sentence for one of those criminal offences but never more than thirty years (Article 57 et seq. CC). Fines may be imposed for any of the concurrent offences.[3] Finally, there is a possibility of combining various principal sentences (Article 9 CC). A prison sentence may be combined with a fine or a community service.

6.2 RULES ON REASONING OF SENTENCES

The choice of sanctions must remain within the broad statutory limits and ultimately lies with the court, but is subject to procedural requirements concerning the reasoning of the sentence. Article 359(5) CCP requires that the verdict states the reasons determining the sentence or measure. Until recently the court often confined itself to a standard phrase limited to the statement that the imposed sentence meets the seriousness of the offence, the circumstances in which the criminal offence has been committed, and the personality of the offender. It was generally known that this reasoning, required by Article 359(5) CCP, was pre-printed on the sentence form, or flowed easily from the word processor when devising the verdict. However, courts have begun to reason their sentence decisions more thoroughly. Article 359(6) CCP furthermore requires that in a

---

[2] See extensively on aggravating and mitigating circumstances in the CC, P.M. Schuyt, *Verantwoorde staftoemeting*, Deventer: Kluwer 2009 (with summary in English).

[3] See J.M. ten Voorde et al., *Meerdaadse samenloop in het strafrecht*, Den Haag: Boom juridische uitgevers 2013 (with a summary in English).

verdict that results in a punishment of measure which entails the deprivation of liberty, particular reasons that led to the choice of a custodial sentence must be given. The judgment shall also indicate the circumstances that were considered in assessing the appropriate length of the sentence. The choice of a suspended sentence does not need further reasoning. Additionally, Article 359(7) CCP requires special reasoning when the court imposes an entrustment order for a crime involving a risk to bodily integrity. Finally, Article 359 (2, second sentence) CCP requires a reasoned response to explicitly stated and substantiated opinions of the defense or the prosecution regarding sentencing.

Dutch procedural criminal law provides for a two-part reasoning in the sentencing of adults (Articles 359 (5) and 359(6) CCP). The first requires a decision on the punishment that is proportionate to the offender's criminal liability and the seriousness of the offence. The second step requires a decision on whether punishment should be imposed as a fine, a suspended sentence or determinate sentence of imprisonment. In this decision, it is not the individual criminal liability or seriousness of the offence that plays a decisive role, but considerations of special or general prevention.

6.3 SENTENCING AIMS AND PRINCIPLES

There is no statutory provision on the aims of sentencing. These aims are quite diverse and include retribution, special or general deterrence, rehabilitation, conflict solution, protection of society and reparation. All the statutory sanctions and measures are based on various sentencing aims. The penalty of community service, for example, combines many aims, but special prevention has a certain priority when imposing the community service. Multiple aims exist also for the withdrawal of illegally obtained profits (reparation, retribution and prevention), the fine (retribution, prevention and reparation), imprisonment (retribution, prevention and protection) and the entrustment order (protection, prevention as well as retribution). The basic notion of sentencing, however, remains the retribution of criminally liable conduct.

The court is free to choose one or more aims it thinks appropriate in each individual case.[4] The chosen aim can often be deduced from the kind of sentence and the extent of the sentence. Courts frequently opt for a combination of sentencing aims, but there are also many examples where one aim is emphasized, e.g. Supreme Court, 26 August 1960, ECLI:NL:HR:1960:33, *NJ* 1960/566: retribution ('…that measures are not, unlike sentences, also beneficial to retribution of the criminal offence and are only aimed at the protection of public order and improvement of the offender…'); Supreme Court, 9 December 1986,

---

4   See for empirical research on the sentencing aims of Dutch judges, J.W. de Keijser, *Punishment and purpose: from moral theory to punishment in action*, Amsterdam: Thela Thesis 2000.

ECLI:NL:HR:1986:AC1152, *NJ* 1987/540: general prevention ('...that foreign criminals, like the defendant, should be deterred from providing for themselves by committing offences in this country...'); Supreme Court, 12 November 1985, ECLI:NL:HR:1985:AC2708, *NJ* 1986/327: protection of society against the defendant ('...in the imposition of a prison sentence, the reason that the Court wished to protect society as far as was possible by doing so is not impermissible...'); Supreme Court, 15 July 1985, ECLI:NL:HR:1985:AC4252, *NJ* 1986/184: special prevention ('...with a view to a proper enforcement of norms, the Court holds that no other sentence but deprivation of freedom shall be imposed...').

Still, as a rule the court does not explicate the aims of the sentence in the verdict at all. Exceptionally however, in a famous case (the murder of Pim Fortuyn, a popular politician, who was killed whilst campaigning for Prime Minister), the court explicitly dealt with the aims of sentencing. The murderer was sentenced to a prison sentence of eighteen years and not to life sentence despite the societal shock that the murder caused and the seriousness of the crime. The Court in first instance ruled that for humanitarian reasons the suspect deserved to have an opportunity to return to society. On appeal, the Appeal Court explicitly referred to the attack on the democratic process and the very restricted recidivism risk, but kept the sentence intact because, as a rule, a first offender murderer, despite the seriousness of the crime and the special circumstances, would not normally be sentenced to life (Amsterdam Court of Appeal 18 July 2003, ECLI:NL:GHAMS:2003:AI0123, *NJ* 2003/580).

A few years later in another famous case (the murder of the media personality Theo van Gogh, who produced the film 'Submission'), which was equal in its shock to society, the Court sentenced the offender to life. In this case, however, the murderer did not show signs of remorse and was more likely to re-offend after being released (Amsterdam District Court, 26 July 2005, ECLI:NL:RBAMS:2005:AU0025).

The question arises here as to the extent to which the level of guilt of the offender puts a further limit on the severity of the sentence, and to what extent the sentence imposed should be in proportion to the degree of criminal liability. The principle 'no sentence without criminal liability' is part of Dutch penal law.[5] That means that a defendant, by reason of insanity, cannot be punished and his case will be dismissed. But if the defendant suffers from a mental disease or defect and poses a danger to others, or to the general safety of persons or goods, the court may order that the defendant be admitted to a secure institution through an entrustment order (Article 37a CC).

However, the principle 'no sentence without criminal liability' does not imply that the sentence is fully determined by this liability. Nor does it mean that a sentence that is disproportionate when measured by the degree of liability is inappropriate. In fact, the nature and severity of the sentence is not

---

[5] De Hullu, *Materieel strafrecht*, Deventer: Kluwer 2018, pp. 214–215.

only determined by the degree of liability, but also by other factors such as: protection of society against recurrence in connection with the danger of the offender; the seriousness of the offence committed; the seriousness of the effects for the legal order; and the general and preventive effect which emanates from such a sentence.[6] In its case law, the Supreme Court has repeatedly accepted a sentence in which a measure (e.g. an entrustment order), due to mental disorder, was combined with a very long prison sentence. Despite diminished liability due to the mental disorder, the court can pass a long-term prison sentence, because it feels the need to keep the offender outside society for a long time, in order to protect society.[7] A combination of an entrustment order and a life sentence, however, is not compatible. When the court imposes a life sentence, it is the intention of the court that the convict does not return into free society. The entrustment order has as main aim that the offender receive treatment and that he, as a consequence, be able to return into society. A combination of these sentences would conflict.[8]

Various personal or contextual factors may be reasons to adjust the actual sentence upwards or downwards.[9] An upward adjustment may be justified by the criminal past of the accused, or by the negative attitude of the accused during the examination in court; for example, an accused who consequently denies having committed the crime, or an accused wanting to evade a sentence by making several false statements, by the motives that compelled him to commit the offence, for instance jealousy and hate, by the circumstance that the accused did not want to cooperate in a psychiatric evaluation, or by the fact that the accused fails to understand that his behavior was wrong. A downward adjustment may be justified by a serious delay between the time of committing the crime and the trial, by voluntarily offering compensation for damages inflicted, by expressions of regret on the part of the accused, by a lack of previous convictions or by positive probation prospects.

6.4 JUDICIAL REVIEW OF SENTENCING

A sentence by a court of first instance can be reviewed by an appellate court. An appeal can be lodged by the defendant or the prosecutor. In appeal, the court enjoys full discretion to determine a new sentence. As a rule, lodging an appeal

---

6   Supreme Court, 15 July 1985, ECLI:NL:HR:1985:AC4252, *NJ* 1986/184.
7   Supreme Court, 10 September 1957, ECLI:NL:HR:1957:2, *NJ* 1958/5 (*Black rider*), Supreme Court, 6 December 1977, ECLI:NL:HR:1977:AB7287, *NJ* 1979/181, and Supreme Court, 12 November 1985, ECLI:NL:HR:1985:AC2708, *NJ* 1986/327.
8   Supreme Court, 14 March 2006, ECLI:NL:HR:2006:AU5496, *NJ* 2007/345.
9   See, in particular on the risk of reoffending as a relevant factor, S.G.C. van Wingerden, *Sentencing in the Netherlands: taking risk-related offender characteristics into account*, Den Haag: Eleven International Publishing 2014.

pays off, but Appeal Courts certainly do not shy away from imposing a higher sentence. Review of sentencing is exercised by the Supreme Court as well, but the review is restricted to the legal questions as to whether the statutory framework on sentencing is respected (i.e. maxima, cumulation and combination of sentences) and as to whether the sentence is sufficiently reasoned, according to the statutory requirements of Article 359 CCP. The Supreme Court, as a rule, accepts as sufficiently reasoned the standard formula that the sentence is proportionate with the seriousness of the crime, the circumstances in which it was committed, and with the personal circumstances of the suspect. However, the Supreme Court does not accept this standard formula when the sentence is surprisingly severe. This is the case when, for example:

- there is an obvious discrepancy between the offence committed and the sentence imposed, e.g. the seizure of a car worth €18,000 for a criminal offence that carried a fine not exceeding €5,000[10];
- on appeal the sentence is augmented considerably without further motivation, which is the case when a suspended prison sentence, imposed in first instance, is replaced by a determinate sentence[11];
- the judge did not respond to an explicit defense as to the sentence at the trial, in which the defendant pointed out a factor for reduction of the sentence in an insisting and confident way[12]; or
- the court imposes a high fine whilst the offender is poor.[13]

Recently the proper reasoning of sentences has been stressed by a reform of Article 359(2) CCP. The Court has to give explicit reasoning for not taking into consideration a well-reasoned and sound argument of the public prosecutor or the defense counsel.

6.5 DISPARITY IN SENTENCING

The absence of mandatory rules for sentencing may contribute to a mild penal climate, but may also result in great disparity in sentencing. Disparity between sentences for crimes that appear similar might be one of the most serious problems in sentencing in the Netherlands. The Court of Appeal or the Supreme Court can, as we have seen, reverse sentences. But neither appellate courts, nor the Supreme Court, can ever realize full equality in sentencing by lower courts. Equality in sentencing has been a major concern over the last decades.

---

[10]   Supreme Court, 13 June 1989, ECLI:NL:HR:1989:AJ5657, *NJ* 1990/138.
[11]   Supreme Court, 2 April 1985, ECLI:NL:HR:1985:AB7969, *NJ* 1985/875.
[12]   Supreme Court, 1 November 1988, ECLI:NL:HR:1988:AB7790, *NJ* 1989/351.
[13]   Supreme Court, 17 February 1998, ECLI:NL:HR:1998:ZD0941, *NJ* 1998/447.

Various proposals have been discussed to improve the equality in sentencing without restricting the judges' discretionary powers to individualize the sentence too much. Those proposals ranged from the establishment of a special sentencing court, to a databank on sentences, or sentencing check-lists or guidelines for courts. For certain types of offences, however, less disparity in sentencing was found. This was not a coincidence, but a result of the fact that for these offences the prosecution service had issued guidelines on what sentence was to be requested at trial in the closing speech. This holds good for drunk-driving, social security fraud, tax fraud, drug crimes, and so on. Those guidelines had a harmonizing effect. It appeared that in practice the Court considered the sanction requested by the prosecutor in his closing speech as a guideline for sanctioning. These guidelines have been issued by the Board of the Prosecutors-General, and were in line with the sentencing policy of individual courts. An individual member of the prosecution service is guidelines in principle bound by these. This obligation stems from the hierarchical structure of the prosecution service, in which someone lower in the hierarchy is committed to instructions emanating from his superior. This commitment is expressed in the law (Article 139 Judicial Organization Act, and Article 140 CCP). Unlike the members of the prosecution service, the Court is not bound by these guidelines. Nor is it obliged to state the reasons for a deviation from the guidelines to the detriment of the offender.[14] In daily practice, however, the guidelines prove to be a guide in its sentencing policy.

Although, since the 1970s, these types of sentencing guidelines for prosecutors have been issued for a large variety of crimes, they did not eliminate disparity in sentencing completely. This was due to the fact that the guidelines allowed a large margin between the highest and the lowest sentence to be requested, without making clear when the highest or the lowest sentence was appropriate. There was also a lack of consistency in the guidelines. The question of whether a weapon was used was very important in the guideline on bodily harm, but the use of a weapon did not play a role in the guideline on sentencing for the use of violence. Another reason why the sentencing guidelines did not eliminate disparity completely was that the prosecutorial guidelines on sentencing left room for public prosecutors to deviate from these guidelines in individual cases.[15]

---

14   Supreme Court, 10 March 1992, ECLI:NL:HR:1992:ZC0567, *NJ* 1992/593.
15   See on disparity in sentencing M. Duker, *Legitieme straftoemeting*, Den Haag: Boom juridische uitgevers 2003 (with a summary in English); and G.K. Schoep, *Straftoemetingsrecht en strafvorming*, Deventer: Kluwer 2008 (with summary in English).

6.6 PROSECUTORIAL SENTENCING GUIDELINES

Since 1999, more than 50 national guidelines for sentencing have been formulated by the prosecution service, which should lead to equality in sentencing for the majority of crimes. The structure of these prosecutorial sentencing guidelines is very clear and is based on the 'Framework for prosecutorial sentencing guidelines' (Aanwijzing kader strafvordering en OM-afdoening) published by the Board of Prosecutors General.

On the basis of this framework, specific guidelines prescribe a certain basis sanction for specific offences. As a result of special circumstances, the prescribed sanction be increased or decreased. For example, the use of weapons or the victim being a public servant leads to a higher sanction (up to 200%). Recidivism generally leads to the prescribed sanction being increased by 50%; multiple recidivism leads to an increase of 100%. The crime committed being one of attempt, on the other hand, leads to a reduction. A prescribed sanction can – after increase and/or decrease – be converted in another sanction or combined with another sanction. For example, a prescribed fine of € 6000 may be increased with 100% due to recidivism and be converted in a prison sentence of 95 days. An individual public prosecutor is allowed to deviate from these guidelines, but he has to give an explicit reason for doing so.

Let us look at guideline on assault as an example (Richtlijn voor strafvordering mishandeling 2015R009). The statutory maximum for assault is a prison sentence of 3 years or a fine of about €20.000 (Article 300 CC). However, the guideline on assault paints a different picture. If the assault merely induced pain but no injury, the basic sentence for a single strike is € 400. If a striking weapon or object is used, the basic sentence is 60 hours of community service. In the case of injury, the use of a striking weapon amounts to a basic sentence of 120 hours of community service. In the case of recidivism, this sentence is raised to 180 hours of community service. If the assault is committed during an event or under the influence of alcohol or drugs, the prescribed sanction is raised by 75%.

6.7 JUDICIAL POINTS OF REFERENCE FOR SENTENCING

The absence of mandatory sentences and the wide discretionary power in sentencing is one of the key characteristics of the Dutch criminal justice system. It is an expression of faith in its judiciary. However, discretion may lead to arbitrary or inconsistent sentences. Therefore, the use of discretion needs to be justified by the Court in its reasoning of the sentence. Nowadays, society expects greater transparency and equality in sentencing.

Unlike public prosecutors, judges cannot be bound by guidelines on sentencing issued by superior courts because of the requirement of independence (Article. 6 ECHR).[16] Judges are however free to develop a non-binding but consistent sentencing system. In recent years, two instruments have been developed in order to support courts in the sentencing process. The first, a database of consistent sentencing case law, was abolished in 2014. The second instrument is a system of judicial points of reference for sentencing. For a number of crimes, points of reference are set by the National council of professionals in criminal law (LOVS). Points of reference for sentencing exist for drug crimes, traffic crimes, various types of theft, injuries and perjury. As a rule, judges seem to apply these points of reference, although they are not bound by them.[17] When a discrepancy arises between the application of the prosecutorial sentencing guidelines and the judicial points of reference for sentencing, the latter usually prevail, as is shown in a decision of the Amsterdam Court of Appeal, 24 July 2007, ECLI:NL:GHAMS:2007:BB0460, *NJFS* 2007/229.

---

16   See recently Supreme Court, 27 may 2014, ECLI:NL:HR:2014:1236, *NJ* 2014/364.
17   Supreme Court, 31 Januari 2017, ECLI:NL:HR:2017:114, *NJ* 2017/199.

7. THE SYSTEM OF SANCTIONS

Henny SACKERS*

7.1 CLASSIFICATION OF PENALTIES

The current Dutch sanction system for adults distinguishes between penalties and measures.

Penalties are aimed at punishment and general prevention. Punishment means that the offender, through the penalty, is made to suffer in reaction to the harm his offence caused to others. Revenge plays a role in the penalty. Due to this element of revenge, the length of imprisonment must be proportionate to the level of blameworthiness.

Measures, on the other hand, are aimed at the promotion of the security and safety of persons or property, or at restoring a state of affairs. A measure differs from a penalty in that it can also be imposed where there is no question of criminal responsibility, in the sense that the person cannot be blamed for having committed a crime.

The Criminal Code furthermore distinguishes between principal penalties and accessory penalties, which could originally only be imposed in conjunction with a principal penalty. Since 1984, accessory penalties may be imposed as principal sentences as well.

7.2 SANCTIONS FOR ADULTS

The various principal penalties are set out in order of severity in Article 9 of the Criminal Code as follows:

- imprisonment (Articles 10–13);
- detention (Articles 18–19);
- task penalties (Articles 22c–22k); and
- a fine (Articles 23–24e).

---

* H.J.B. Sackers (Ph.D.) is professor of Criminal and Administrative Sanctions at Radboud University Nijmegen. He is also a judge *at litem* at the district court of 's-Hertogenbosch.

For all offences, the maximum statutory penalty is specified by the Act which defines the particular offence. This maximum penalty reflects the gravity of the worst possible case and is thus high for the most serious offences, e.g. life or thirty years imprisonment for murder, twelve years for rape, nine years for extortion, six years for domestic burglary and four years for simple theft.

7.3   CAPITAL PUNISHMENT

Capital punishment for ordinary crimes was abolished in 1870. For military crimes and war crimes, capital punishment was abolished in 1983 (Article 114 Dutch Constitution), but in practice had not been used since 1950. The Netherlands ratified Protocol no. 6 to the European Convention of Human Rights on the abolition of the death penalty which entered into force in 1985.

7.4   PRINCIPLE PENALTIES

Imprisonment

The most severe penalty in the Dutch penal system is imprisonment, which can only be imposed for crimes. The most severe form is life imprisonment, which is rarely imposed (since 1950, on approximately 60 occasions). Around twenty crimes carry life imprisonment as a statutory penalty, but the Criminal Code does not prescribe compulsory life imprisonment in any circumstances. Crimes, such as murder or manslaughter under aggravating circumstances that carry a tariff of life imprisonment also carry a fixed-term prison sentence of up to thirty years. Furthermore, since 1983 a fine may be imposed as the sole sanction for any crime, even those which carry life imprisonment as statutory sanction.

A life sentence is deprivation of liberty for an indeterminate period. Parole or early release arrangements are not applicable in the case of a life sentence. A life sentence as a rule lasts until the death of the prisoner. However, having served twenty years of imprisonment, life sentences may be converted by way of pardon into a fixed-term prison sentence. After such a pardon, the offender may be considered for early release. A conversion by way of pardon is very rarely granted. In 2016 and in accordance with the case law of the European Court of Human Rights (e.g. ECtHR, *Vinter v. the United Kingdom*, 7 July 2015, appl. nos. 66069/09, 130/10 and 3896/10) the Dutch government submitted a legislative proposal for an interim test after 25 years of prison. According to the Supreme Court, this proposal provides for a system of reassessment to allow for the shortening of life imprisonment in the appropriate cases. This means that imposing a life sentence is not in itself contrary to Article 3 European Convention (HR 19th December 2017, ECLI:NL:HR:2018:3185).

The fixed-term prison sentence is the most frequently applied form of imprisonment. The statutory minimum is one day and the statutory maximum is fifteen years. For designated crimes and in certain circumstances, the maximum may be thirty years. Unlike the situation in other countries, no offences carry a special statutory minimum term of imprisonment. Thus, for example for murder, a minimum prison sentence of one day is theoretically possible.

Where an offender is sentenced to imprisonment for several offences committed concurrently or consecutively, the court may impose a prison sentence which may exceed by one third the maximum statutory prison sentence for the severest offence. A prison sentence, however, may never exceed thirty years.

Detention

Detention is the custodial sentence for infractions. The minimum duration of detention is one day and the maximum duration is one year. In special cases, e.g. in cases of recidivism, the maximum can be increased to sixteen months. Originally intended as a *custodia honesta*, detention is deemed a lighter sentence on the sentencing scale than imprisonment, although the two hardly differ in the manner of their implementation.

Task penalty

The task penalty is one type of community sentences increasingly used to reduce the incidence of custodial sentences. Additional forms of community sentences such as electronic monitoring and penitentiary programs are alternative forms to the deprivation of liberty (*executiemodaliteiten*).

The development of community sentences started in the seventies with the establishment in 1974 of the Committee on alternative penal sanctions. This Committee was set up to advise the Government on new sentencing options in order to reduce the number of short-term prison sentences.

Resolution (76)10 of the Committee of Ministers of the Council of Europe and positive experiences in England and Scotland suggested the community service order (CSO) as a sentencing option.

In 1979, the Committee on alternative penal sanctions proposed a CSO experiment, which was initiated on 1 February 1981.

Ministerial guidelines directed that the experiments take place within the existing statutory framework. Therefore, CSO could be imposed by the prosecution service as a condition for waiving prosecution, or by the court as a condition attached to a decision to suspend a sentence.

At the end of the experiment, statutory provisions governing the CSO for adult offenders were introduced in the Criminal Code on 1 December 1987. Statutory provisions on CSO for juvenile offenders followed in September 1995.

The criminal court could impose a CSO only when it would otherwise impose an unconditional prison sentence of six months or less or a part suspended/part unconditional prison sentence of which the unconditional part is six months or less. Community service could not be used as an alternative to a suspended prison sentence, a fine, or a fine-default detention.

The number of CSOs imposed on adult offenders increased rapidly from 2,000 in 1983 to over 32,000 in 2018.

In 2001, the provisions on the CSO were considerably reformed. The CSO has been replaced by the task penalty (*taakstraf*) which is no longer a substitute for a short-term prison sentence but a distinct sanction option considered to be a restriction of a person's liberty that is less severe than the custodial sentence, and more severe than a fine. A task penalty may consist of a work order, a training order or a combination of both orders.

From 2012 the court is no longer allowed to impose a task penalty on a person who, during the previous five years, had already been sentenced to a task penalty (Article 22b CC).

A task penalty may not exceed a total of 240 hours. The task penalty must be completed within twelve months. Extension of this term is possible.

When imposing a task penalty, the court has to state the term of default detention in case the task penalty is not complied with. The default detention is at least one day and the maximum is eight months. Every two hours of task penalty count for one day default detention. When part of the task penalty is complied with, the length of the default detention is thus reduced proportionally.

The prosecution service is responsible for overseeing compliance with the task penalty, and information may be requested from individuals and organizations involved in probation work for this purpose. In appropriate cases, the prosecution service may change the nature of the work to be carried out, or the kind of education to be followed.

When the prosecution service is satisfied that the task penalty has been carried out properly, it must notify the person convicted as soon as possible.

If the person convicted has not carried out the task penalty properly, the prosecution service may order execution of the default detention mentioned in the sentence, taking into account the number of hours of the task penalty that has been carried out properly. The person convicted can file an appeal against the order to implement the default detention. The appeal is dealt with by the court which imposed the task penalty. The order to implement the default detention must be given within three months of the end of the completion period.

The probation service is responsible for administering task penalties and coordinators have been appointed in each of the eleven jurisdictions who canvass for workplaces where the work order can be carried out. The work order must benefit the community. It can be with public bodies such as the municipality, or private organizations involved in health care, the environment and the protection of nature, or social and cultural work.

A training order is of a different nature. It means that the offender is sentenced to follow a training course in order to learn specific behavioral skills or in order to be confronted with the consequences of his criminal behavior for the victim. Training orders are mainly imposed on offenders from whom it is expected that they are motivated to change their behavior by attending courses or other activities aiming to improve communicative or social abilities.

Fine

The fine is the least severe of the principal penalties. Originally, it was exclusively intended for infractions and minor crimes.

Since the 1983 Financial Penalties Act all offences, including those subject to life imprisonment, may be sentenced with a fine.

The 1983 Act furthermore expresses the principle that fines should be preferred over prison sentences. Article 359 CCP requires the court to give special reasons whenever a custodial sentence is ordered instead of a fine.

The 1983 Act was the final part of a major reform of the fines system, which started in the mid-1970s with a view to creating better opportunities to reduce the use of imprisonment.

The law reform was prepared by the Financial Penalties Committee established in 1966. The reform of the fines system was launched in 1976, by enacting the Financial Penalties Enforcement Act. The main purpose of this Act was to improve the enforcement of fines so that fines could function as a better alternative to the short-term prison sentences. This Act introduced the installment fine and other opportunities for paying fines in installments, simplified the recovery procedures in cases of non-payment, and reduced the maximum fine default detention.

The next step was the adoption of the 1983 Financial Penalties Act. This Act replaced the old fine system, in which every offence carried its own statutory maximum fine, with a more simple and convenient system of fine categories. The minimum fine for all offences is three Euros. The maximum fine depends on the fine category into which a crime or infraction is placed.

The 1983 Act created six fine categories with (at present) maxima of €415, €4,150, €8,300, €20,750, €83,000 and €830,000 (Article 23 CC). Infractions come under the first three categories and crimes under categories II through V. Category VI fines can only be imposed on corporate bodies and on individuals under a few special criminal laws, such as the Economic Offences Act and the Narcotic Drug Offences Act.

When the fines system was reformed in 1983, the old system of fixed sum fines was retained. Following the advice of the Financial Penalties Committee, the introduction of a day-fine-system, as known in an increasing number of European criminal law systems, was rejected on theoretical as well as practical grounds.

The Act urges courts to take into account the financial position of the offender when imposing a fine sentence in as far as this is necessary to arrive at an appropriate sentence without the offender being disproportionately affected in his income and capital (Article 24 CC). There must be a two-pronged proportionality test, between the crime and the fine and between the fine and the ability to pay.

The court may decide that the payment of fines be done in installments to be determined by the court. The total fine has to be paid within two years.

7.5 FINE DEFAULT DETENTION

The implementation of fines and other judicially imposed financial penalties rests entirely with the prosecution service. Fines are collected by the Central Fine Collection Agency. If the person convicted does not pay the fine, the fine may be recovered from the offender's property. If the prosecution service rejects recovery as an option, default detention will be enforced. The term of the default detention is set by the court when imposing the original fine. In practice, a conversion rate of €50 for one day default detention is usually applied.

The statutory minimum duration of fine default detention is one day, and the maximum is twelve months. A fine default detainee can be released if he pays the fine while in prison.

In order to reduce the need for prison capacity for fine default detention, a more effective way of recovering fines imposed for crimes forms part of the present sentence implementation policy. The aim of this policy is to recover 95% of the fines within a year after being imposed.

There are at present no alternatives for fine default detention. The early release regulations are not applicable to fine default detention.

7.6 OTHER COMMUNITY SANCTIONS

Electronic monitoring

Electronic monitoring (EM) is the latest new community sentence that may gain a statutory basis in the near future. EM is a restriction of liberty that can be imposed as a sentence in case a full deprivation of liberty is considered to be too severe and inappropriate. At present EM is still regulated in an instruction by the Board of Prosecutors General (1 March 2015, State Journal 2015, 5390). Electronic monitoring is considered to be a viable substitute to imprisonment or any other form of deprivation of liberty (e.g. pre-trial detention).

Electronic monitoring is applied either in the last phase of the duration of the prison sentence as part of a penitentiary program, or in combination with a suspended sentence. By applying EM in the last phase, the actual period spent in the prison can be reduced.

The public prosecutor may request the court to impose a suspended sentence and to order EM as a condition. Electronic monitoring in combination with a suspended sentence can be applied as condition attached to a suspended sentence.

Candidates for EM are selected by the probation service. The probation service is in charge of supervision and control. The decision to allow persons to serve their sentence through EM is made by the court in as far as it concerns the combination with a suspended sentence and is vested with the prison administration in as far as it concerns the last phase of the detention.

7.7   ACCESSORY PENALTIES

The possibility to impose accessory penalties is limited to certain kinds of offences. The accessory penalties are:

–   deprivation of rights and disqualification from practicing professions;
–   forfeiture; and
–   publication of the judgment.

The deprivation of rights concerns: the right to hold a public office, the right to serve in the army, the right to vote and to be elected, the right to serve as an official administrator and the right to practice specific professions (Article 28 CC).

Forfeiture consists of deprivation of objects or money (Article 33 CC). Objects that may be forfeited are those obtained by means of the criminal offence, or in relation to which the offence was committed or which are manufactured or intended for committing the crime.

The court may order that the judgment be published in a newspaper or a specialist journal or through a billboard. The expenses for the publication are to be borne by the convict. Publication of the judgment (Article 36 CC) is only rarely imposed.

Some special criminal law codes contain specific accessory penalties such as revocation of one's driving license (Article 179 of the 1994 Road Traffic Act) or closure of a company (Article 7 Economic Offences Act). These specific accessory penalties are more frequently imposed.

7.8   MEASURES

Measures can be imposed on offenders regardless of whether they can be held criminally responsible for having committed an offence, since measures are not aimed at punishment but at the promotion of safety and security of persons or property or at restoring a state of affairs. Measures can be imposed as a distinct sentence or in combination with sanctions.

A range of measures is laid down in the Criminal Code:

Withdrawal from circulation (Article 36b CC)

During a police investigation, objects may be seized. Certain objects which are dangerous or whose possession is undesirable may be confiscated. This concerns: objects obtained entirely or largely by means of or derived from the offence, objects in relation to which the offence was committed, objects used to commit or prepare the offence, objects used to obstruct investigation of the offence, and objects manufactured or intended for committing the offence.

If the uncontrolled possession of the objects in question would be in conflict with the law or contrary to public interest, they can be withdrawn from circulation, regardless of whether the offender is convicted of a criminal offence. These are for example drugs, firearms, discriminatory texts, child pornography, etc.

This measure can also be imposed in addition to a penal order.

Confiscation of illegally obtained profits (Article 36e CC)

Since the 1993 Criminal Code law reform (the so-called Strip-them Act) the court may impose an obligation to pay the State Treasury an amount that equals the financial gain obtained through the commission of criminal offences. The measure was introduced in order to improve the fight against organized crime such as drug trafficking, fraud, environmental crime and money laundering.

Not only the profits from a crime for which the offender was sentenced, but also the profits from similar offences for which a fine of the fifth category may be imposed, and where there is sufficient evidence that they have been committed by him, may be confiscated.

The court must assess the net value of the illegally obtained profits. In case of non-compliance with the obligation of full recovery, the court may order civil imprisonment, i.e. imprisonment for debt. Only full recovery can lead to release from civil imprisonment.

Obligation to pay compensation (Article 36f CC)

The 1996 Compensation Order Act introduced the possibility for the court to impose an obligation upon a person convicted of a criminal offence to pay the

State Treasury a sum of money for the benefit of the victim of the crime. The Treasury shall remit the money received to the victim without delay. In cases of non-recovery of the full amount due, the court can order default detention of one year maximum.

This measure was introduced in order to improve the legal position of the victim in the criminal procedure

This measure can also be imposed in addition to a penal order.

Psychiatric hospital order (Article 37 CC)

If a defendant cannot be held criminally liable for the crime of which he is accused by reason of a mental defect or disorder, the court may not impose a penalty, but may order that the defendant be committed to a psychiatric hospital for up to one year, provided that the person is a danger to himself, to others, to the general public or to property in general. The court shall only issue the order after submission of a reasoned, dated and signed opinion of at least two behavioral experts – one being a psychiatrist – who have examined the defendant, except in cases where the defendant is unwilling to cooperate in a psychiatric examination.

Entrustment order (Article 37a CC)

If the court considers that a defendant, despite his mental defect or disorder, can be deemed responsible, it may, in order to protect the safety of other people, the general public or property, impose a penalty in combination with an entrustment order with compulsory nursing care. An entrustment order may be imposed for crimes carrying a statutory prison sentence of at least four years.

The order may only be issued after submission of opinions by two behavioral experts who have examined the defendant, except when he refuses to cooperate in such an examination. The order is carried out in a special secure private or state institution were the person is treated, the so-called *terbeschikkingstelling* (TBS).

The order lasts for two years but may be extended by one or two years on application of the prosecution service. For certain violent offences, further extension is possible as long as the safety of others so requires. Every six years, a review of the entrustment order has to take place. A recent opinion of behavioral experts has to be available to the court.

Decisions of the court to extend the entrustment order, or to refuse to extend, may be appealed by the detained psychiatric patient or by the public prosecutor (Article 509v CCP). Appeals are heard by the penitentiary division of the Court of Appeal in Arnhem. The division consists of three professional judges, and two experts in behavioral sciences who are not members of the judiciary (Article 73 Judicial Organization Act).

Decisions by the Penitentiary Division of the Arnhem Court of Appeal are final. Judicial review by the Supreme Court is not available (Article 509x CCP). In recent years, the entrustment order institutions have been under great pressure. The courts have increasingly imposed entrustment orders but the number of detained psychiatric patients being released has decreased. The main reason for this trend is a rise in the number of serious crimes, mainly violent crimes and sexual offences, and the increase in the number of severely mentally disordered offenders due to alcohol and drug addiction. These factors have led to an increased average length of the term of treatment (in 1995: 59 months, in 2006: 89 months). Even after the regular term of treatment (six years), many detained psychiatric patients are still not ready to return to society, and courts continue to extend their entrustment orders with nursing care.

Despite long-term treatment, these mentally disordered delinquent psychiatric patients continue to pose a high risk to society.

For these persistently dangerous delinquent psychiatric patients, long-stay wings have been opened. It is estimated that one third of the total population in the entrustment order institutions are eligible for long-stay wings. With the establishment of long-stay wings, it is accepted by psychiatrists and by the courts that the entrustment order in effect means a detention for life.

In the long-stay wing, the psychiatric treatment is of lower priority. The day-to-day regime in a long-stay wing aims to prevent delinquent psychiatric patients from deteriorating as much as possible by providing them with a meaningful existence. For delinquent psychiatric patients who are eligible for the long-stay wing, the prognosis is rather bad. Those who have been treated for more than twelve years have a tendency to become chronic delinquent psychiatric patients.

Patients who, after being treated, are no longer considered to pose a danger gradually receive leave permissions and eventually the nursing care will be conditionally terminated. The conditional termination of nursing care (Article 38g CC), introduced in 1997, offers the possibility of a smooth transition from the nursing care in the entrustment order institution to complete freedom and a return to society. A gradual transition and an increase in freedom are made possible. The conditional termination period is one year and may be extended twice for one year. During the conditional termination of the nursing care, the entrustment order is still valid and may even be extended by the court.

The conditional termination of nursing care is not widely applied because the three-year probation period is considered to be too short. After the expiry of that period, there is no possibility to assist, supervise or treat the patient in order to monitor the use of psycho-pharmacy and to reduce recidivism. A bill to extend the probation period and to increase the supervision is in 2015 approved (State Journal 2015, 460).

Out-patient hospital order (Article 38 CC)

If the court considers that the requirements for an entrustment order are met but compulsory nursing care in a secure institution is not necessary, it can order an entrustment in combination with conditions. The delinquent psychiatric patient is not treated in a closed entrustment order treatment institution but in a regular mental hospital or in society provided that the patient complies with the conditions such as to place himself under the treatment of a psychiatrist or to use psycho-pharmacy. If the patient does not comply with these conditions, or if otherwise the safety of others or the general safety of persons or property so requires, and on request of the prosecution service, the court may order that the entrustment order be implemented in a secure institution (Article 38c CC). The court orders that the probation service shall offer the necessary help and support.

When a custodial sentence is also imposed, the entrustment order shall not be for more than three years. The instructions attached to the entrustment order may not limit the freedom to profess religious or other beliefs or curtail constitutional freedom.

The persistent offender detention order (Article 38m CC)

Persistent offenders (mainly drug addicted offenders) are responsible for a disproportionately large share of property crimes and nuisance in the major Dutch cities. In order to enhance security and to reduce this nuisance, the court has, since 2001, the power to impose a detention order. The major aim of the detention order is to enhance the security and to stop the re-offending by the offender. The court may, at the request of the public prosecutor, impose the order when the following conditions are met:

- the offence with which the offender is charged allows for pre-trial detention;
- the offender has been sentenced to imprisonment or community service at least three times in the previous five years;
- the offender is likely to re-offend; and
- the safety of persons or property is at stake.

The order may only be issued after submission of an opinion on the recidivism risks, the causes of recidivism and the receptivity for interventions. A risk assessment instrument has been developed in order to properly prepare such an opinion. Such an opinion need not be submitted in cases where the offender refuses to cooperate in the risk assessment examination.

The order may last two years regardless of the seriousness of the crime. The order is implemented in a closed setting.

Where the problem of persistent re-offending is related to drug or alcohol addiction or to a mental disorder, the detention order may lead to a treatment for drug and alcohol rehabilitation provided that the offender is motivated to participate in a re-socialization and reintegration program. In a number of cases, no program is offered because the offender is not motivated or is unsuited. The re-socialization and reintegration program is regulated in the Prison Rules (chapter 9A) and consists of skills training in relation to self-care and hygiene, labor, education, financial administration, unsupervised living and social attitude.

The court may suspend the order under certain conditions, e.g. the condition that the offender accepts medical treatment for his addiction as an out-patient. A probation officer specialized in the rehabilitation of drug addicts supervises the offender.

The court may assess the effect of the order halfway through the execution and may decide that there is no longer any need to continue the implementation of the order.

The measure restricting freedom (Article 38v CC)

Since 2012, the court may impose a measure restricting liberty of movement. This measure may mean that the defendant is ordered that he should not come in a certain area. Also, it can impose a restraining order and / or a liability at certain times to be present at a certain location to report. The measure may be imposed for a period of five years. In special cases (e.g. in case of serious stalking) the measure can be declared immediately enforceable.

7.9 SANCTIONS FOR JUVENILES (ARTICLES 77A–77HH CC)

In 1995, a major reform of juvenile criminal law took place in response to criticisms on the juvenile criminal law adopted in 1965. The 1965 juvenile criminal law was considered too paternalistic and no longer in line with the increased emancipation of the youth. Furthermore, the legal position of juveniles was too weak and the juvenile criminal law was perceived as too complex and outdated.

The 1995 juvenile criminal law was simplified and modernized by introducing various substitutes to imprisonment, and by taking into consideration the increased emancipation of adolescents.

Only a restricted number of crimes committed by juveniles are tried by juvenile courts, since both the police and the prosecution service can settle juvenile cases out of court.

The conditions for a transaction are different from those for adults (Article 77f CC). The conditions may be:

–   compliance with the instructions issued by the Child Care and Protection Board during a probationary period not exceeding six months;
–   performance of non-remunerated labor or for forty hours maximum to be completed within three months;
–   reparation of the damage caused by the offence;
–   attending a training project for forty hours maximum to improve behavioral skills; and finally
–   the payment of a sum of less than € 4,150 to the Treasury.

For minor crimes such as vandalism, shoplifting and theft, the police may even settle the case through a so-called *Halt-maatregel* (Stop measure), provided that the juvenile offender takes part in a crime prevention project of maximum twenty hours (Article 77e CC). This settlement is regarded as a conditional waiver. The public prosecutor supervises the Stop measures and may give instructions to the police.

The Stop measure is applicable to all juveniles even those who because of their age (younger than twelve years old) cannot be held criminally responsible. For those younger than twelve years, the measure must be of a pedagogic nature (e.g. writing an essay and offering an apology to the victim).

Where the crime is too serious to be settled out of court, the juvenile court may impose juvenile detention, a task penalty or a fine.

The aim of the detention is correction. The pedagogical effect of the detention is mainly the result of the deterrent effect of the sanction. Although the treatment of the juvenile offender is not a major point during the execution of the detention, much attention is paid to formative activities such as education, work and sport.

The minimum term of juvenile detention is one day. The maximum term is twelve months for juvenile offenders under sixteen years of age and 24 months for those over sixteens. Juvenile detention is implemented in special juvenile penitentiary institutions where offence-related treatment can take place. In 2017, approximately 420 young people (96% of them were boys) were daily detained in the correctional institutions for juvenile offenders, where they receive support from staff during their stay. They are detained in one central government institution (part of the Ministry of Justice and Security) and four private institutions (subsidized by the Ministry, but privately managed).

The task penalty may consist of:

–   a community service order or work contributing to the repair of the damage caused by the offence of 200 hours maximum;

- a training order (attendance at a training center in order to follow courses or training programs) of 200 hours maximum; or
- a combination of a community service order and a training order of 240 hours maximum.

Non-compliance with a task penalty may lead to a default detention in a juvenile detention center of a maximum of four months.

For many juveniles, a fine is an effective sanction provided that the fine is not paid by their parents. The minimum fine is €3, the maximum is €4,150, which may be paid in installments. The total fine must be paid within two years. When neither full payment nor recovery of the amount due is possible, the court may order a fine default detention in a juvenile detention center for three months maximum or a task penalty.

7.10 MEASURES FOR JUVENILES

Six measures may be imposed by a juvenile court:

- the committal to an institution for juveniles;
- the re-education order;
- withdrawal from circulation;
- confiscation of illegally obtained profits;
- compensation for the damage and
- the restricting freedom.

The latter four measures are governed by the same rules on measures applicable in adult criminal law.

Committal to an institution for young persons is a very radical measure, and may only be imposed where it concerns a serious offence for which pre-trial detention is allowed, where the safety of others or the general safety of persons or of property requires such a measure to be imposed, and where the measure is in the interest of the future development of the offender.

The main objective of the measure, besides the protection of the community, is to provide young persons with the education and the care which is considered necessary.

The duration of the measure is not fixed in advance but is rather determined by the degree to which the young person in question requires residential education. For this reason, the juvenile court may only impose the measure after submission of a reasoned, dated and signed opinion by no fewer than two behavioral scientists of different disciplines. One such expert must be a psychiatrist if the juvenile suffered from mental defect or mental disease at the time of the commission of the offence.

The measure lasts for two years. It can be terminated by the Minister of Justice and Security at any time throughout upon consultation with the Childcare and Protection Board. It may also be extended by the Juvenile Court. Extensions can be requested for a maximum of two years upon request of the prosecution service. Extension is only possible if the measure was imposed in case of a violent offence or a sexual offence. Extension of the term of the measure by a further two years is only possible when the juvenile offender at the time of the offence was suffering from a mental defect or mental disease. The security and development criteria must once again be met before extension is allowed. This means that a juvenile offender receiving such a measure at the age of 17 years can be, at the maximum, detained until he is 23. However, if the disturbance (mental illness) is still present, conversion into an entrustment order can follow. A request for an extension of the measure of committal to an institution is heard by a three-judge bench of the district court.

The re-education order is imposed for six to twelve months, during which time the juvenile has to follow special treatment programs such as Multidimensional Treatment Foster Care. Juveniles showing a chronic anti-social or criminal behavior or suffering of serious emotional disorders may be placed in a foster family that has undergone special training in how to deal with disturbed youngsters.

The order may be extended for one year maximum only once. Before the order may be imposed, an opinion by the Child Care and Protection Board has to be submitted to the prosecution service.

7.11 SPECIAL SANCTIONS FOR MILITARY PERSONNEL

Neither the Criminal Code nor any other statute provides special sanctions for civil servants or other special groups. The Military Criminal Code, after the reform on 1 January 1991, contains sanctions similar to those noted in the Criminal Code. The custodial sanctions imposed on military personnel are enforced in a military penitentiary facility, where the regime differs from that in ordinary penal facilities.

7.12 THE SUSPENDED SENTENCE

Articles 14a–14k CC deal with the suspension of sentences. The Dutch suspended sentence is a hybrid form of the Belgian-French *sursis* and the Anglo-Saxon probation.

The suspension of a sentence involves the non-execution of (a part of) an imposed sentence. Since its introduction in 1915, the rules for the suspension have been radically revised a number of times. The last major reforms took place in 1986 and 2006, when the scope of application of the suspension of sentences was substantially expanded.

The reforms were strongly influenced by the need to reduce the pressure on prison capacity. The 1986 reform simultaneously responded to a need, which had long been recognized in practice, to make a partial revocation of a suspended sentence possible.

Since the 2006 law reform, suspension of a sentence is possible for all principal sentences. A prison sentence of up to two years, detention and fines may all be suspended completely or in part. A prison sentence between two years and four years may be suspended for a part not exceeding two years. A prison sentence of over four years may not be suspended.

Suspension can be applied to all offences. Accessory penalties may be suspended as well.

7.13 PARTLY SUSPENDED SENTENCES

The court may impose a sentence that is suspended only in part. Since a sentence may consist of a combination of various principal penalties, a partly suspended prison sentence in combination with a task penalty or a fine is possible. The suspended sentence is very widely applied.

Conditions

The suspension of the sentence is always subject to the general condition that the convicted person shall not commit another offence during the period of probation.

In addition to the general condition, the court may impose one or more special conditions, such as:

– compensation for all or part of the damage caused by the offence;
– admission to an institution of nursing care for the duration of the period of probation;
– deposit of bail (an amount of money equal to the statutory fine);
– the donation of a certain sum of money not exceeding the maximum statutory fine to the Criminal Injuries Compensation Fund or to other organizations interested in the protection of the interests of the victims of crime;
– prohibition to be at or in the immediate vicinity of a certain location;

- obligation to be present at a certain location at specific times or during a specific period;
- obligation to report to a specific authority at specific times;
- prohibition on the use of narcotics or alcohol and the obligation to cooperate with blood testing or urinalysis in order to comply with this prohibition; and
- other special conditions concerning someone's behavior and attitude.

The special conditions may not restrict the freedom to practice one's religion or personal beliefs or one's civil liberties.

The court determines the length of the probation period at the time of the sentencing. The probation period for the pecuniary conditions is two years, and for the other conditions three years maximum. The probation period can be extended to ten years maximum where there exist serious indications that the convict will again commit a serious crime involving bodily harm.

Control over compliance with conditions

The effectiveness and credibility of the suspended sentence depends very much upon the control on the compliance with the conditions of the suspension. The prosecution service has to exercise control over compliance and the probation service may be ordered by the court to help and assist the convicted person to comply with the conditions imposed. The probation service keeps the prosecution service and the court informed about the progress of the suspended sentence through progress reports (Article 12 Probation Rules).

Compulsory probation supervision was abolished in 1973 under pressure from the probation service, which increasingly had come to feel that this task conflicted with its proper social role. With the abolition of the supervision by the probation service, the judiciary's confidence in the effectiveness of the special conditions plummeted and gradually less 'creative' behavioral conditions were attached to the suspension of a sentence.

Revocation

In case of violation of one or more conditions, the public prosecutor can order the immediate arrest of the convicted person. Non-compliance with the conditions of the suspension may lead to a revocation by the court of the suspension at the request of the public prosecutor. The court may decide to partially revoke the suspension, to extend the probation period or to add or change the condition attached to the suspension of the sentence.

When the court considers revocation of a suspension of a sentence or part of it, it may order the performance of a task penalty instead (Article 14g CC).

7.14 PUNITIVE SANCTIONS IN ADMINISTRATIVE LAW

In the past decades punitive sanctions in administrative law have increasingly been developed alongside criminal sanctions. Because these sanctions can be applied simultaneously to or in conjunction with criminal offenses, they are briefly discussed.

Administrative sanctions are not imposed by a judge, but by the administration. It is possible to have the sanction subsequently assessed by the judge.

In the case of criminal behavior that has seriously disrupted public order, the mayor may impose prohibitions on territories, group bans, contact prohibitions and reporting obligations on the suspect (Municipal Act). In the case of drug law offenses that refer to drugs dealing, the mayor may close a building (Narcotic Drug Offences Act). If there is a suspicion that an adult is guilty of domestic violence, the mayor may expel him from his home and order a cooling-off period (Temporary out-of-home placement Act). Furthermore, the government can impose fines in many cases (General Administrative Law Act). The Central Bureau for Driving Licenses can withdraw a driving license as a punishment and impose training sentences (1994 Road Traffic Act). Other punitive sanctions under administrative law are the revocation of Dutch citizenship in sentencing terrorist offenses (Kingdom Act on Dutch nationality), a prohibition to travel by public transport or a station prohibition (2000 Passenger Transport Act), and the order to leave a house due to domestic nuisance caused by antisocial behavior (Municipal Act). Legislative proposals are being prepared that will allow the imposition of even more administrative sanctions.

8. CONDITIONAL RELEASE, PARDON AND AFTERCARE OF PRISONERS

Geert PESSELSE[*]

8.1 INTRODUCTION

The origins of conditional release

Conditional release provisions were incorporated in the Criminal Code as early as 1886. At that time, conditional release (*voorwaardelijke invrijheidstelling*) was intended as a gesture of leniency for good conduct, to be applied only in exceptional cases and only to prisoners who had served rather long sentences. This concept of conditional release was expressed in the legal prerequisites for conditional release, and the granting of release lay within the discretion of the prison administration. In 1915, the regulations on release were changed considerably. Conditional release became a means of improving the rehabilitation of the offender into free society. The objective of the conditional release was to improve the offender's future conduct by means of supervision by the probation service and by attaching conditions to the release.

Following the 1915 reform, prisoners were eligible for conditional release after having served two-thirds of their sentence and at least nine months. The period of parole lasted for a minimum of one year. The release decision was taken by the administration (the Prison and Probation Department of the Ministry of Justice and Security) at the request of the local prison board. The prosecution service was given the power to ensure compliance with the conditions. In addition to the mandatory general condition, the administration could attach special conditions to the release. The general condition was that the released prisoner would not commit further offences during the probation period and would not misbehave in other ways. Special conditions related to the conduct of the released prisoner, but were not further specified. In practice, the special condition most applied was that the released person should accept special supervision by a probation officer. The prosecution service was vested with the right to control compliance

---

[*]   G. Pesselse (Ph.D.) is a member of the scientific staff of the Court of Appeal in 's-Hertogenbosch. He is also a judge *ad litem* at the District Court of Gelderland.

with the conditions and the right to require revocation of the release. A breach of conditions had to be reported by the supervising probation officer.

Decline of conditional release

In the 1960s and 1970s, the importance of the conditional release as an instrument of rehabilitation decreased. This was partly a result of the decrease in the number of long prison sentences, which meant that the number of prisoners eligible for conditional release declined as well.

Far more important, however, was the fact that the professionalization of probation work and the adoption of new probation work methods led to tension between the probation work philosophy and the statutory tasks for the probation service, particularly concerning the post-release supervision. The essence of this tension was that in the relationship between a probation officer and a client there is no room for any authoritarianism or for any compulsory supervision which, however, formed basic parts of the statutory probation tasks. One consequence of this probation work philosophy was that reporting non-compliance with the conditions did not fit with the probation officer's duty as a supporting agent. Thus, since the early seventies such reporting was officially abolished in the Netherlands.[1]

As conditional release was no longer considered a reward for good behavior in prison or as an instrument of rehabilitation, it became increasingly difficult for the Prison and Probation Administration to refuse parole to an eligible prisoner. As a result, the release percentages went up from 50% in the early fifties to more than 90% in the early seventies and 99% in 1981. Since release was granted in most cases and only refused in very specific cases, the need was felt to create the possibility for a prisoner to appeal to a court when his request for release was turned down. Since 1976, prisoners eligible for release could lodge an appeal with the special penitentiary division of the Arnhem Court of Appeal against a decision to reject, suspend or revoke conditional release. The Court's case law was critical to the Prison and Probation Administration's release policy, and due to this case law the percentage of parole refusals dropped from 11% in 1975 to 1% by 1986.[2]

The conditional release law reform committee

Gradually, conditional release changed from being a favor to an almost automatic right. Against this background, a Committee was set up in 1980 to advise the

---

[1]   See on (the history of) conditional release F.W. Bleichrodt, *Onder voorwaarde*, Deventer: Gouda Quint 1996 (with a summary in English), pp. 177–198.

[2]   See on these developments F.W. Bleichrodt & P.C. Vegter, *Sanctierecht*, Deventer: Kluwer 2013, pp. 153–155.

Minister of Justice as to whether conditional release should be retained and if so, whether it would be advisable to include the right of eligible prisoners to be paroled in the penal code?

The Committee did not support the idea of an automatic release. Although automatic release would save on government costs since the release procedure was time consuming and very bureaucratic, and although automatic release would stop prisoners feeling uncertain, it also has considerable drawbacks. With automatic release there is a risk that courts will take the release into account when deciding on the length of the sentence; automatic release would mean that dangerous prisoners would be released as well; with automatic release there is no longer any incentive for good contact between the prisoner and the wardens, and finally, automatic release would constitute a need for remission to be deserved for good conduct. The conclusion of the Committee was that the conditional release regulations should be reformed. The criminal code should not regulate the grounds on which conditional release would be granted but the grounds on which it should be refused. The Committee advocated retaining the possibility of attaching special conditions in order to provide the conditionally released prisoner with the possibility of continuing with his probation contacts.

The Government, however, preferred a system which would reduce the pressure on the prison system, get rid of red tape, and save a great deal of money and time by introducing a system of automatic early release. New legislation came into force in 1987. Early release could be postponed at the request of the public prosecutor. Unlike the former conditional release, the power to refuse or postpone early release rests not with the Prison and Probation Administration, but directly with the penitentiary division of the Court of Appeal in Arnhem. Refusals or postponements were both rather rare. One of the disadvantages of this de facto early release policy is that an ex-prisoner cannot be supervised or monitored after the date of his release because his release is in practice unconditional. However, in the first months after the release social integration and the prevention of re-offending is of great importance and might be improved if conditions could be attached to his early release.

8.2 CURRENT EARLY RELEASE PROVISIONS

Due to continuing criticism on early release as a *de facto* unconditional right, a reform in 2008 re-introduced conditional early release (Article 15 et seq. CC). The essence of the new provisions is as follows: prisoners serving an unconditional prison sentence of more than one, but less than two years will be conditionally released after having served one year and one third of the remaining term; prisoners serving a sentence of more than two years will be conditionally released after having served two thirds. The release is truly conditional: special and general conditions apply. The general condition holds that the convicted offender does not commit a criminal offence before expiration of the probation period and cooperates with probation service supervision. Furthermore, special conditions may be imposed by the public prosecutor, such as:

- a prohibition to contact, directly or through a third party, specific persons or organizations;
- an obligation to report at specific times to a specific agency;
- a prohibition to use drugs or alcohol and the obligation to cooperate with a blood or urine test for the purpose of verifying compliance with this prohibition;
- an obligation to receive treatment from a professional or healthcare institution for a specific period of time at least equal to the probation period.

Special conditions may not restrict the freedom to practice one's religion or personal belief or one's civil liberties. No appeal against the imposition of special conditions is possible. The prosecution service supervises the compliance with the special conditions, and the probation service can be ordered to provide help and assistance to the parolee as well as reporting breaches of conditions to the prosecution service.

Early release may be postponed or refused when, for example:

- the convicted offender has been admitted by reason of mental disease or defect to a custodial institution for the treatment under an entrustment order;
- it has been shown that the convicted offender seriously misbehaved after the start of his sentence, as evidenced by a criminal conviction or disciplinary sanction;
- after the start of the convicted offender's sentence, he seeks or makes an attempt to avoid serving this sentence;
- the setting of conditions cannot sufficiently reduce the recidivism risk for serious offences or if the convicted offender does not state that he is prepared to comply with the conditions for release.

The decision on postponement or refusal of conditional release is taken by a criminal court, following a demand by the prosecution service. Appeal is not possible.

Once released, non-compliance with the general or special conditions may lead to a full or partial revocation of the conditional release. The decision on revocation is taken by a criminal court, following a demand by the prosecution service. Appeal is not possible. Prior to handling the demand for revocation by the criminal court, the prosecution service can arrest the conditionally released convict.

8.3   PARDON

The 1998 Pardon Act, which was revised in 2003, empowers the King – *de facto* the Ministry of Justice and Security – to grant a pardon (*gratie*) when petitioned either by the person sentenced or by the prosecution service. Only clearly reasoned petitions will be processed by the Pardon Office of the Ministry of Justice and Security.

Under Article 122 of the Constitution and the provisions in the Pardon Act, pardon may be granted for all prison sentences, fines and custodial sentences, as well as for certain measures imposed by Dutch courts. Pardon may furthermore be granted for all sentences imposed by foreign courts but implemented in the Netherlands, provided that the foreign sentence is converted into a Dutch sentence or the prisoner is transferred to the Netherlands on the basis of a treaty.

There are two statutory grounds to grant pardon. The first is that the court when sentencing did not – or could not – take account of circumstances that, if the court had been aware of them, would have led to a different sentence or to no sentence at all. The second ground for pardon is that the (continuation of the) execution of a sentence reasonably cannot serve the purpose for which the sentence was intended.

The prosecution service and the court that imposed the sentence are, generally, to be consulted before pardon may be granted. Pardon may involve a complete or partial remission of the sentence, the suspension of the execution of the sentence or the conversion of the sentence into a less serious one, such as a community service. A pardon decision may be conditional. The possible conditions of a pardon are similar to the conditions of a suspended sentence. The probation service can be ordered to support and assist the conditionally pardoned offender. In recent years, the number of pardon requests has declined, from about 3,500 in 2006 to about 1500 in 2014. However, the percentage of (conditional) pardon remains about 30%.[3]

8.4   AFTERCARE OF RELEASED PRISONERS

When the sentence has been served, the ex-convict cannot be obliged to stay in contact with the probation service. Of course, under the conditional release regulations, the conditionally released prisoner can be obliged to stay in contact with the probation service, which supervises the compliance with the imposed conditions but also supports and advises the ex-convict. In 2019 legislation was enacted that enables so called 'lifelong supervision' for certain sex and violence offenders. When a released prisoner asks for help on his or her own initiative,

---

[3]   Www.cbs.nl.

the probation service will transfer the client to other organizations outside the criminal justice system, such as social services or health care services. These services provide all kinds of material help such as assistance in housing, employment, and debt relief. For the resettlement of released prisoners, aftercare projects have been set up in which volunteers play an important role.

REFERENCES

BOOKS

I. Andriessen, H. Fernee & K. Wittebrood, *Ervaren discriminatie in Nederland*, Den Haag: Sociaal en Cultureel Planbureau, 2013.

B. Bieleman, R. Mennes & M. Sijtstra, *Coffeeshops in Nederland 2016*, Groningen-Rotterdam, 2017.

F.W. Bleichrodt & P.C. Vegter, *Sanctierecht*, Deventer: Kluwer 2013.

F.W. Bleichrodt, *Onder voorwaarde*, Deventer: Gouda Quint 1996.

J. Boksem, *Op den grondslag der telastelegging. Beschouwingen naar aanleiding van het Nederlandse grondslagstelsel*, Nijmegen: Ars Aequi Libri 1996.

M.J. Borgers, I.M. Koopmans & F.G.H. Kristen (eds.), *'Verwijtbare uitholling van schuld?'*, Nijmegen: Ars Aequi Libri 1998.

P.T. Bovend'Eert & C.A.J.M. Kortmann, *Constitutional Law in the Netherlands*, Alphen aan de Rijn: Kluwer Law International, 2018.

S. Brinkhoff, *Startinformatie in het strafproces*, Deventer: Kluwer, 2014.

G.J.M Corstens, M.J. Borgers & T. Kooijmans, *Het Nederlands strafprocesrecht*, Deventer: Wolters Kluwer, 2018.

De Hullu, *Materieel strafrecht*, Deventer: Wolters Kluwer 2018.

J.W. de Keijser, *Punishment and purpose: from moral theory to punishment in action*, Amsterdam: Thela Thesis 2000.

B. de Wilde, *Stille getuigen: het recht belastende getuigen in strafzaken te ondervragen (artikel 6 lid 3 sub d EVRM)*, Deventer: Wolters Kluwer 2015.

W.H.B. Dreissen, *Bewijsmotivering in strafzaken*, Den Haag: Boom Juridische uitgevers 2007.

M.J. Dubelaar, *Betrouwbaar getuigenbewijs. Totstandkoming en waardering van strafrechtelijke getuigenverklaringen in perspectief*, Deventer: Kluwer 2014.

M. Duker, *Legitieme straftoemeting*, Den Haag: Boom juridische uitgevers 2003.

D.M.H.R. Garé, *Het onmiddellijkheidsbeginsel in het Nederlandse strafproces*, Arnhem: Gouda Quint 1994 (with summary in English).

D.M.H.R. Garé & P.A.M. Mevis, *Over het oproepen van getuigen ter terechtzitting en getuigenbewijs in strafzaken*, Nijmegen: Ars Aequi Libri 2000.

A.N. Kesteloo, *De rechtspersoon in het strafrecht*, Deventer: Kluwer 2013.

B.M. Kortenhorst, *De motiveringsverplichting in strafzaken. Een analyse van de artikelen 358 en 359 van het Wetboek van Strafvordering*, Arnhem: Gouda Quint 1990.

M. Krabbe, *Complete defenses in international criminal law*, Cambridge [etc.]: Intersentia, 2014.

S. Lestrade, *De strafbaarstelling van arbeidsuitbuiting in Nederland*, Deventer: Wolters Kluwer 2018.

A.R. Lodder, N.S. van der Meulen, T.H.A. Wisman, L. Meij and C.M.M. Zwinkels, *Big Data, big consequenses. Een verkenning naar privacy en big data gebruik binnen de opsporing, vervolging en rechtspraak*, WODC-report 2014.

J.S. Nan, *Het lex certa-beginsel*, Den Haag: Sdu Uitgevers 2011.

D. Roef, *Strafbare overheden*, Deventer: Kluwer 2001.

G.K. Schoep, *Straftoemetingsrecht en strafvorming*, Deventer: Kluwer 2008.

P.M. Schuyt, *Verantwoorde staftoemeting*, Deventer: Kluwer 2009.

J.M. ten Voorde *et al.*, *Meerdaadse samenloop in het strafrecht*, Den Haag: Boom juridische uitgevers 2013.

M. Timmerman, *Legality in Europe. On the principle* nullem crimen, nulla poena sine lege *in EU law and under the ECHR*, Cambridge [etc]: Intersentia 2018.

P.P.J. van der Meij, *De driehoeksverhouding in het strafrechtelijk vooronderzoek. Een onverminderde zoektocht naar evenwicht in de rolverdeling tussen de rechter-commissaris, de officier van justitie en de verdediging*, Deventer, Kluwer, 2010.

A.A. van Dijk, *Strafrechtelijke aansprakelijkheid heroverwogen*, Antwerp: Maklu 2008.

P.T.C. van Kampen, *Expert evidence compared. Rules and practices in the Dutch and American criminal justice system,* Antwerpen: Intersentia 1998.

P.H.P.H.M.C. van Kempen & M.I. Fedorova, *International Law and Cannabis I. Regulation of Cannabis Cultivation for Recreational Use under the UN Narcotic Drugs Conventions and the EU Legal Instruments in Anti-Drugs Policy*, Cambridge/Antwerp/Portland: Intersentia 2019.

P.H.P.H.M.C. van Kempen & M.I. Fedorova, *International Law and Cannabis II. Regulation of Cannabis Cultivation and Trade for Recreational Use: Positive Human Rights Obligations versus UN Narcotic Drugs Conventions*, Cambridge/Antwerp/Portland: Intersentia 2019.

P.H.P.H.M.C. van Kempen and M.I. Fedorova, *'Foreign terrorist fighters': strafbaarstelling van verblijf op een terroristisch grondgebied? Een toetsing aan materieel strafrechtelijke, mensenrechtelijke en volkenrechtelijke parameters*, Deventer: Kluwer 2015.

P.H.P.H.M.C. van Kempen & M.G.M. van der Staak, *Een meewerkverplichting bij grootschalig DNA-onderzoek in strafzaken?*, Deventer: Kluwer 2013.

S.G.C. van Wingerden, *Sentencing in the Netherlands: taking risk-related offender characteristics into account*, Den Haag: Eleven International Publishing 2014.

S.G.C. van Wingerden, M. Moerings & J. van Wilsem, *De praktijk van schadevergoeding voor slachtoffers van misdrijven,* Den Haag: Boom Juridische uitgevers, 2007.

K. Veegens, *A disrupted balance? Prevention of terrorism and compliance with fundamental rights and principles of law – the Dutch anti-terrorism legislation*, Cambridge [etc.]: Intersentia, 2012.

P.A.M. Verrest, *Raison d'etre. Een onderzoek naar de rol van de rechtercommissaris in ons strafproces*, Den Haag: Boom juridische uitgevers 2011.

E.M. Witjens, *Strafrechtelijke causaliteit*, Deventer: Kluwer 2011.

BOOK CHAPTERS

L. Besselink, 'The Kingdom of the Netherlands', in: P.T. Bovend'Eert, H. Broeksteeg, R. de Lange en W. Voermans (Eds.), *Constitutional law of the EU member states*, Kluwer: Deventer, 2014.

J.W. Fokkens & N. Kirkels-Vrijman, 'The Dutch system of legal remedies', in: M.S. Groenhuijsen & T. Kooijmans, *The reform of the Dutch code of criminal procedure in comparative perspective*, Leiden: Nijhoff 2012.

E.J. Koops, Cybercrime legislation in the Netherlands, in: J.H.M. van Erp, & L.P.W. van Vliet (Eds.), *Netherlands Reports to the Eighteenth International Congress on Comparative Law*, Antwerp, Intersentia, 2010.

C. Peristeridou, The principle of *lex certa* in national law and European perspectives, in: *Substantive Criminal Law of the European Union*, A. Klip (ed.), Antwerp [etc]: Maklu 2011.

J. Simmelink, 'The law of evidence and substantiation of evidence', in: M.S. Groenhuijsen & T. Kooijmans, *The reform of the Dutch code of criminal procedure in comparative perspective*, Leiden: Nijhoff, 2012.

J.P. Tak, 'Women in prison in the Netherlands', in: P.H.P.H.M.C. van Kempen & M.J.M. Krabbe (eds.), *Women in Prison. The Bangkok Rules and Beyond*, Cambridge/Antwerp/Portland: Intersentia 2017.

J. Terpstra, Towards a National Police in the Netherlands – Background of a Radical Police Reform, in: N.R. Fyfe, J. Terpstra & P. Tops (eds.), *Centralizing Forces?*, The Hague: Eleven International Publishing, 2013.

L.F. Zwaak, 'The Netherlands', in: R. Blackburn & J. Polakiewicz (eds), *Fundamental Rights in Europe: The ECHR and its Member States*, 1950–2000, Oxford, Oxford University Press, 2001.

JOURNAL ARTICLES

M.J. Borgers & L. Stevens, 'The use of illegally gathered evidence in the Dutch criminal trial', *Electronic Journal of comparative law*, 2010, vol. 14.3.

Y. Buruma, 'Dutch Tolerance: On Drugs, Prostitution, and Euthanasia', *Crime and Justice* 2007, vol. 35, no. 1.

M. Fedorova, 'De "achterdeur-problematiek" van de coffeeshop in de rechtspraak: wetgever help de strafrechter uit de spagaat', *Delikt en Delinkwent* 2016, vol. 46, no. 7.

K. Greenawalt, 'The perplexing borders of justification and excuse', *Columbia Law Review*, 1984, 8.

M.S. Groenhuijsen & H. Selçuk, 'The principle of immediacy in Dutch criminal procedure in the perspective of European Human Rights Law', *ZSTW* 2014, 126.

B.F. Keulen, E. Gritter, 'Corporate Criminal Liability in the Netherlands', in: M. Pieth & R. Ivory (eds), *Corporate Criminal Liability: Emergence, Convergence, and Risk*, Ius Gentium-Comparative Perspectives on Law and Justice, Dordrecht: Springer 2011, vol. 9.

P. Mevis, L. Postma, M. Habets, J. Rietjens & A. van der Heide, 'Advance directives requesting euthanasia in the Netherlands: do they enable euthanasia for patients who lack mental capacity?', *Journal of Medical Law and Ethics* 2016, vol. 4, no. 2.

Stichting Farmaceutische Kengetallen, 'Palliatieve sedatie vaker ingezet bij levenseinde', *Pharmaceutisch Weekblad*, 16 februari 2017, vol. 152, no. 7.

J. Terpstra, 'Police reform in the Netherlands and Scotland compared', *Scottish Justice Matters*, 2015.

J. Terpstra & N.R. Fyfe, 'Mind the implementation gap? Police reform and local policing in the Netherlands and Scotland', *Criminology & Criminal Justice*, 2015.

J. Terpstra & N.R. Fyfe, 'Policy processes and police reform: Examining similarities and differences between Scotland and the Netherlands', *International Journal of Law, Crime and Justice*, 2014, volume 42, issue 4.

L. van den Akker, L. Dalhuisen & M. Stokkel, 'Fitness to stand trial: A general principle of European criminal law?', *Utrecht Law Review* 2011.

S. van der Aa & M.S. Groenhuijsen, 'Slachtofferrechten in het strafproces: drie stapjes naar voren en een stapje terug?' *Ars Aequi* 2012.

P.H.P.H.M.C. van Kempen, 'The Protection of Human Rights in Criminal Law Procedure in The Netherlands', *Electronic Journal of Comparative Law*, 2009, Vol. 13.2.

P.H.P.H.M.C. van Kempen, 'De ondergrens van culpa. Opmerkingen over de eis van 'grove schuld' bij artikel 6 WvW 1994 mede in relatie tot de wederrechtelijkheid en de verwijtbaarheid, *Delikt en Delinkwent*, 2004, pp. 996–1014.

M. van Ooyen-Houben & E. Kleemans, 'Drug Policy: The 'Dutch Model'', *Crime & Justice* 2015, vol. 44.

A. van Verseveld, 'Noodweer: de Hoge Raad geeft een overzicht', *Delikt en Delinkwent*, 2016, 5.

COMMENTARIES

J.M. ten Voorde, *Tekst & Commentaar Strafrecht*, commentaar op titel III Sr, Inleidende opmerkingen, par. 11 sub (e), 2018 (On Kluwer Navigator).

PARLIAMENTARY DOCUMENTS

Kamerstukken II 2017–2018, 34 997.
Kamerstukken II 2014–2015, 34 165.
Kamerstukken II 1995–1996, 24 072.
Kamerstukken II 2015–2016, 29 279.

INTERNET PUBLICATIONS

B. Bieleman & R. Mennes, 'Steeds minder coffeeshops in Nederland', Secondant, Platform voor maatschappelijke veiligheid, 2016.

CASE LAW

EUROPEAN COURT OF HUMAN RIGHTS (ECtHR)

European Court of Human Rights, *Vinter v. the United Kingdom*, 7 July 2015, appl. nos. 66069/09, 130/10 and 3896/10.

European Court of Human Rights, *Contrada v. Italy (No. 3)*, 14 April 2015, appl. no. 66655/13.

European Court of Human Rights (GC), *Rohlena v. The Czech Republic*, 27 January 2015, appl. no. 59552/08.

European Court of Human Rights (GC), *Del Río Prada v. Spain*, 21 October 2013, appl. no. 42750/09.

European Court of Human Rights, *Vidgen v. the Netherlands*, 10 July 2012, appl. no. 29353/06, *NJ* 2012/649.

European Court of Human Rights, *Lalmahomed v. the Netherlands*, 22 February 2011, no. 26036/08, *NJ* 2012/306.

European Court of Human Rights, *Salduz v. Turkey*, 27 November 2008, appl. no. 36391/02, *NJ* 2009/214.

European Court of Human Rights, *Pelladoah v. the Netherlands*, 22 September 1994, appl. no. 16737/90.

European Court of Human Rights, *Lala v. the Netherlands*, 22 September 1994, appl. no. 14861/89, *NJ* 1994/733.

European Court of Human Rights, *Kruslin/Huvig v. France*, 24 April 1990, appl. no. 11801/95 and 11105/84, *NJ* 1991/523.

European Court of Human Rights, *Hauschildt v. Denmark*, 24 May 1989, appl. no. 10486/83, *NJ* 1990/627.

European Court of Human Rights, *Kostovski v. the Netherlands*, 20 November 1989, appl. no. 11454/85, *NJ* 1990/245.

European Court of Human Rights, *Kamasinksi v. Austria*, 19 December 1989, appl. no. 9783/82, *NJ* 1994/26.

European Court of Human Rights, *Brogan and others v. United Kingdom*, 29 November 1988, appl. no. 1266/84, 11234/84 and 11209/84, *NJ* 1989/815.

European Court of Human Rights, *De Cubber v. Belgium*, 26 October 1984, appl. no. 9186/80, *NJ* 2012/649.

UN HUMAN RIGHTS COMMITTEE

UN Human Rights Committee, *Mennen v. the Netherlands*, 27 July 2010, no. 1797/2008, *NJ* 2012/305.

SUPREME COURT OF THE NETHERLANDS (HOGE RAAD DER NEDERLANDEN)

Supreme Court, 16 April 2019, ECLI:NL:HR:2019:598 (*Heringa case*).

Supreme Court, 6 November 2018, ECLI:NL:HR:2018:2050.

Supreme Court, 29 May 2018, ECLI:NL:HR:2018:718, *NJ* 2019/103.

Supreme Court, 14 March 2017, ECLI:NL:HR:2017:418, *NJ* 2017/269 (*Heringa case*).

Supreme Court, 31 January 2017, ECLI:NL:HR:2017:114, *NJ* 2017/199.

Supreme Court, 26 April 2016, ECLI:NL:HR:2016:742, *NJ* 2016/388.

Supreme Court, 22, March 2016, ECLI:NL:HR:2016:456, *NJ* 2016/316 (*Overview judgment on self-defense*).

Supreme Court, 22 December 2015, ECLI:NL:HR:2015:3608, *NJ* 2016/52.

Supreme Court, 16 December 2014, ECLI:NL:HR:2014:3637, *NJ* 2015/391 (*Overview judgement on participation*).

Supreme Court, 1 July 2014, ECLI:NL:HR:2014:1563, *NJ* 2015/114 en 115.

Supreme Court, 1 July 2014, ECLI:NL:HR:2014:1496, *NJ* 2014/441.

Supreme Court, 27 May 2014, ECLI:NL:HR:2014:1236, *NJ* 2014/364.

Supreme Court, 17 December 2013, ECLI:NL:HR:2013:2013, *NJ* 2014/204.

Supreme Court, 2 July 2013, ECLI:NL:HR:2013:7, *NJ* 2013/563 (*Checkpoint case*).

Supreme Court, 19 February 2013, ECLI:NL:HR:2013:BY5321, *NJ* 2013/308 (*Unauthorized auxiliary prosecutor*).

Supreme Court, 29 January 2013, ECLI:NL:HR:2013:BX5539, *NJ* 2013/145, ECLI:NL:HR:2013:BX5539 (*post-Vidgen*).

Supreme Court, 13 November 2012, ECLI:NL:HR: 2012:BW9338.

Supreme Court, 24 January 2012, ECLI:NL:HR:2012:BT1856, *NJ* 2012/82.

Supreme Court, 12 July 2011, ECLI:NL:HR:2011:BP6878, *NJ* 2012/78.

Supreme Court, 30 June 2009, ECLI:NL:HR:2009:BG7746, *NJ* 2009/496.

Supreme Court, 30 June 2009, ECLI:NL:HR:2009:BH3079, *NJ* 2009/349.

Supreme Court, 28 October 2008, ECLI:NL:HR:2008:BE9611, *NJ* 2008/570.

Supreme Court, 8 April 2008, ECLI:NLHR:2008:BC4459, *NJ* 2008/312 (*Testicle squeezer*).

Supreme Court, 14 March 2006, ECLI:NL:HR:2006:AU5496, *NJ* 2007/345.

Supreme Court, 11 October 2005, ECLI:NL:HR:2005:AT5772, *NJ* 2006/548 (*Trunk*).

Supreme Court, 15 June 2004, ECLI:NL:HR:2004:AO9639, *NJ* 2004/464.

Supreme Court, 1 June 2004, ECLI:NL:HR:2004:AO5822, *NJ* 2005/252 (*Blackout*).

Supreme Court, 30 March 2004, ECLI:NL:HR:2004:AM2533, *NJ* 2004/376 (*Drainage pipe*).

Supreme Court, 21 October 2003, ECLI:NL:HR:2003:AF7938, *NJ* 2006/328 (*Slurry*).

Supreme Court, 25 March 2003, ECLI:NL:HR:2003:AE9049, *NJ* 2003/552 (*HIV-I*).

Supreme Court, 24 December 2002, ECLI:NL:HR:2002:AE8772, NJ 2003/167 (*Brongersma case*).

Supreme Court, 31 October 2000, ECLI:NL:HR:2000:AA7954, *NJ* 2001/14.

Supreme Court, 21 March 2000, ECLI:NL:HR:2000:AA5254.

Supreme Court, 26 May 1998, ECLI:NL:HR:1998:ZD1050, *NJ* 1998/713.

Supreme Court, 17 February 1998, ECLI:NL:HR:1998:ZD0941, NJ 1998/447.

Supreme Court, 6 January 1998, ECLI:NL:HR:1998:AA9342, *NJ* 1998/367 (*Pikmeer II*).

Supreme Court, 24 June 1997, ECLI:NL:HR:1997:ZD0773, *NJ* 1998/70.

Supreme Court, 3 June 1997, ECLI:NL:HR:1997:ZD0733, *NJ* 1997/584.

Supreme Court, 19 December 1995, ECLI:NL:HR:1995:ZD0328, *NJ* 1996/249.
Supreme Court, 21 June 1994, ECLI:NL:HR:1994:AD2122, *NJ* 1994/656 (*Chabot case*).
Supreme Court, 25 January 1994, ECLI:NL:HR:1994:ZC9616, *NJ* 1994/598 (*Air base Volkel*).
Supreme Court, 26 October 1993, ECLI:NL:HR:1993:ZC9475, *NJ* 1994/51 (*Klaver Fashion*).
Supreme Court, 10 March 1992, ECLI:NL:HR:1992:ZC0567, *NJ* 1992/593.
Supreme Court, 13 June 1989, ECLI:NL:HR:1989:AJ5657, *NJ* 1990/138.
Supreme Court, 1 November 1988, ECLI:NL:HR:1988:AB7790, *NJ* 1989/351.
Supreme Court, 16 December 1987, ECLI:NL:HR:1986:AC9607, *NJ* 1987/321 (*Slavenburg II*).
Supreme Court, 9 December 1986, ECLI:NL:HR:1986:AC1152, *NJ* 1987/540.
Supreme Court, 12 November 1985, ECLI:NL:HR:1985:AC2708, *NJ* 1986/327.
Supreme Court, 15 July 1985, ECLI:NL:HR:1985:AC4252, *NJ* 1986/184.
Supreme Court, 2 April 1985, ECLI:NL:HR:1985:AB7969, *NJ* 1985/875.
Supreme Court, 27 November 1984, ECLI:NL:HR:1984:AC8615, *NJ* 1985/106 (*Schoonheim case*).
Supreme Court, 24 October 1978, ECLI:NL:HR:1978:AC6373, *NJ* 1979/52 (*Employment agency Cito*).
Supreme Court, 6 December 1977, ECLI:NL:HR:1977:AB7287, *NJ* 1979/181.
Supreme Court, 26 August 1960, ECLI:NL:HR:1960:33, *NJ* 1960/566.
Supreme Court, 10 September 1957, ECLI:NL:HR:1957:2, *NJ* 1958/5 (*Black rider*).
Supreme Court, 8 February 1932, ECLI:NL:HR:1932:BG9439, *NJ* 1932/617 (*Fear judgement*).
Supreme Court, 15 October 1923, ECLI:NL:HR:1923:243, *NJ* 1923/1329 (*Optician*).

APPEAL COURT

Amsterdam Court of Appeal, 24 July 2007, ECLI:NL:GHAMS:2007:BB0460, *NJFS* 2007/229.
Amsterdam Court of Appeal, 18 July 2003, ECLI:NL:GHAMS:2003:AI0123, *NJ* 2003/580.

DISTRICT COURT

The Hague District Court, 9 December 2016, ECLI:NL:RBDHA:2016:15014.
Amsterdam District Court, 23 June 2011, ECLI:NL:RBAMS:2011:BQ9001, *NJ* 2012/370.
Amsterdam District Court, 26 July 2005, ECLI:NL:RBAMS:2005:AU0025.
Rotterdam District Court, 1 December 1981, ECLI:NL:RBROT:1981:AB7817, *NJ* 1982/63 (*Wertheim case*).
Leeuwarden District Court 21 February 1973, ECLI:NL:RBLEE:1973:AB5464, *NJ* 1973/183 (*Postma case*).

CPSIA information can be obtained
at www.ICGtesting.com
Printed in the USA
LVHW060836061222
734648LV00002B/6

9 781780 689623